EUROPEANIZATION OF NATIONAL SECURITY IDENTITY

This book provides an understanding of how the EU functions as a security actor, and how and to what extent the EU affects national security identities.

Since the early 1990s the EU has gradually become more important as an independent security provider. The special character of the EU – being something between an international organization and a federal state – makes it different from other existing security actors. It is this particularity that makes it interesting to study the impact of the EU on national security approaches. The aim of this book is therefore twofold. First, it provides an understanding of how the EU functions as a security actor. Second, it analyses how and to what extent the EU affects national security identities of both member states and states that are closely linked to the Union. The empirical focus here is a comparison of the processes of change and adaptations in the Nordic countries. But the topic of the book has also wider implications and the analysis combines integration theory, security studies and studies of Europeanization. Still, the main aim of this volume is to contribute to increased understanding of how national security identities change. The EU is a security actor and due to its level of integration, it exerts a powerful influence on member state security approaches and identities.

Pernille Rieker is senior researcher at the Norwegian Institute of International Affairs (NUPI), where she is co-ordinating a research programme on European security and transatlantic relations within the department of international politics. Her research interests include European integration, European security policy and transatlantic relations.

CONTEMPORARY SECURITY STUDIES

PROPAGANDA, THE PRESS AND CONFLICT
The Gulf War and Kosovo
David R. Willcox

MISSILE DEFENCE
International, regional and national implications
Bertel Heurlin and Sten Rynning (eds)

GLOBALISING JUSTICE FOR MASS ATROCITIES
A revolution in accountability
Chandra Lekha Sriram

ETHNIC CONFLICT AND TERRORISM
The origins and dynamics of civil wars
Joseph L. Soeters

GLOBALISATION AND THE FUTURE OF TERRORISM
Patterns and predictions
Brynjar Lia

NUCLEAR WEAPONS AND STRATEGY
The evolution of American nuclear policy
Stephen J. Cimbala

NASSER AND THE MISSILE AGE IN THE MIDDLE EAST
Owen L. Sirrs

WAR AS RISK MANAGEMENT
Strategy and conflict in an age of globalised risks
Yee-Kuang Heng

MILITARY NANOTECHNOLOGY
Potential applications and preventive arms control
Jurgen Altmann

NATO AND WEAPONS OF MASS DESTRUCTION
Regional alliance, global threats
Eric R. Terzuolo

EUROPEANIZATION OF NATIONAL SECURITY IDENTITY
The EU and the changing security identities of the Nordic states
Pernille Rieker

INTERNATIONAL CONFLICT PREVENTION AND
PEACE-BUILDING
Sustaining the peace in post conflict societies
T. David Mason and James D. Meernik (eds)

CONTROLLING THE WEAPONS OF WAR
Politics, persuasion, and the prohibition of inhumanity
Brian Rappert

EUROPEANIZATION OF NATIONAL SECURITY IDENTITY

The EU and the changing security identities of the Nordic states

Pernille Rieker

Routledge
Taylor & Francis Group

LONDON AND NEW YORK

First published 2006
by Routledge
2 Park Square, Milton Park, Abingdon, Oxon OX14 4RN

Simultaneously published in the USA and Canada
by Routledge
270 Madison Ave, New York, NY 10016

Routledge is an imprint of the Taylor & Francis Group

Transferred to Digital Printing 2009

© 2006 Pernille Rieker

Typeset in Times by
RefineCatch Limited, Bungay, Suffolk

British Library Cataloguing in Publication Data
A catalogue record for this book is available from the British Library

Library of Congress Cataloging in Publication Data
A catalog record for this book has been requested

ISBN10: 0–415–38022–7 (hbk)
ISBN10: 0–415–54494–7 (pbk)

ISBN13: 9–78–0–415–38022–5 (hbk)
ISBN13: 9–78–0–415–54494–8 (pbk)

CONTENTS

CONTENTS

ACKNOWLEDGEMENTS

A number of people have contributed significantly to this book. First of all, I would like to thank Martin Sæter for convincing me that I should continue with research and for sharing his knowledge about the European integration process. I am particularly grateful to Walter Carlsnaes for his skilled guidance and support throughout the whole process. I have also benefited from the good advice and many constructive comments from Clive Archer, Karin Dokken, Ole Elgström, Adrian Hyde-Price and Janne Haaland Matlary. Several other people have also given me valuable advice: special thanks to Magnus Ekengren, Trine Flockhart, Peter Viggo Jakobsen, Pertti Joenniemi, Knud Erik Jørgensen, Morten Kelstrup, Bjørn Olav Knutsen, Hanna Ojanen, Helene Sjursen, Peter Strandbrink, Teija Tiilikainen, Ola Tunander, and Ole Wæver.

While completing this manuscript I have been employed by the Norwegian Institute of International Affairs (NUPI) in Oslo and the project has been funded by the Norwegian Research Council (NFR). I am particularly grateful for the support from the director, Sverre Lodgaard, and my colleagues in the Department for International Politics. I would also like to thank Hazel Henriksen, Dagfrid Hermansen and Tore Gustavsson in the NUPI library, who have been extremely helpful in finding literature and documents not easily available, as well as Susan Høivik for correcting the language.

I am thankful to the Norwegian Ministry of Foreign Affairs for financially supporting my research visits to the other Nordic states. I am also very grateful to the Swedish Institute for International Affairs (UI), the Finnish Institute for International Affairs (UPI), the Danish Institute for International Affairs (DUPI) and the EU Institute for Security Studies (EU ISS) for providing me with an interesting working environment during my research visits. My learning was enhanced by discussing my work with many researchers during these visits. I also want to thank the many officials who have had a positive attitude and found the time to be interviewed. They have represented different ministries, various governmental institutions, the European Commission and the Council of the EU.

Finally, I am also most thankful for the grant from the Norwegian

ACKNOWLEDGEMENTS

Ministry of Defence that made it possible to convert my initial manuscript into a book, and to Professor Helen Wallace for giving me the opportunity to finalize this work as a visiting researcher at the Robert Schuman Center for Advanced Studies at the European University Institute (EUI) in Florence. On a personal note, I would like to thank my friends and family for their support. In particular, I would like to thank Ulf for his patience and many constructive comments.

Needless to say, any errors are all mine.

Pernille Rieker
Oslo/Florence April 2005

ABBREVIATIONS

CFSP	Common Foreign and Security Policy
CIMIC	Civil–Military Co-operation
CJTF	Combined Joint Task Forces
COREU	Correspondance européenne
CSCE	Conference on Security and Co-operation in Europe
DCI	Defence Capability Initiative
DIIS	Dansk Institut for Internationale Studier (Danish Institute for International Studies)
DUPI	Dansk Udenrigspolitisk Institut (Danish Institute of International Affairs) (now DIIS, q.v.)
EC	European Community
ECSC	European Coal and Steel Community
EDC	European Defence Community
EEA	European Economic Area
EEC	European Economic Community
EFTA	European Free Trade Area
EMP	European Mediterranean Partnership
EMU	Economic and Monetary Union
EPC	European Political Co-operation
ESDP	European Security and Defence Policy
ESS	European Security Strategy
EU	European Union
FCMA	Friendship, Co-operation and Mutual Assistance Treaty (USSR–Finland)
IGC	Intergovernmental Conference
IR	International Relations
ISAF	International Stabilization Force
JHA	Justice and Home Affairs
KBM	Krisberedskapsmyndigheten (Swedish Emergency Management Agency)
MC	Military Committee
NACC	North Atlantic Co-operation Council

ABBREVIATIONS

NATO	North Atlantic Treaty Organization
NSM	Nasjonal Sikkerhetsmyndighet (Directorate for National Security)
ÖCB	Överstyrelsen for Civilt Beredskap (former Swedish Agency for Emergency Planning)
OSCE	Organization for Security and Co-operation in Europe
PARP	Planning and Review Process
PfP	Partnership for Peace
PSC	Political and Security Committee
SDA	Scandinavian Defence Association
SEA	Single European Act
SIPRI	Stockholm International Peace Research Institute
SNU	Nedrustningspolitisk Udvalg (Danish Commission on Disarmament and Security Affairs)
SPF	Styrelsen for Psykologisk Försvar (Swedish National Board for Psychological Defence)
SWEDINT	Swedish Armed Forces International Centre
SWERAP	Swedish Rapid Reaction Force
UI	Utrikespolitiska Institutet (Swedish Institute of International Affairs)
UPI	Ulkopoliittinen Instituutti (Finnish Institute of International Affairs)
WEU	Western European Union

PREFACE

Since the early 1990s the European Union (EU) has increasingly become a more important security policy actor. This has triggered interest in two key questions. How is the EU functioning as a security actor? How and to what extent is the EU affecting national security identities?

This book aims to shed light on these two questions. It does so by comparing the processes of adaptation and change in four Nordic states (Denmark, Finland, Norway and Sweden). Comparing these countries is interesting since they have different relationships to the EU and different security policy traditions. In fact, during the Cold War period, the security policies of the Nordic states were referred to as the 'Nordic balance' – a combination of different policies aimed at preserving a balance between the two superpowers.

This book argues that the EU has developed into special kind of security actor that, due to its level of political integration, has had an important influence on national security approaches and identities. The analysis applies a combination of integration theory, security studies and studies of Europeanization. It relates to the branch of this literature, which is concerned with how change outside the borders of the nation-state impacts on and leads to changes and adaptations at the domestic level.

I argue that while the end of the Cold War paved the way for a different and more complex security approach, it took some time before the Nordic states responded to this new security context. Rather than adapting to the changing conditions created by the end of the Cold War, the Nordic states changed their security approaches in response to the European integration process. I show how different phases in the post-Cold War European integration process have influenced the national security approaches of Sweden, Finland, Denmark and Norway. While all four security approaches have to some extent been Europeanized, the speed and the character of these changes vary due to a combination of differing ties to the EU and differing security policy traditions.

1

INTRODUCTION

This book deals with the relationship between European integration, security and national identity change. How and to what extent has the development towards a specific European Union security view – understood as a *comprehensive security identity* – led to adaptations and changes in national security approaches and identities?

The theoretical point of departure is an interest in national identity changes in response to community norms. The book argues that national security approaches are adapted to the norms defined by a community to which they are closely linked. This adaptation evolves over time, through a socialization process, and may also lead to a change in national security identities. These observations challenge two common assumptions in conventional International Relations (IR). First, the idea that national security is primarily about the nation-state defending its national territory against military threats, making military means the central tool of security policy (see for instance Walt 1991). Second, the assumption held by rationalists that both national identities and interests are fixed and independent of structural factors such as international norms.

This book argues in favour of a broader approach to security and that the development of an EU security identity affects national identities and interests. The empirical focus will be restricted to changes in the national security approaches and identities in Denmark, Finland, Norway and Sweden after the end of the Cold War. I show that the security approaches in these countries have been influenced by the development of a specific EU security identity. However, the character and the degree of Europeanization depend both on the country's traditions in security policy and on its relationship to the Union.

This introductory chapter is divided into three main parts. First, the main research questions are presented. Second, some key concepts are clarified. Finally, the analytical framework and research design are introduced.

1

Research questions

Focusing on the Europeanization of the security identities of the Nordic states, the analysis in this book is closely related to other studies of the Union's impact on various policies and institutions in different nation-states. In addition, it helps to fill an important gap in this literature, since little or no research has been done on the Europeanization of national security identities. There are also few recent comparative studies of the relationship between the EU and the Nordic countries.

Most of the research on the EU and the Nordic countries[1] within the field of IR has focused on individual Nordic countries and their attempts at achieving EU accession. Thus, there are few comparative studies of the Nordic states and their relationship with the EU. However, after Sweden and Finland joined the Union in 1995 whereas Norway and Iceland decided not to, interest in such comparative work has increased. One comprehensive treatment of the relationship between the EU and the Nordic countries was a volume edited by Lee Miles (Miles 1996), in which EU–Nordic relations were studied through chronological, state-centred and issue-based approaches.[2] While each chapter in the Miles study provides important insights into this relationship, the volume as a whole lacks a clear theoretical focus. More recent work has tried to highlight differences between the attitudes of the Nordic countries towards the European integration process, by focusing either on differences in economic and material factors (Ingebritsen 1998), or on differences in national identity formation (Hansen and Wæver 2002). Thus, while the main argument in Christine Ingebritsen's study is that the specificities of the economic structure of each country explain the differences, the study by Lene Hansen and Ole Wæver emphasizes the differences in national identities, and especially how the relationship between concepts like *state, nation* and *Europe* becomes elaborated in the national discourse.

The focus of this book is somewhat different. Instead of seeking to explain why the Nordic countries have chosen differing approaches to the EU, this study has a more specific ambition. It aims at assessing *how and to what extent the development of a distinct EU security identity has influenced the security approaches and identities of the four largest Nordic states – Denmark, Finland, Norway and Sweden.* In order to illustrate this relationship, it may be useful to present the Union's security identity as the *independent variable,* national security identity change as the *dependent variable* and Europeanization as one important *process* of change.

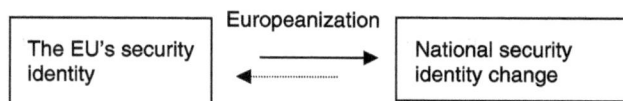

```
                          Europeanization
┌──────────────────┐    ──────────────▶    ┌──────────────────┐
│ The EU's security │                       │ National security │
│ identity          │    ◀ · · · · · · · ·  │ identity change   │
└──────────────────┘                       └──────────────────┘
```

Figure 1.1 Europeanization of national security identity.

This is *not* to say that this is a one-way process. In reality the EU member states also influence the development of an EU security identity. Still, the aim of this particular study is to investigate to what extent the development of an EU security identity has challenged also the national security identity. This means that while a state promotes a certain security policy at the EU level, it does not mean that this particular policy is adopted at the national level. For instance, while Sweden has promoted a comprehensive security approach in the EU, it has until recently upheld a rather traditional national security and defence policy, dominated by non-alignment and territorial defence.

I am well aware that there are also other factors, institutions and actors, be they national or international, which might impact on national security identities. However, since the EU is such an important and large entity it is interesting to try to examine its specific impact on national security identities. I also argue, and hopefully show, that it is possible to separate the effects of the EU from other institutions and actors if one uses the method of process-tracing, carefully examining the temporal order of the various changes and the arguments used for these changes. That being said, I think that a more comprehensive understanding of the dynamics of national security identities would benefit further by also supplementing such studies with the impact of NATO, the US and other external factors and crises arising. In addition various internal factors could also be included. In this analysis I have limited the focus to the impact of the EU. In fact, the EU is assumed to have a decisive influence on the nation-state's security identities, and the study is based on the following three assumptions:

- First, that the European security context has changed radically since the end of the Cold War, giving the concept of security a different and broader meaning.
- Second, that the European Union has developed a security identity in tune with this new security context.
- Third, that this security identity influences the national security identities of EU member states as well as other states closely linked to the integration process, through a process of Europeanization.

The first assumption is given a more extensive presentation in the second part of this chapter (under 'key concepts'). Let us now move on to examine the other two.

The security identity of the EU

In order to understand the importance of studying the Europeanization of nation-state security identities, the character of the independent variable has to be clarified. Assuming both that the EU is an actor and that it has a distinct security approach is in fact controversial. For a long time the main opposition stood between those who perceived European integration solely as an arena for intergovernmental bargaining, and those who saw it as a continuous process towards a supranational state.[3] The argument put forward in this book, however, is that the European integration process has gradually consolidated parts of Europe as a political actor, but without having become a supranational state. The establishment of a political union (EU), the implementation of the Economic and Monetary Union (EMU), the Common Foreign and Security Policy (CFSP) and increased co-operative policies in the area of justice and home affairs (JHA) have been important steps in that direction. This is not to say that the European Community (EC) never acted as such, but rather that the Maastricht Treaty represented a qualitative step towards the establishment of a European political *actor*.[4]

In addition, whether or not the EU has a distinct security approach depends on how one defines 'security'. While it is generally agreed that there is a relationship between integration and security, those who defend a traditional definition of security may tend to ignore the EU as a security actor. The EU's lack of effective military capabilities makes it difficult for them to characterize it as a security actor (Bull 1982; Walt 1991; Hill 1993; Regelsberger and Wessels 1996; Hoffmann 2000; Kagan 2003). To those who understand security in a broader sense, however, the situation will look quite different. For them, the Union's potential to *co-ordinate diverse tools of security policy* – economic, political and military – makes it a major security actor of the post-Cold War context (Wæver 1995a; Smith 1999; Ginsberg 2001; White 2001; Sjursen 2001b; Manners 2002; Smith 2002; Rieker and Ulriksen 2003; Smith 2003; Krahmann 2003; Cooper 2003). Not surprisingly, it is the latter view that is emphasized by the EU itself through its official documents and speeches.

This understanding of security has also moved beyond the rhetorical level, as the EU has begun to transform these ideas into concrete policy. This has been the case in international crisis management, where a civilian component has been established in parallel to the military one, and where the need for improved co-ordination between the two has been emphasized. For several decades, considerable attention has also been given to developing an effective policy for curtailing crime and terrorism within the EU. Initially this threat was considered as an internal one, so the EU's policy focused on security within the EU area, by strengthening co-operation in justice and home affairs. More recently, the traditional distinction between internal and external security has become less clear-cut, and there is now general agreement within the EU that a combination of external and internal tools is necessary in order to respond to today's security challenges. All this indicates that the EU has begun to adopt a security political approach that goes beyond the CFSP, including the Community policies linked both to economic integration (pillar I) and to justice and home affairs (pillar III). This approach is referred to as a *comprehensive security approach*. Used on the EU, this means that the EU focuses on the potential of the EU for co-ordinating a broad spectre of security threats (both internal and external) and a wide range of security policy tools (both civilian and military).[5]

The development of a comprehensive approach to security has occurred gradually, and as a response to the dramatic changes in the European security context in the early 1990s. Existing multilateral security policy frameworks, such as NATO and the Organization for Security and Co-operation in Europe (OSCE), have also adapted to the new security context. However, the most radical transformation has occurred within the EU – the only multilateral framework with no security policy legacy from the Cold War period. While the fact that the EU has no clear security legacy is a consequence of earlier reluctance of the part of the member states to relinquish national sovereignty in this area, it seems that this reluctance has actually facilitated the development of an innovative security approach. Using Robert Cooper's terminology, this is what one may call a *post-modern security approach*.[6] Cooper argues that the EU must be considered as the most developed post-modern system, since the dividing line between foreign and domestic policy is being erased, states are giving up their traditional monopoly on violence and [internal] borders are increasingly irrelevant (Cooper 2003: 36–7).

According to this logic, one may argue that it is the special character of the EU – the fact that the EU is an institutional hybrid between an international organization and a federal state,[7] and the fact that it lacks a clearly defined security policy legacy from the past – that makes it post-modern. While the first opens up a path to forms of governance other than the ones we are used to, the second makes it easier to develop an innovative (comprehensive) security approach. Thus, rather than being the result of the influence of a particular member state or a particular group of member states, the Union's current security approach seems to be a result of the special character of the integration process and the fact that the EU did not have an institutionalized security policy from the past. As Craig Parsons argues, one idea of European integration becomes institutionalized rather than another simply because it is easier to institutionalize or because it fits better with elements of the environment (Parsons 2003: 20).

It is possible to distinguish between three important formative phases in the development of the EU security identity:

- The establishment of a political union and the CFSP in the early 1990s;
- The process towards the establishment of a European Security and Defence Policy (ESDP) at the end of the 1990s, with the focus on the development of both a military and a civilian capacity for international crisis management;
- The intensified efforts of integrating civilian and military instruments in relation to both internal and external security. Such a comprehensive

security approach has received increased attention at the turn of the century, and is explicitly emphasized in the European Security Strategy (ESS).

The development towards a specific EU security identity is discussed in further detail in the next chapter.

Europeanization of the security identities of the Nordic states

The close link between security and identity makes radical changes in national security policy difficult. This means that only minor adaptations are likely to take place. Due to the high level of political integration in the EU compared to other multilateral frameworks, however, one may expect that the development of a comprehensive security approach will also, in turn, influence the security approaches and/or identities of the individual European nation-state. The empirical focus of this study is the changes in security approaches and identities in the four largest Nordic countries – Denmark, Finland, Norway and Sweden.[8] A comparative study of these countries is interesting since they differ both with respect to their individual national security approaches and in their formal relationship to the EU.

During the Cold War period, the security approaches of the Nordic states were based on the different security policy choices made in the late 1940s: Denmark, Iceland and Norway joined the newly established Atlantic alliance, NATO; Finland became non-aligned but signed the FCMA (Friendship, Co-operation and Mutual Assistance) Treaty with the USSR, and Sweden remained neutral and non-aligned. By the early 1960s it had become normal to use the concept of 'balance' to describe the Nordic security policy context (Brundtland 1966, 1981; Holst 1983). For the most part 'Nordic balance' has been portrayed as a description of the Nordic pattern, providing an understanding of how the mechanisms of security work; but it has also been presented as a model, a system or doctrine – and ultimately, as a 'theory' (Joenniemi 1992: 58).

In the context of research, the primary purpose of the concept of 'Nordic balance' has been to provide an explanation for the prevailing conditions of peace and stability in the Nordic area. The concept rests on assumptions of a bipolar East–West system, with the Nordic region as one of its components, and a perception of an interplay between regional policies and those of a larger system of blocs and major powers. As a rule 'Norden' was not considered to be part of a traditional *military* balance. Rather, the argument was that it constituted a system of political deterrence, a balance of potential options for keeping the superpowers out of 'Norden' as much as possible and for preventing them from applying maximalist policies of confrontation in the region. The perspective focused particularly on Norway and Finland, each of which had its own superpower to keep in check. This conceptualization of Nordic balance was originally elaborated by analysts within the Realist school of thought, seeking to fit 'Norden' into the normal world of power politics (Brundtland 1966, 1981; Holst 1983, 1994).

With the end of the Cold War, this special Nordic identity characterized by a security community and 'Nordic balance' disappeared, and the Nordic countries became involved in a new European security discourse (Joenniemi 1992). The acceleration of the European integration process in the immediate wake of this dramatic and profound change in European security presented 'Norden' with complex challenges. While the rivalry between the superpowers had led to a situation that could easily be discussed within the framework of traditional security analysis, the security dimension of this more recent European integration process is more complex, evading analysis based on concepts such as balance, stability or credibility (Wæver and Wiberg 1992). Rather than building a political identity by being different from the other European states, the main challenge has seemed to be how to integrate the Nordic countries into the new European security context (Knutsen 2000).

In this book the following assumptions are investigated:

* The emergence of a distinct European security identity influences the security approaches and identities of the Nordic countries.
* The character and the strength of the Europeanization process vary according to national security policy traditions and the character of the relationship to the EU.

Thus, it is assumed that the Union will influence all four countries, but with greatest impact on the security identities of those countries that are the most integrated into the EU. In addition, some security policy traditions are expected to lead to a stronger degree of Europeanization than others. While 'recent' war experiences and a continued perceived vulnerable geopolitical position might reduce the degree of Europeanization, the converse would favour such a process. This may be illustrated as follows:

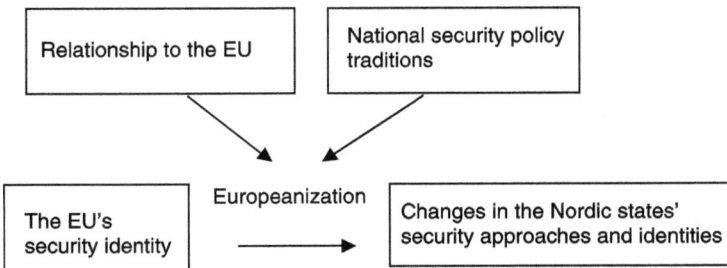

Figure 1.2 Europeanization of the security approaches and identities of the Nordic states.

7

Before turning to the analytical approach on which the ensuing analysis is based, we need to clarify some key concepts.

Key concepts

In the literature, concepts such as 'security', 'identity' and 'Europeanization' are used with a variety of different interpretations. In order to follow the main argument in this book it is necessary to clarify how these concepts are applied.

Security

In this book, security is in the first place limited to what two specific actors – the EU and the Nordic states – *present* as security issues through a process of securitization (Buzan *et al.* 1998: 24–6) or desecuritization (Wæver 1995b). This way of approaching security distinguishes itself from more conventional approaches that apply a less flexible definition of security. For a long time it was common to understand 'security' as equivalent to territorial defence against military threats. This was the main use during the Cold War, when national security first became a central concern within the field of IR. Recently, the importance of territorial defence has been toned down, but interest in the military aspects of security still dominates the field (Baldwin 1995).

In contrast to traditional security analyses, the approach applied here argues that it is the actor itself (the so-called *securitizing actor*)[9] and not the analyst who decides whether something is to be handled as an existential threat, and thus justifies the use of 'extraordinary measures' to handle it (Buzan *et al.* 1998: 21). A discourse that takes the form of presenting something as an existential threat to a referant object, however, does not by itself create securitization. This is what Buzan *et al.* call a 'securitizing move'. An issue is securitized only when this 'move' is accepted by society.

While the theory of securitization (or speech acts) is successful in avoiding the 'intellectual incoherence' of the issue-driven widening of the security concept in the 1980s,[10] it tends, however, to elevate 'security' into a kind of universal 'good'. As Wæver (1995b) has argued, this is a dangerously narrow view because the word 'security' might extend the call for state mobilization to a broad range of issues. Although in international relations security may generally be preferable to insecurity, it might be better, as Wæver argues, to aim for *desecuritization* – shifting issues out of the emergency mode and into the normal bargaining processes of the political sphere.

However, it is not sufficient to decide whether an issue is being securitized/desecuritized. Rather, it is also important to study the extent to which there is a match or a mismatch between discourse and policy. Recently there has been an increased emphasis on the need to develop a *comprehensive* or holistic approach to security. While the concept is generally referred to in relation to studies of environmental security (Westing 1989; Dokken 1997), it will here be used to refer to a holistic security approach that includes both internal and external security mechanisms. This is in accordance with Katzenstein (1996a: 3), who emphasizes the social, economic and political aspects of security rather than focusing narrowly on the explicitly coercive dimensions of state policy. While the implementation of such a holistic approach has proved difficult, the argument in this book is that the integration process has facilitated such a development.

As we shall see in the next chapter, the EU has desecuritized the traditional security issues of territorial defence, securitized new issues and put increased emphasis on the need for a comprehensive security approach. Interestingly, a similar development can be identified in the Nordic countries, and it is argued here that these changes to some extent must be seen as a result of a process of Europeanization.

Nation-state security identity

The widening of the concept of security has brought renewed interest to questions of culture and identities in security studies (Lapid and Kratochwil 1996), and in this book it is the *security identity of the nation-state* that is in focus.

In general the concept of 'collective identities' refers to the idea that groups of individuals with a perception of common or shared factors will form an 'imagined community' (Anderson 1991). This is then accentuated by a sense of difference with regard to other communities, which is often referred to as the 'other' (Neumann 1999). Thomas Risse argues that 'while political elites are constantly in the business of identity constructions, only some of these constructions are consensual at any given point in time' (Risse 2001: 201). The part that is consensual could be termed *nation-state identity*. Nation-state identity distinguishes itself from other components of collective identity by the fact that it takes a longer time to construct and that it is deeply embedded in both institutions and a certain political culture (ibid.: 201–2). Various components of this nation-state identity are invoked, depending on the policy area in question.

The nation-state security identity, however, can be identified by uncovering the *dominant security discourse* undertaken by the political leadership in a given nation-state. By 'dominant discourse' I mean the general understanding of security shared by the majority of the political elites at a given point in time.[11] This dominant discourse, however, is influenced by a set of shared beliefs or a certain 'cognitive structure' within a particular nation-state. It is this cognitive structure that establishes the boundaries for the discourse, which in turn puts limits on possible policy options (Hopf 2002: 10). This explains why a nation-state security *identity* has to be distinguished from nation-state security *policy*. A stable and durable change in security policy, however, depends on a change in security identity, but changes in policy may also have the character of instrumental adaptations within an unchanged 'cognitive structure'. This means that it is possible to have a change in policy without a change in identity.

For those who see the international system of states as an anarchic system of unified nation-states that always acts strategically on the basis of given interests, this difference between identity and policy is irrelevant. For these scholars (often referred to as rationalists), a state will always seek to maximize its (absolute or relative) power and influence through various strategies, and these interests are therefore fixed and independent of their identities (Waltz 1979). However, for those who hold that national identities and interests may change, this distinction is important. For these scholars (often referred to as social constructivists), a change in identity might lead to a change in interest and in the end also to a more lasting change in policy. According to this logic, a significant and lasting change in national security policy will always be dependent on changes in the national security identity (Jepperson *et al.* 1996).

However, studying *nation-state identity* has also been criticized by some for being too state-centric. Such an approach, it has been claimed, differs from the rationalist analyses only in that it includes identity as an independent variable and that it does not show how and under what conditions these identities occur in the first place (McSweeney 1996, 1999), However, since the aim of the present study is not to explain identity formation but rather to provide an increased *understanding of how changes in identities take place*, it makes sense to choose such an approach. The fact that there are many more security actors other than just the nation-state does not mean that the nation-state has become an uninteresting unit of study. The changes in a nation-state's identity are an appropriate and necessary topic to study if we are to make sense of actions which flow from, and carry with them, the power and resources of the state.[12]

Nation-state security identities are shaped over time, and in response to changes in the environment. The various national security identities in Western Europe towards the late 1980s were largely coloured by the Cold War period and its emphasis on military territorial defence against a potential attack from the East. In the Nordic states these identities were central to the conception of the 'Nordic balance'. Then, when the Cold War ended, the European security environment was radically altered, and these identities came under considerable pressure. However, a nation-state's security identity is embedded in institutions and a specific political culture, and change therefore tends to be slow.

One way to identify changes in a nation-state's security identity is by studying the language used in official documents and speeches presented by the government. It could be argued, however, that in order to identify the national security identity, ideally what is needed is a much broader approach, based on the study of parliamentary debates and the public debate in general. Due to limitations of time and capacity, such an approach is not always possible. Nor is it so important in a study of nation-state security identity, which is a result of an achieved common understanding of security that is not easily changed. A study of official documents over a relatively long period of time[13] should thus provide a good account. With Norway, for instance, its nation-state security identity during the Cold War was dominated by the country's membership in NATO, and is characterized here as *Atlanticism*. This is not to say that there was no opposition to this policy, but this was the compromise that Norwegian politicians had managed to reach. As to the case of Sweden, few would disagree that neutrality remained an important part of the Swedish security identity up to the late 1980s, even though it is now well known that the country also had close ties to NATO throughout most of the period.

In studying the nation-state's dominant security discourse, what is interesting is 'neither what individual decision-makers really believe, nor what are shared beliefs among a population, but which codes are used when actors relate to each other', as Wæver argues (Wæver 2002: 26). These *codes* can, he holds, be identified through a systematic study of a nation-state's official documents and the speeches of its political leadership, and will produce what we will term the *dominant national security discourse*. Basing the current study on this level rests on three assumptions: first, that these codes put relatively narrow limits on possible policies; second, that the codes are sufficiently stable so that they can be seen as 'causal' factors; and third, that it is possible to locate the most important discursive space in which the actor in question is operating (ibid.: 30).[14] In order to identify a nation-state security identity, we therefore have to 'decode' the political language. Identifying the nation-state's dominant security discourse and identity will in turn make it possible to determine the nation-state's interests (Hopf 2002: 19).

How then can the security identity of the European Union be identified? In contrast to the nation-state, the EU's security identity is of recent date. However, it is also possible to identify 'codes' at the EU level that are defining for the Union's dominant discourse on security. As we shall see in the next chapter, the European Community started to develop a distinct security policy view only after the end of the Cold War. The result has been what we may call a *comprehensive security identity*, whereby the EU emphasizes a co-ordinated approach to security.[15] The high level of political integration that came with the Maastricht Treaty rendered nation-state security identities more exposed to influence from this community than from other multilateral frameworks. This influence and the changes that this produced at the national level is referred to as *Europeanization*.

Europeanization

The concept of 'Europeanization' has been used to signify various things, and several scholars have tried to provide a systematic categorization of these different conceptualizations (Radaelli 2000; Featherstone and Kazamias 2001; Featherstone 2002; Olsen 2002). These can be summarized with reference to five different groups of interpretations. The first group sees Europeanization as the export of cultural norms from Europe to other parts of the world. The second group uses the term as a synonym for the integration process as such, or for development towards a unified and politically stronger Europe. The third views Europeanization as the development of a special system of governance on the EU level. A fourth focuses on the development of a collective European identity. And finally, there is a large group which takes Europeanization to mean the adaptation of domestic political structures (institutions, public administration, intergovernmental relations, the legal structure, structures of representation, cognitive and normative structures) to European pressure.

As already indicated, this study will fit into the latter group. While there are several scholars who use this conceptualization of Europeanization, most of their work has focused on how EU activities have influenced national administrative systems, the political institutions and the policy-making styles of member states (see for instance Rometsch and Wessels 1996; Hanf and Soetendorp 1998; Sverdrup 2000; Featherstone and Kazamias 2001). Less work has been done on how EU has affected national identities (some exceptions: Boekle *et al.* 2001; Risse 2001).[16] In addition, in most analyses of European security, the term 'Europeanization' is employed differently. The most common use is with reference to the possible emergence of a European pillar within NATO, often referred to as 'the Europeanization of NATO' (see for instance Croft 2000). It is only recently, and especially with the emergence of a common European Security and Defence Policy, that more and more studies have begun to use the term in relation to the impact of the ESDP on the foreign and security policies of EU member states (Manners and Withman 2000; Tonra 2001; Featherstone 2002).

However, few studies deal with more radical changes in these actors' understanding of security, threats and security policy means. To this end what is needed is a more open analysis, one not limited to what is traditionally considered to be foreign and security policy in a certain period of time. This book aims to fill that gap by focusing on the impact of the security approach of the European Union on the *security identities of nation-states*. It will analyse domestic adaptations to the development of an EU security identity, expressed through the nation-states' dominant discourse. I will argue that national security identities are constituted by discourses of this kind, which are also defining for national policies, practices and formal institutions. Chapter 3 will present this process of Europeanization (understood as a process of socialization) in greater detail.

Analytical approach, methodology and sources

The analysis in this book is based on a 'social constructivist' approach. Since there are various interpretations of *social constructivism*, this section starts with a brief clarification concerning the meta-theoretical foundation of the analysis to follow. Then I will discuss methodological questions and show why the use of interpretative case studies and a 'soft' version of discourse analysis is an appropriate way of studying changes in national security identities of nation-states.

A social constructivist approach

Within the field of International Relations, the debate between neo-realists and neo-liberalists – about whether institutions matter in international politics and whether 'co-operation under anarchy' is possible – has now been replaced by a debate between rationalist institutionalist and social constructivist approaches, centring on *why* and *how* institutions matter in world politics (Adler 1997b, 2002). Social constructivists have sought to understand the full array of systematic roles played by ideas, norms and values in world politics, rather than specifying *a priori* roles based on theoretical presuppositions and then testing for those specified roles. While neo-liberals study how institutions affect a state's behaviour, they do not think that institutions change a state's identity and interests. Constructivists, by contrast, want to know how norms constitute the identities and interests of international actors in particular cases (Katzenstein 1996a). When the aim is to find out whether and how a specific European security view has affected and affects national security identities, a social constructivist approach is thus the most natural choice.

While rationalists have been criticized for paying too much attention to agents, constructivists are now being criticized for putting too much emphasis on structure (Checkel 1999). Focusing on the impact of the EU on the security identities of nation-states, this study has a structural starting point that might leave it open to the same criticisms that many have directed at other social constructivist studies. But when the aim is to understand how the European integration process influences the security identity of a nation-state, there is no avoiding a structural approach. On the other hand, the focus on *how* nation-states comply with the community's security norms reduces the structural dominance (more on this in Chapter 3).

Let us now move from very this brief presentation of the meta-theoretical basis to the more concrete methodology to be applied in the following analysis. In social science it is always important to be explicit about the method that is used and the potential problems related to the approach chosen. This is particularly important with a social constructivist approach, since this approach has often been criticized for lacking an appropriate methodology to enable the conduct of fruitful empirical research.

Comparing speech acts

While it has been argued that 'methodology is the major missing link in constructivist theory and research' (Adler 2002: 109), this does not mean that constructivist analysts ignore the importance of method – but rather that no common methodological approach exists. In fact, social constructivist epistemology is situated at the crossroads of explaining and understanding (Hollis and Smith 1990). It does not reject causality, but has an interpretation of causality different from that of most neo-positivist researchers. Instead of studying what *x* causes *y*, these studies are more preoccupied with the *process* that leads to *y*. In this study, which focuses on the process of Europeanization of the nation-state's security identity, I will use a combination of comparative interpretative process-tracing case studies and a soft version of discourse analysis.

Interpretative case studies

Because of its flexibility, a case-study approach seems an appropriate design for a social constructivist study. However, this flexibility is also problematic, since it means that there is no universally accepted definition of a case study, and that this research approach can be misused as a catch-all research category for anything that is not a survey, an experiment or statistical in nature. Many qualitative researchers use the case-study approach as a guide to their investigations. By concentrating on a single phenomenon or entity, they seek to uncover the interaction of significant factors or characteristics of the phenomenon. In general, however, *any* phenomenon can be studied by case-study methods, whereas other qualitative research traditions, although compatible, are limited to a particular category of phenomena.

The epistemological orientation of constructivist case studies is *interpretative*. This means that knowledge is gained from a mode of inquiry not based on deduction and hypothesis- or theory-testing. In traditional qualitative research, the alternative to this method is an inductive, hypothesis- or theory-generating research. In this study, however, the interpretative case-study approach is understood as a strategy in which *the main objective is an in-depth understanding of the particular*. This is not to deny the existence of causal relationships and the possibilities for obtaining generalizable knowledge; however, they are not seen as ends in themselves. A case study is not undertaken primarily because the case represents other cases or because it illustrates a particular trait or problem, but because, in all its particularity and ordinariness, *this* case is of interest. The reason for studying the security identities of the Nordic states is therefore less because it is assumed to provide generalizable knowledge of Europeanization, and more because these cases are interesting in themselves due to their particular security policy traditions and relationships to the EU. This does not rule out the possibility of achieving greater insight into how the EU influences nation-state security identities in general, but it is not the main aim of the analysis.

The major challenge is how to assess the effects of EU's security identity on nation-state security identities. Alexander George (George 1979) delineated the process-tracing approach when attempting to trace the process by which norms, ideas and beliefs influence behaviour. Considerable research in the constructivist tradition has been devoted to process-tracing (Checkel 1998, 2001; Finnemore and Sikkink 1998). Amy Gurowitz states: 'the impact of international norms varies across time and place, and it is only through detailed process tracing that we can understand the matter' (quoted in Björkdahl 2002: 35). This indicates that such an approach might reveal the impact of the EU's security identity on the nation-state's security approaches and identity.

As interpretative research is inductive, it may be confusing to think of it as also starting from theory. However, since no study can be designed without some question being asked explicitly or implicitly, theory is present in all qualitative research. Theories are only used to structure the study in order to provide a starting point, and are often vaguely formulated. Still, they may take a firm shape in cases that normally are pieced together inductively (Ragin and Becker 1992). Towards the end of Chapter 3 a five-phase model for how the Europeanization process is expected to happen is presented. Even though this model will not structure the presentation in the following case studies which is based on a categorization revealed 'inductively' through the analysis of the collected empirical material and structured according to three main dimensions in the EU's security identity (the establishment of a political union, the development towards an ESDP and the development towards a comprehensive security identity), the five-phase model is discussed towards the end of each case study set out here.

Process-tracing and comparison

All research is concerned with producing valid and reliable knowledge, and constructivist case studies are no exception. Regardless of the type of research, validity and reliability are concerns that can be approached through careful attention to a study's conceptualization and the way in which the data are collected, analysed and interpreted. *Reliability* refers to the extent to which the research, if studied repeatedly, will yield the same results; *validity* concerns how one's findings match reality (internal validity) and to what extent the findings of one study can be applied to other situations (external validity). If an in-depth *understanding* of the phenomenon under study is the primary rationale for the investigation, the criteria for trusting the study is somewhat different than if the objective is to discover a law or test a hypothesis. Obviously, reliability and validity are problematic for researchers who do not share the assumption that there exists a single and objective reality, and who instead view reality as a social construction.

One way of resolving the (internal) validity question is to reject objectivity as a validity criterion and focus instead on interpretative validity. This can be variously determined by factors such as usefulness (the extent to which a case study is enlightening or liberating); contextual completeness (in which comprehensiveness is a standard of credibility); the researcher's positioning (a demonstrated sensitivity by the researcher to how he or she relates to the case at hand); the reporting style (the ability to reconstruct the participants' reality credibly and authentically); triangulation (the use of multiple data-collection methods, sources, analyses or theories to check validity); member checking (the corroboration of data by participants in the case study); chain of evidence (meaningful links between research questions, raw data and findings); outlier analysis (the use of exceptions to test and strengthen the basic findings); pattern-matching (the extent to which patterns discovered in case-study data correspond to predictions from a predetermined set of theoretical propositions); long-term observation (collecting data over a long period, with repeated observations of the phenomenon); and representativeness check (the extent to which a finding is typical of the field site from which it is obtained) (Merriam 1998). But even with such factors in focus, this book does not escape some general methodological difficulties involved in examining processes of Europeanization. How can we control for the fact that different independent variables might lead to the same result on the dependent variable? It is a difficult challenge to isolate the effects of Europeanization from other internal or external dynamics. In order to cope with this problem this book seeks to identify the independent impact of the integration process by process-tracing and by carefully examining the temporal order of various changes.

The external validity concern is even more problematic for social constructivist studies. In fact, interpretative case studies are often understood to be studies that do not aim at contributing to empirical generalizations, and hence have no value in theory-building (Lijphart 1971: 692). Since it is the understanding of the complexity and the uniqueness of the case(s) that is of importance, many qualitative researchers also consider the search for general knowledge inappropriate. However, generalizability is often reframed to reflect the assumptions underlying interpretative inquiry, and is seen as a process arrived at by recognizing similarities of objects and issues in and out of context and by sensing the natural co-variations of events. To enhance the possibility of generalizing from an interpretative case study, the investigator must either provide a detailed description of the context of the study or incorporate a comparative dimension.

Even though obtaining generalizable knowledge for theory-testing is not the main aim of this study, a comparative case study might enhance the possibilities of obtaining some insights of general value. Studying several cases along the same lines increases the potential for generalizing beyond the particular case without losing the complexity or the in-depth understanding of the cases. While a single case study often samples from sub-units (people, events or documents) within the case in collecting data, a multiple case study involves collecting and analysing data from several cases. Each case in such a study is first treated as a comprehensive case in and of itself. Data are gathered to provide as much information as possible about the contextual variables that have a bearing on the case. By comparing cases, one can establish the range of generality of a finding or explanation/understanding, and at the same time, pin down the condition under which that finding will occur. A qualitative, inductive and multiple case study, as undertaken in this book, seeks to build generalizations *across cases*. This means that the aim is to build a general explanation that fits each of the individual cases, even though the cases will vary in their details. The researcher attempts to see processes and outcomes that occur across many cases or sites, and to understand how such processes are affected by specific contextual variables.

In discussing comparative case studies, Alexander George notes that taking account of the unique aspects of individual cases forces the investigator to develop more comprehensive theory – the uniqueness of the explanation is recognized but it is described in more general terms, as a particular value of a general variable that is part of a theoretical framework (George 1979: 47). This means that the difference between a-theoretical and more theoretical grounded studies may be less clear in comparative case studies, since a systematic comparison often leads to a focus on some central variables and the connection between them. In this book, the nation-state's security identity from the Cold War period constitutes the starting point for each case study. Next, the impact of three dimensions of the EU's security identity – the establishment of a political union, the ESDP process and the development of a comprehensive security approach – are investigated. Each case study concludes with a discussion of the character and degree of the Europeanization process; the main findings are analysed and we ask how the case fits into the five-phase socialization model presented in Chapter 3.

Even though external validity is frequently seen as the ultimate aim of good research, and the added value of using comparative case studies is precisely that it increases the chances of obtaining generalizable knowledge, some will argue that generalization across cases should be discarded, and that causes instead should be identified within each case, without any presumptions of generality and applicability across cases. The added value of comparative studies should rather be that they make it easier to identify *possible causes*. The actual causes must then be identified empirically on the basis of studies of each case. In accordance with this view, interpretation of meanings and causal explanation must be the main goals of social science, and the added value of comparative studies is only that such studies make it easier to construct better interpretations and causal explanations (Sundstøl 2002).

In my view, however, a descriptive display of data from multiple sites or cases can make it possible to advance to higher levels of analysis. This makes it more than a unified description across cases; it can build categories, themes or typologies that conceptualize the data from all the cases, or lead to the construction of substantive theory that offers an integrated framework covering multiple cases. The choice of studying the Nordic countries in the 1990s also avoids the problems associated with comparing observations within different system frames. It is often argued that in order to be able to produce results as valid and reliable as possible, one has to choose comparable cases, and, according to Ragin, the major criterion for comparability is that the cases are limited in both time and place (Ragin 1987).

A 'soft' version of discourse analysis

A comparative case-study approach based on process-tracing is appropriate for studying the topic of this book. But this research design can only provide an overall framework for the analysis. It gives few indications as to how to collect and analyse data, and there are various ways of actually pursuing such a study. In this book I apply a soft version of discourse analysis. *Soft* is then distinct from the version used by scholars who argue that intersubjective meaning *cannot* be apprehended in or by itself, and that it is constituted by language (Larsen 1997; Neumann 2001a).

Thus, I will argue that discourse analysis is an appropriate approach for identifying the dominant security discourse that expresses collective identities. Discourse analysis can show which values and elements of identity are basic to a society's self-perception and which values and elements of identity are significant in a given context (Boekle *et al.* 2001: 8). This means that a discursive approach stresses frameworks of meaning and defines the range of possible policy options. In this book the dominant security discourse expressed by a nation-state's political leadership is seen as an expression of the security identity of that country. In order to identify possible changes in the security identities of the Nordic states in the post-Cold War period, it is therefore not sufficient to study policy outcomes alone. It is through the language or speech acts of the securitizing actors that we can decode the security identity of the nation-state in question.

Making empirical claims about identity is always difficult. Identity is an intersubjective concept that is manifested in group consciousness. It is not a material entity that easily can be measured by quantitative standards. It is therefore difficult to argue that a particular actor has a certain identity. Moreover, unlike material-based variables, intersubjective ones are essentially constitutive rather than causal. That is they do not cause behaviour, but instead influence action by helping to define social situations and the nature and quality of the actors with whom individuals come into contact. This makes it difficult to assign a direct link between the identity of the actors and their political preferences. Another question is how strong an identity has to be before it produces change in attitude and behaviour. Recognizing these potential problems, we must rely on systematic observation and interpretation. There are at least two ways to determine, in any given case, whether a group identity exists and whether this identity affects subsequent political choices (Cronin 1999).

First, one can examine the *nature of discourse* that characterizes the interactions among specified political actors. As Carlsnaes argues:

> ideas do not simply reflect policy processes [but] are constitutive of the latter, since they are used, invoked and elaborated upon by individuals in a given time and space in order to make actions intelligible and decisions authoritative. It is in this sense that they play such a central role in the analysis of change, and why a discursive focus is deemed essential to it.
>
> (Carlsnaes 1993a: 28)

The surest sign of identity change and socialization is the development of a *new vocabulary* in terms of which the identity can then be publicly articulated. This means that a researcher studying changes in security identity should look for consistent patterns in the way the actors define security threats and instruments of security policy. Some have argued that discourses and ideas mask deeper material interests (Krasner 1993). While this may be true in some cases, it does not refute the idea that the dominant national security discourse will give an indication of a nation-state's security identity. As Bruce Cronin has put it: 'assuming that an actor's words reflect her or his true intentions is no more presumptuous than divining what her true "deeper interests" really are' (Cronin 1999: 16).

A second, or rather complementary, method for determining the existence and constitutive power of a given social identity is through analysis and interpretation of *individual and group behaviour*. The researcher then seeks to determine if the actors behave in a manner consistent with their identities in circumstances where they would be expected to do so. This approach raises the problem of causation mentioned above. How can we know that a particular action or behaviour is the result of one's identity, and not of some other variable? For instance, how can we know that a change in national security policy is the result of a change in identity (learning through socialization) and not of other 'material' factors such as national economy, domestic politics or international agreements (adaptation)? Cronin proposes one way of attacking the problem: to stipulate in advance what actions we should expect an actor to take (1999: 16).

In this book I apply a combination of these two methods. First, I study dominant security discourse in order to find out whether a new vocabulary has been introduced. Second, I investigate a set of assumptions for the expected changes in the security approaches and identities of the Nordic countries, which will determine whether the changes in the discourse can be identified as instrumental adaptation or identity changes. The assumptions are developed on the basis of a five-phase socialization model presented towards the end of Chapter 3.

Sources

The analysis in this book builds on various sources. First of all it relies on official documents and speeches produced by the European Commission, the European Council and the Council in the EU, and the political leadership in each country.

As it is the government that normally defines national security policy, a study of the government's discourse over a decade should give us a good idea of developments in the security identities of these countries. However, what is not obvious is which part of the government expresses the dominant security discourse. This book applies a broad approach to security, focusing on speech acts, with no distinction between a nation-state's foreign policy discourse, its security policy discourse, and its defence policy discourse. What interests us here is what issues are being securitized or desecuritized in the discourse, regardless of what policy they are considered to be part of.

But since this book seeks to identify the nation-state security identity through the dominant discourse, I have to clarify what part of the government is the most likely to express this particular discourse. In fact, the choice of documents will have major implications for the results of the study, since the security discourse undertaken by officials in the ministries of foreign affairs, for instance, is likely to be different from that of officials in the ministries of defence (Andersen 2000). Traditionally, foreign policy and security policy have been the responsibility of the ministries of foreign affairs, while defence policy has been the responsibility of the ministry of defence (Skogan 2001). In general, defence policy was considered as one (and the most important) instrument of security policy. This is changing, with security and defence policy more interlinked than before. This has resulted in the creation of security policy departments in most defence ministries, and greater importance being given to other security policy tools. In turn, this has led to an ongoing debate concerning who defines a nation-state's security policy (Andersen 2000).

Since the ministries of foreign affairs have long experience in a broad approach to conflict prevention and security-building through various foreign policy instruments, it is only natural that the incorporation of a comprehensive discourse also in the security field is most easily introduced here.

For the ministries of defence this is a totally new dimension, and thus also more difficult to incorporate. However, this does not mean that these ministries have been more conservative in every respect. In fact, these ministries have tended to be in the forefront (also compared to the ministries of foreign affairs) when it comes to the modernization of the military instrument – direct experiences from various military operations throughout the 1990s being of importance here (Frantzen 2003). Still, the military have paid less attention to the civilian dimension and the need for developing a comprehensive security approach in relation to both external and internal (domestic) security. The concept of CIMIC (Civil–Military Co-operation) has been introduced, but this is often seen an additional task and not given top priority (Jakobsen, forthcoming).

In addition, CIMIC is understood in various ways. The concept was first introduced by NATO in 1997, but has a different interpretations in the UN and yet another at the national level. While the NATO definition gives priority to military operations,[17] the UN emphasizes CIMIC as a mechanism for creating a common understanding and approach.[18] Thus, while CIMIC in NATO is seen as a *means* to achieve a clearly defined goal, it in the UN perceived as an *end* in itself in order to achieve a common goal. There is also a third use of the concept, related to the total defence concept and linked to national defence (Jensen 2003: 3–10). In this book we will in general use the concept of *comprehensive security* and distinguish between internal and external security in this respect. This concept defined above (pp. 8–9) is most closely linked to the definition used by the UN. CIMIC is seen as a move towards a comprehensive security approach, and is referred to only when the concept is used in the official documents studied.

It is in the official statements made by the ministries of defence that one can identify a nation-state's *dominant* security discourse or nation-state security identity. This is based on the assumption that it is the ministries of defence that are expected to be among the last institutions to incorporate a totally new security thinking – a thinking that also involves other security policy tools than the military. While alterations in the discourse undertaken by other parts of the political leadership may indicate the beginning of a change, it is not until the discourse within the ministries of defence has changed that it is possible to claim that a nation-state has reached the final stages in the socialization process, which is characterized by a change in identity.[19]

In addition to official documents, a series of interviews were conducted in the four countries and in Brussels. In the four countries, officials in the ministries of foreign affairs and of defence were interviewed. In Brussels, interviews were undertaken in the four national delegations to the EU and NATO, and in the EU with officials working for the European Commission and the Council. The interviews, conducted between April 2001 and June 2002, have been systematically used as background information for better understanding the security thinking in both the EU and in each of the four Nordic states.

Secondary sources in forms of relevant books, journal articles and newspapers articles have also been carefully studied, and have provided the necessary background information and understanding of security thinking in the EU and in the Nordic countries. Two-week research visits to each country as a guest researcher at the research institute for international affairs of each of the countries (UI in Stockholm, UPI in Helsinki and DUPI in Copenhagen) have also been very useful for understanding the broader cultural setting in which to analyse the primary sources.

The structure of the book

The aim of this book is to investigate how and to what extent changes in the dominant national security approaches and identities in the Nordic area can be understood as the result of a *process of Europeanization*. The first step must therefore be to identify the European security identity. Chapter 2 sets about this through a study of official publications and speeches by EU officials, and second, asks to what extent the ideas inherent in this discourse have been transformed into concrete policy.

Chapter 3 presents a model for investigating how this EU approach may be expected to influence the security approaches and identities of both member states and states that are closely linked to the EU. The Europeanization process is understood here as a process of socialization and learning, in terms of which a five-phase socialization model is presented. Five assumptions, to be investigated in the ensuing chapters, are formulated towards the end of Chapter 3.

In the following four chapters (Chapters 4–7) developments in the Swedish, Finnish, Danish and Norwegian security discourses from 1990 to December 2004 are analysed. Towards the end of each chapter the model presented in Chapter 3 is applied in order to see whether it is possible to speak of a 'Europeanization' of the security identities of these four Nordic countries. The case studies are presented in the order indicated above, starting with Sweden and Finland, both of which became members in 1995, followed by Denmark, a member since 1973 but with a special status since 1993 due to its 'opt-outs', and ending with Norway, which rejected membership in 1994 but has developed a close relationship to the Union in the years after the referendum.

In the final chapter (Chapter 8) some comparative considerations are presented, the main findings are summarized, and some possible implications for further research are discussed.

2

THE EU

A comprehensive security actor

While security has always been the main reason behind the integration process in Europe, and few would question the link between integration and security, the two have usually been studied as separate topics. Integration specialists have paid more attention to the economy than to the security aspect, and security experts have studied traditional security institutions and generally overlooked the EU. In this chapter, I combine these two theory traditions, to show both how the European Union has become a security actor, and how it functions.

It is not in fact immediately apparent whether the EU *is* an actor, and there is in European integration theory a large literature that discusses precisely that question. For a long time the main opposition stood between those who perceived European integration as solely an arena for inter-governmental bargaining, and those who saw it as a continuous process towards a supranational state.[1] Today, this debate has become less dominant in the integration literature, and most scholars agree that the EU should be characterized as something in between an international organization and a federal state. The consequence of this compromise has been that 'the study of the EU has, to a large extent, shifted from the study of integration to the study of governance (. . .) defined as being about the exercise of authority with or without the formal institutions of government' (Rosamond 2000: 109). Thus, more emphasis is put on the complexity of Euro-policy – on how the EU functions as an actor in various policy areas – and concepts like 'multi-level governance'[2] and 'policy communities' have been introduced for this purpose. This complexity of decision-making and competences also indicates a special kind of 'actorness', with behaviour varying according to the policy area in question.

In order to understand how the EU functions as a security actor, I have chosen to draw on Adler and Barnett's interpretation of Karl Deutsch's classic concept of pluralistic security communities (Adler and Barnett 1998). While Deutsch understood integration as the creation of security communities among states in a region without formal statehood, Adler and Barnett's concept of *tightly coupled* pluralistic security communities captures the EU's special kind of 'actorness', characterized by a high level of political integration without being a federation.

The literature on the EC/EU's security dimension can be divided into four groups. The first discusses whether or not the EC/EU needs military capabilities (Duchêne 1972, 1973; Bull 1982; Hill 1993; Lodge 1993; Whitmann 1998; Zielonka 1998; Maull 2000; Smith 2000; Duchêne 2002). The second group tends to focus exclusively on second-pillar issues – the CFSP and the ESDP – when referring to the EU's security dimension (Lodge and Flynn 1998; Peterson and Sjursen 1998; Duke 2000; Heisbourg 2000; Howorth 2000; Kupchan 2000; Larsen 2002b; Youngs 2002; Smith 2004). A third group consists of those who focus on EU's foreign policy, or first-pillar issues (external relations). While some of these scholars seem to reject or at least downplay the need for a military dimension (Smith 1999; Smith 2002; Smith 2003) others have a more holitistic approach (White 2001; Ginsberg 2001; Krahmann 2003). A final group of scholars is more interested in understanding the normative basis of the EU's foreign and security policy (Ehrhart 2001; Manners 2002) or the driving forces behind it (Sjursen 2001a; Aggestam 2004; Sjursen 2004).

While there are important differences between the groups mentioned above, they all tend to focus exclusively on the *external dimension* of the Union's security approach. The analysis in this book has a somewhat different approach. By drawing on a broader concept of security, it is more open to what security is all about. The EU as a tightly coupled security community[3] actor is understood as a securitizing actor that defines threats and appropriate security policy tools. Thus, the analysis is not limited to one specific policy area, and as we shall see in this chapter, the EU may be characterized as a *comprehensive security actor*.

This chapter is divided into three main parts. First, I discuss the relationship between security and integration in general, and the EU as a tightly coupled security community in particular. Second, I show the phases through which this security community has passed. Finally, I discuss the EU's security approach both in discourse and in practice.

Security and integration

Viewing integration as a possible security system points to the importance of overcoming the sub-disciplinary separation between integration theory and security studies. The reason why few scholars have referred to European integration as a security system or security actor is perhaps, as Ole Wæver (1997) has argued, that in contrast to traditional security systems such as collective security and collective defence, it does not fit the model of 'sovereign equality'. Wæver claims that an emerging European post-sovereign security system includes the EU as neither state nor international organization. Regions of various kinds and non-members relate to the EU, not as to an external, imperial threat but because they see the EU as holding some legitimacy on behalf of Europe and also in relation to themselves as not (yet) members. This system of overlapping authorities, asymmetries and non-like units naturally produces security in ways that deviate from classical security models (ibid.: 23–4).

While one might talk about the European region as a 'heterogeneous security complex', the EU can be characterized as a tightly coupled security community (Adler and Barnett 1998: 56–7). As we shall see in this chapter, it is possible to claim that this tightly coupled security community is increasingly becoming a securitizing (or perhaps rather a desecuritizing) actor with referent objects varying according to sector (see endnote 9, p. 194).

Europe as a heterogeneous regional security complex

Since insecurity is often associated with proximity, the regional level seems appropriate for security analyses. It is for that reason Barry Buzan (1991) has developed the concept of 'regional security complexes'. The main assumption of this first (and rather traditional) version of regional security complex theory is that, although the great powers may form a kind of global security complex amongst themselves, taking the whole planet as their region, lesser states usually find themselves locked into a regional security complex with their neighbours. According to Buzan (1991: 197), such a regional security complex may exist in four different forms:

1   A *'normal' complex* characterized by a regional pattern of power rivalry;
2   A situation where great-power interests dominate a region so heavily that the local pattern of security relations virtually ceases to operate (*overlay*);
3   *Centralization* of power in a region to the point where it is primarily to be seen as an actor in the global security constellation among the greatest powers;
4   A situation characterized by *a low level of security interdependence*, where the local states have domestically directed security perspectives, and where there are not enough security interactions between them to generate a local complex.

Since neither a security complex characterized by overlay (a renewed 'Cold War situation') nor one characterized by a low level of security interdependence is currently likely to evolve in Europe, it is the European integration process that will determine which of the two other European patterns (integration or fragmentation) will unfold. Following this logic, the EU becomes the most important security institution in Europe (Wæver 1997: 16). As Buzan *et al.* point out:

Regional integration will eliminate a security complex with which it

25

is coextensive by transforming it from an anarchic subsystem of states to a single, larger actor within the system. Regional integration among some members of that complex will transform the power structure of that complex.

(Buzan *et al.* 1998: 12)

In this book Buzan and his associates move beyond classical security complex theory by introducing a less state-centred version of the theory (ibid.: 201). The more general concept of 'unit' is used instead of 'state', and instead of looking at the interdependence of security interests they study the interdependence of processes of securitization/desecuritization. This means that the analysis is not reduced to only the political and military sectors. Whereas classical security complex theory addressed this issue simply in terms of patterns of amity and enmity, Buzan *et al.* take an explicitly constructivist approach in order to understand the process by which issues become securitized or desecuritized. Following this logic, integration is important not only in order to prevent the re-emergence of a European security complex characterized by balance-of-power behaviour between the European states, but also because it provides a framework for handling the new security challenges.

Buzan *et al.* (1998) distinguish two ways of moving beyond classical security complex theory. The first is by introducing what they call *homogeneous complexes*. A homogeneous complex theory retains the 'classical' assumption that security complexes are concentrated within specific sectors and are therefore composed of specific forms of interaction among similar types of units. This logic leads to different types of complexes that occur in different sectors; thus, while military complexes are made up predominantly of states, societal complexes consist of various identity-based units and the like. The second way of opening up the analysis is to introduce *heterogeneous complexes*. Heterogeneous complex theory abandons the assumption that security complexes are locked into specific sectors; instead, it assumes that the regional logic can integrate different types of actors interacting across two or more sectors. While homogeneous security complex analysis offers the possibility of isolating sector-specific security dynamics, heterogeneous complex analysis has the advantage of linking actors across sectors, thus enabling the analyst to keep the entire picture within a single frame, as well as keeping track of the inevitable spillovers between sectors such as the military, the environmental, the societal and the political. With its multiple actors and threats, post-Cold War Europe will here be characterized as such a heterogeneous security complex.

The most important characteristic of this security complex is the European integration process. The close links that have developed between the members of the European Community/Union since the beginning of the integration process seem to have many of the characteristics of what the recent literature on security communities refers to as a 'tightly coupled security community'. Such a security community is the result of political and economic integration and pooled sovereignty, and represents, in my view, a useful perspective from which to understand the security mechanisms of the EU.

The EU as a tightly coupled security community

According to Deutsch, 'security communities' arise out of a process of regional integration characterized by the development of transaction flows, shared understandings and transnational values (Deutsch 1957: 58). These transaction flows involve the regular, institutionalized interaction of not only national governments but also members of civil society. In Deutsch's view, this interaction leads to dependable expectations of peaceful change, where states believe that disputes among members of the community will not be settled by force. Security communities, however, are not defined merely by the absence of war. They are also characterized by what Deutsch has called a 'we-feeling', or shared identity. As states move toward community, they no longer need to rely on balance-of-power mechanisms to protect their security. In such a community, states focus on assurance rather than on deterrence. Collective security, joint military planning and integration, unfortified borders, free movement of people across borders and common definitions of both external and internal threats – these are all hallmarks of security communities.

Deutsch distinguishes between security communities that are 'amalgamated' and those that are 'pluralistic'. An amalgamated community implies that two or more states formally merge into an expanded state; a pluralistic security community involves integration between independent states to the point where they entertain 'dependable' expectations of peaceful change. A pluralistic security community develops when its members possess a compatibility of core values derived from common institutions and mutual responsiveness – a matter of mutual identity and loyalty, a sense of 'we-ness', or a 'we-feeling' among states (ibid.: 5–7). Despite its theoretical potential, Deutsch's 'security community' has not been seen as an important theoretical contribution either to the history of security studies or to integration theory (McSweeney 1999: 47). To recent scholars of security studies it has proven more attractive for its label than substance, and as a theory of integration it has been overtaken by the advent of neo-functionalism.

The cornerstone of neo-functionalism and the basis of its theory of security is the idea that co-operation in technical and economic areas will eventually spill over into high politics (foreign and defence policy) (Haas 1958). The novel, and contended, part of the neo-functionalist model is that the need to initiate and sustain co-operation can be managed and controlled by non-state actors, and that states are forced by the spillover mechanism to acquiesce in the pooling of sovereignty and the practice of co-operation. Even though neo-functionalism has been widely criticized, especially because neither states nor their polities have shown themselves to be willing puppets in the roles assigned to them by neo-functionalists, it still remains 'the sole attempt to fashion a coherent and comprehensive theory of European integration' (Sæter 1998: 11). While there is little doubt that neo-functionalism remains the major contribution to the conceptualization of how and why states pursue integration, it still does not give any precise explanation of how this integration process functions as a security system.

Even though Deutsch's 'security community' has been overshadowed by neo-functionalism as a theory of integration, the concept of 'pluralistic security communities' has recently made a constructivist comeback that may be useful for understanding the security dynamics of the EU. In an article published in 1997, Emanuel Adler argues that such communities are 'socially constructed "cognitive regions" or "community-regions" whose people imagine that, with respect to their own security and economic well-being, borders run, more or less, where shared understandings and common identities end' (Adler 1997a: 250). In other words, security communities rest on shared practical awareness of the peaceful resolution of conflicts and are socially constructed because shared meanings, constituted by interaction, engender collective identities.

According to Adler, a constructivist approach is helpful in identifying this phenomenon, as well as in discerning the many 'strong' multilateral institutional attributes, processes and consequences that might otherwise escape attention. Shifting the focus of security studies away from states and towards transnational social, political, economic, ecological and moral forces, Adler finds that the concept of pluralistic communities, coupled with a constructivist approach, offers a way to re-order our thinking about international security in the post-Cold War period (ibid.: 276). Once established, a community is based on an 'inside-out model', where states see their interests as best served by being inside the community (Adler and Barnett 1998: 119). Security is no longer defined exclusively as the protection of sovereign national borders from military threat: rather, security is achieved through the benefits accrued from participating in a 'mature security community'.

According to Adler and Barnett, a mature security community develops through three phases. In the initial (*nascent*) phase, governments do not explicitly seek to create a security community, but instead begin to consider how they might co-ordinate their relations in order to increase mutual security. The second (*ascendant*) phase is characterized by the establishment of new institutions and organizations, reflecting both a tighter military co-ordination and a decreased fear that the 'other' represents a threat. In turn, these networks result in cognitive structures that deepen the level of mutual trust and lead to the emergence of collective identities. In sum, this second phase is defined by an intensive and extensive network pattern between states that is likely to be produced by, and be a product of, various international institutions and organizations. A core state, or a coalition of states, remains important for stabilizing and encouraging the further development of the security community. Finally, in the third (*mature*) phase, it becomes increasingly difficult for the members of this 'region' to think solely in instrumental ways and/or to prepare for war against one another (ibid.: 50–8). The emergence of such a community can be found in various indicators that reflect a high degree of trust, a shared identity and a common vision of the future. It is also important that there be low or no probability that conflicts will lead to military encounters, and that there be a clear differentiation between those within and those outside the security community.

While these indicators represent the conditions for a mature security community to emerge, Adler and Barnett also distinguish between two ideal types of pluralistic security communities: 'loosely coupled' and 'tightly coupled' (ibid.: 56–7). The former observes the minimal definitional properties – a transnational region made up of sovereign states whose people maintain dependable expectations of peaceful change, whereas the latter type is more demanding in two respects. First, it constructs collective security system arrangements. Second, it possesses a system of rules somewhere between a sovereign state and a regional, centralized government, which means a post-sovereign system endowed with common supranational, transnational and national institutions. According to this definition, the transatlantic community (NATO) should be characterized as a loosely coupled security community, while the EU is a tightly coupled one, especially now that its CFSP is becoming increasingly institutionalized. The OSCE cannot yet qualify as a mature security community, but since it is important in contributing to the development of regional security communities it might be characterized as a 'security community-building institution'.

The concept of a 'tightly coupled security community' is interesting in relation to the integration process, since it takes into account the special character of the Union as something more than an international organization but less than a supranational federation. This means that the EU can be characterized as a 'pluralistic security community' combined with a dimension of 'tight' political co-operation/integration without becoming an amalgamated security community à la Deutsch. This special institutional character combined with a comprehensive security approach, covering both internal and external security mechanisms, also gives it an unique *atout* for the practical realization of a vision of 'holistic' or comprehensive security policy (Pastore 2001: 20).

Ole Wæver, however, has claimed that the three phases that Adler and Barnett identify in the introduction to their edited volume, *Security Communities*, do not fully correspond with the history of the European integration process (Wæver 1998: 91). Instead, he understands the achievement of a security community as happening through a process of *desecuritization*

(Wæver 1998, 2000). While it is true that these phases cannot capture all the specificities of the integration process, they might still be helpful for showing how European integration has developed into a tightly coupled security community. There are many ways of presenting the history of European integration, and each approach emphasizes different aspects of this process. The added value of presenting it as a process towards a tightly coupled security community is that it highlights some interesting aspects related to the EU as a security actor, aspects that take into account both the special institutional character of the Union and its comprehensive focus. First, the integration process in itself contributes to security and stability by binding current and future member states more closely together. Second, the level of political integration over a range of different policy areas makes it possible to talk about the EU as an active and comprehensive security actor. Here we should note that this framework is not necessarily in contradiction with Ole Wæver's processes of securitization and desecuritization. In fact, the two are complementary in the sense that the security community framework can account for the EU as a security actor, and the other helps us in identifying what this actor considers to be a question of security.

It is this special character of the Union that makes traditional approaches inadequate for providing an accurate explanation of how the EU functions as a security actor. The reason is that the development of a security community leads to a new form of post-sovereign security thinking difficult to grasp through traditional approaches. As Wæver claims:

> Without war, security becomes much more complex, and the identities built on this kind of security pose challenges not only to security analysis but generally to international relations theory, unprepared as it still largely is for structured thinking about post-sovereign politics.
>
> (Wæver 1998: 105–6)

The problem with most of the literature is precisely that it studies the EU without taking into account this special character of the Union.[4] This, combined with the fact that a traditional definition of security is often used, explains why most studies on integration and security have been limited to the second pillar, or the Common Foreign and Security Policy (Hill 1993; Duff 1994; Eekelen 1998; Peterson and Sjursen 1998; Bretherton and Vogler 1999; Soetendorp 1999; Bertelsmann Foundation 2000; Duke 2000; Wallace and Forster 2000; Larsen 2002b). After the St Malo process many studies have become even more specialized, focusing on the recent development towards a common ESDP (Lodge and Flynn 1998; Duke 2000; Heisbourg 2000; Howorth 2000; Kupchan 2000; Larsen 2002b; Youngs 2002).

This chapter seeks to provide an alternative understanding of the EU as a security actor. By identifying the dominant security discourse expressed by various EU officials, this analysis is more open to what the EU considers to be a security issue, and thus seems better suited to capture the Union's 'real' security approach.

In the next section we will explore how the EU has developed into a tightly coupled security community. In my view, this process has gone through all three of the phases identified by Adler and Barnett, but it is the second phase that is most important. The first phase is the one during which the heads of the European states and governments considered how to increase their mutual security, and corresponds to the first years after the Second World War. The second phase is characterized by institution-building and the development of a collective identity, and corresponds to the integration process during the Cold War. The last period is characterized by a mature security community and corresponds to the period after the end of the Cold War. With the Maastricht Treaty and the establishment of a political union, this mature *European security community* can now be characterized as *tightly coupled*.

Towards a tightly coupled security community

Increasing mutual security between European states

The initial or 'nascent' phase in the development of a security community is characterized by considerations by heads of states and governments in a specific region concerning how they might co-ordinate their relations in order to increase their mutual security (Adler and Barnett 1998: 50).

This first phase corresponds well with the situation in Western Europe during the first years after the Second World War. This period saw several initiatives and consultations between the European states, motivated by mutual and common security concerns aiming at avoiding another war. From 1945 to 1949 the Western European countries and their North American allies viewed with concern the expansionist politics and methods of the USSR. Having fulfilled their own wartime undertakings to reduce their defence establishments and to demobilize forces, Western governments became increasingly alarmed as it became clear that the Soviet leadership intended to maintain its own military forces at full strength.

Moreover, in view of the declared ideological aims of the Soviet Communist Party, it was evident that appeals for respect for the United Nations Charter, and for respect for the international settlements reached at the end of the war, would not guarantee the national sovereignty or independence of democratic states faced with the threat of outside aggression or internal subversion. The imposition of non-democratic forms of government and the repression of effective opposition and of basic human and civic rights and freedoms in many Central and Eastern European countries, as well as elsewhere in the world, added to these fears. Between 1947 and 1949 a series of dramatic political events[5] brought matters to a head, and led to discussions between the Western European states on how to increase security in Europe.

The first result of these discussions led to the signing of the Brussels Treaty in March 1948. This initiative marked the determination of five Western European countries (Belgium, France, Luxembourg, the Netherlands and the United Kingdom) to develop a common defence system and to strengthen their mutual ties in a manner which would enable them to resist ideological, political and military threats to their security. As the first step in the post-war reconstruction of Western European security, the Brussels Treaty brought into being the Western Union and the Brussels Treaty Organization.

The next step in this post-war period came with negotiations with the United States and Canada regarding the creation of a single North Atlantic Alliance based on security guarantees and mutual commitments between Europe and North America. Denmark, Iceland, Italy, Norway and Portugal were invited by the Brussels Treaty powers to become participants in this process, and negotiations culminated in the signature of the Treaty of Washington in April 1949. This important treaty brought into being a collective security system based on partnership among its member countries[6] (NATO 1998).

In summary, this first part of the post-war period was characterized by several initiatives, European and transatlantic, aimed at increasing the security of Western Europe. As such it can be seen as constituting the first phase in a security community-building process. In the next phase this process is taken one step further, leading to the emergence of new institutional structures.

Institution-building and the development of a common identity

According to Adler and Barnett, this second or 'ascendant' phase in the development of a security community is characterized by the establishment of new institutions and organizations that reflect a tighter military co-ordination, the existence of a core state or a coalition of states that remains important for stabilizing and encouraging the further development of the security community, decreased fear that the 'other' represents a threat, and the emergence of a collective identity (Adler and Barnett 1998: 53).

In Europe this phase was less a question of reducing the threat among the member states (already basically non-existent due to the bipolar structure of the international system that had unified the Western European states in the face of a common external threat), and more one of deepening the level of political co-operation through the establishment of institutions and organizations and the emergence of a collective identity. However, the importance of the 'German question' must not be ignored. With the prospect of Germany returning to the scene, the answer both in Germany and among the American and European countries was one of *Einbindung* into NATO as well as to the European integration process (Wæver 1998: 82). In the following I will take a closer look at some aspects of the integration process that seem to indicate the existence of an 'ascendant' security community: the first integration initiatives, the role of France and Germany and the emergence of a collective European identity.[7]

The first integration initiatives

While the first phase in the security community-building process involved consultations among the European states concerning how to increase European security, this second period was characterized by the establishment of common agreements and institutions. The Atlantic Treaty was the most obvious result of this first phase, but the Brussels Treaty shows that even at this stage there were independent European approaches to integration. Since France was the European country most in favour of such approaches, it was not surprising that the first initiatives for European integration were also promoted by France. The very first of these was announced on 9 May 1950, when the French Foreign Minister, Robert Schuman, proposed the establishment of a European community for coal and steel. This initiative led to the signing of the Paris Agreement in 1951, resulting in the establishment of the European Coal and Steel Community (ECSC). The so-called Schuman Plan marked the beginning of the European integration process; its main intention was to prevent renewed Franco–German hostility. The ECSC aimed not only at an economic community but also at an eventual political union, based on a far more intensive set of mutual commitments. Such commitments would imply an institutional system where collective interest, as well as majority voting, would be adopted as the norm. The fact that the ECSC was originally intended as part of a more comprehensive federal community with common military forces and a political union explains the second important initiative for further European integration, proposed on 24 October 1950 by the French Minister of Defence, René Pleven, concerning the establishment of a European army – the European Defence Community (EDC).

This initiative came as a reaction to the American idea of re-establishing a West German army. Since the French were not yet psychologically ready for this, the Pleven Plan proposed a European army in order to reduce the perceived danger involved in the creation of West German forces (Duval 1996). This army was intended to be placed under the command of a European defence minister, who would get his mandate from a common decision taken by the participating governments and would be responsible to a European assembly. While member states with national armies were expected to put parts of these under the common European command, Western Germany should do so with whatever forces it finally established. Including these forces under a common European structure was meant to prevent the creation of an independent national West German army; and as such was a clear alternative to the US Secretary of State's idea of bringing Western Germany into an integrated[8] transatlantic alliance. This, combined with French scepticism towards such a US-dominated integrated military structure, led to the French proposal for an independent European army. This initiative was not made in competition with NATO, but it aimed at creating a more balanced transatlantic alliance between an integrated Europe and the USA (Sæter 1971: 240).

When the French understood that the other allies were less ambitious about the EDC, French parliamentarians answered by rejecting it in 1954.[9] As an alternative, the Brussels Treaty countries, together with Western Germany and Italy, went on to establish the Western European Union (WEU) in 1955. However, little attention was paid to this organization at the time, and European defence integration was brought to a halt.[10] With traditional security policy excluded from the European integration process, economic integration through a common market and customs union came to head the agenda. While NATO created the common framework for the Six in security and defence policy, the European integration process continued with the establishment of the European Economic Community (EEC) and the European Atomic Energy Community (Euratom) in 1957.

The role of France and Germany

Another feature of this second phase in the development towards a mature security community is the existence of a core state or a coalition of states that can stabilize and encourage the further development of the security community (Adler and Barnett 1998: 532). In the beginning of the integration process France was such a country: contrary to what is often believed, even Charles de Gaulle (1958–69) supported the initial integration initiatives. The reason for this common misunderstanding concerning de Gaulle is that he strongly opposed any sector-based federal integration process that would not include foreign and security policy. In order to prevent such a development, which in his opinion would lead to an undesirable US dominance in Europe, de Gaulle supported a 'comprehensive intergovernmental' strategy rather than a federal integration which would have been limited to a few sectors only (Sæter 1971: 383–407; Rieker 1998b: 35–42).

The next integration initiative, the Fouchet Plan, represented de Gaulle's ideas on how to further the integration process. A detailed treaty draft for political union based on intergovernmental co-operation rather than federal integration was presented, but prevailing differences between the member states concerning the inclusion of security and defence policy issues prevented an agreement. The disagreement was closely linked to the question of British membership. Whereas the Netherlands and Belgium feared that such a confederal structure would lead to French dominance of the union, de

Gaulle refused to accept British membership, which he saw as equivalent to accepting a US-dominated Europe.

A movement towards closer French–German co-operation also took place during this period. After negotiations between the Six had failed, bilateral consultations between the two countries were intensified. This close relationship resulted in a French–German co-operation agreement (the Elysée Agreement), which included all policy areas from culture to defence, and which institutionalized regular summits between heads of states and governments. This rapprochement between the two countries was, especially in France, viewed as an alternative to the unsuccessful attempts at that time to create a unified Europe. The period after the failure of the Fouchet Plan was characterized by conflicts between the member states, and de Gaulle's veto against British membership in January 1963 led to a crisis within the EC,[11] where there were two sharply opposed views on further integration: one 'European' and one 'Atlantic'. Seeing no prospect of rapid political integration that could include foreign and security policy, France started a seven-month boycott of the community institutions during the summer of 1965.[12] In order to return to the EC, de Gaulle demanded a guarantee that qualified majority voting would not be applied against any of the member states' interests in vital questions. This led to the Luxembourg Compromise of 1966.[13] When co-operation with France, and an opening to the East, became the priorities of Western Germany after the creation of the great coalition in Bonn in 1966, an EC dominated by a French–German axis became an important aspect of the integration process. In such a situation, Great Britain feared that it could become marginalized in European policy, and this explains the renewed British offensive in favour of EC membership. The Luxembourg Compromise had also helped to assuage British doubts, and was seen as a possibility for Great Britain to avoid an unwanted development in Europe. However, in December 1967 de Gaulle once again rejected British membership.

The Hague Conference in December 1969 represented a breakthrough for French views concerning European integration, and it was a general French–German agreement on long-term goals that made this possible. At The Hague, the EC countries finally agreed that progress towards a political union had to start with foreign policy, and that security and defence policy should not be excluded from the future integration process. Foreign and security policy were to be gradually harmonized through European Political Co-operation (EPC). The foreign ministers of the member states now started to meet regularly, and in 1974 these meetings were institutionalized through the establishment of the European Council. Despite continuing disagreement on how to institutionalize this co-operation, small steps towards further integration in security and defence were taken throughout the 1980s. Most important were the 1981 German–Italian initiative (the Gensche/Colomb Initiative) to include security policy in EPC, the reactivating of the Western

European Union in 1984 and the signing of the Single European Act (SEA) in 1985, which integrated EPC and the EC in one single Treaty. The SEA also gave the European Council the authority to define principles and general guidelines for community development as a whole (Nuttal 1992: 50–80).

France and Germany must be characterized as the *core states* of the integration process. As we have seen, this second phase in the security community-building process was characterized by various efforts to deepen the level of political integration. Institutions were established and the Franco–German coupling became the main driving force in stabilising and encouraging the further development of the security community. In fact, during this period, Europe became an increasingly powerful political symbol, especially with the emergence of a collective *European identity* – an identity formalized in the Declaration on European Identity adopted in 1973. This Declaration defined the community's identity goals with respect to three dimensions: (1) a common European heritage and unity; (2) a common European identity in world politics; and (3) development of the character of the future political union (European Commission 1973). This document formalized the existence of a certain European identity, but confined itself to general statements, postponing a more specific definition of a European identity. As we shall see in the next section, this identity was to become more pronounced with the emergence of a *mature* security community.

A mature security community

The third and final phase in the development of a 'mature' security community is characterized by political integration reaching such a level that it becomes increasingly difficult for the members of a region to see each other as a threat (Adler and Barnett 1998: 55). While it is difficult to determine precisely where the line between the two last phases should be drawn in the case of the European integration process, the fact that the end of the Cold War has not resulted in new hostilities between the European states may be a good indicator that the EU has become a mature security community. The end of the Cold War led some scholars to believe that forty years of stability were over and that the risk of major crises and wars among European states was likely to increase (Mearsheimer 1990). In fact, the opposite has been the case, and there has been a strengthening of the European integration process.

In view of the uncertainties in respect of a reunified Germany and the reduced US will to protect Europe, Helmut Kohl and François Mitterrand felt the need to strengthen European integration. This resulted in an initiative to set up an intergovernmental conference on the possibility of creating a political union in Europe. In questions concerning security and defence, conference participants found themselves divided into two camps – one led by Great Britain, the other by France and Germany. The former group wanted intergovernmental European co-operation and a strong NATO, whereas the latter group favoured a strong independent European security and defence policy. The result, achieved in Maastricht in 1992, was an uneasy compromise in the shape of three-pillar structure with two inter-governmental pillars: in addition to that of the EC (pillar I), there was one for foreign, security and defence policy (pillar II), and a third one for justice and home affairs (pillar III) (Duff 1994). Now that the integration process had moved beyond economic co-operation and developed into a political union, it also became the first and indeed only example of a *tightly coupled* security community.

According to Adler and Barnett, an important aspect of a tightly coupled security community is that its members share a common perception of internal and external threats (1998: 56). If, in addition, the community can formulate a vision of how to meet these threats, it will fulfil Bretherton and Vogler's requirement for being an actor (Bretherton and Vogler 1999: 29). However, the *capacity to formulate goals* is not the same as the *capacity to act*, or 'actorness'.[14] Bretherton and Vogler argue that actorness is a function of both external opportunities (those associated with the international legal and institutional framework) and internal capabilities (the availability of policy instruments and the capacity and legitimacy of decision-making processes) (ibid.: 29).

I will argue that the capacity to act depends on the community's ability to institutionalize and implement the ideas inherent in the dominant security discourse. In the next section we will look into the special character of the Union's post-Cold War security approach, to determine to what extent the EU has managed to move beyond the level of discourse.

Towards a comprehensive security approach

The unique character of the EU has been a major challenge to scholars, as it has proved difficult to accommodate a multi-faceted entity which is neither an international organization nor a state, but which operates globally across a range of policy areas. The temptation to use the state as comparator when discussing the EU has proven difficult to resist. However, as Bretherton and Vogler note, 'comparisons between the EU and other actors in the global system are likely to produce only limited insights' (ibid.: 44). While the previous section presented the EU as a security actor based on the framework of Adler and Barnett and their concept of a *tightly coupled security community*, this section will use Bretherton and Vogler's distinction between actor (capacity to formulate goals) and actorness (capacity to act), to see whether it makes sense to characterize the Union as an operational comprehensive security actor.

The Union's capacity to formulate goals

As noted, it has been argued that the major security aspect of the integration process has been to avoid renewed hostilities between the major European powers. This was the main reason behind the early phase of the integration process, and long remained the most powerful argument for further integration. According to Buzan *et al.* (1998) this argument is the one used most consistently throughout the EU, and is also the most strongly securitized. For instance, in a speech held at Louvain University in February 1996, Helmut Kohl stated:

> The policy of European Integration is really a question of war and peace in the twenty-first century. I know that some do not wish to hear this. My warnings may contain an unpleasant truth. But it is no use burying your head in the sand. We have no wish to return to the nation-state of old times. Nationalism has brought great suffering to our continent; just think of the first fifty years of this century. We need Europe to give weight to our collective influence in the world. We can only achieve our common interest if we speak with one voice and combine our strength.
>
> (Quoted in Rea and Wright 1997: 139)

By adding the security argument, integration gains urgency because its alternative is, as Wæver argues, 'a self-propelling process that by definition will destroy "Europe" as a project' and thereby reopen the previous insecurity caused by balance of power, nationalism and war (Wæver 1996: 123). Such arguments have also been used in relation to the Economic and Monetary Union, where it has been held that the EMU can fall into a speculative rush because it is embedded in the volatile global financial system. At the same time, however, EU officials are careful about claiming explicitly that the whole integration process is threatened if the EMU fails (Buzan *et al.* 1998: 182). While a potential fragmentation of the integration process is often used to defend the importance of further integration, it has become increasingly common to argue that such a risk no longer exists. In the words of Jacques Delors: 'the watchword of post-1945 politics, "we must never go to war with each other again" [. . .] has been achieved' (Delors 1991).

According to Delors, the relationship between the European states became desecuritized with the establishment of the European Union in the early 1990s. From then on, the European security discourse moved beyond this aspect of security and towards other threats and other referent objects.

Throughout the 1990s, there was growing interest within the EU in both internal and external security and the link between the two. As early as in 1991, in a speech at the International Institute for Strategic Studies in London, Jacques Delors emphasized the importance of the wider notion of security:

[. . .] the defence issue is being raised in a very different context today from forty years ago, when the founding fathers believed that a European Defence Community could lead to a political Europe.

(Ibid.: 2)

Here Delors sees 'security' as an all-embracing concept, dependent on the ability to create an attractive, harmonious society. In his view, security covers not only problems of defence, but also problems of society at large. On the basis of this understanding, he evaluates the security dynamics of the integration process and distinguishes between *internal* and *external* security dynamics. Besides the main objective of the integration process – to avoid another European war – Delors defines the internal security dynamics of the integration process to include efforts to combat 'new' threats such as crime, terrorism, drug-trafficking and pollution, and also to handle such social and economic problems as economic recession, unemployment and social exclusion. External security mechanisms, on the other hand, are defined as efforts by the EU to avoid conflicts in its 'near abroad', which might represent a threat to the stability of the continent as a whole. In addition to the Union's external relations at large, these efforts include the enlargement process and the development towards the creation of both a non-military and a military crisis-management capability (ibid.).

More recently, the importance of both internal and external security was also emphasized by Romano Prodi:

Europe needs security. External security must be achieved by reducing unrest and tension on our borders. Internal security must be achieved by combating crime, including organized crime. Crime needs to be tackled at its source which often lies in institutional disorder, poor education, social injustice and the soullessness of inner cities and suburbs. Security should also mean a safe environment and safe consumer products, in particular safe food.

(Prodi 2000)

The need 'to develop targeted common approaches to countries and regions at risk of conflict, taking account of CFSP, development, trade and justice and home affairs issues' was also noted in a joint report from the Commission and the High Representative, submitted to the European Council in Nice in December the same year (Secretary General/High Representative and European Commission 2000). In a speech held at the Institut Français des Relations Internationales (IFRI) in Paris, the former Commissioner on external relations, Chris Patten, pleaded for 'the indivisibility of European foreign policy, which cannot be confined to one pillar of the Treaty' (see Missiroli 2001b: Annexe A). Patten also pointed out that there was an increasing will among member states to strengthen this aspect of European security policy:

> [. . .] in recent years they [the Member States] have begun to fashion a Common Foreign and Security Policy, which can be more than just declaratory. And they have recognized that this needs to integrate three stands: national policies, community policies [the EC or the first pillar], and CFSP itself (the so-called 'second pillar'). European foreign policy must combine all three, and will become stronger as that combination becomes seamless.
>
> (Quoted in Missiroli 2001b: Annexe A)

'The Communication on Conflict Prevention' (see Missiroli 2001b: Annexe F), presented by the Commission in April 2001, the 'European Programme for the Prevention of Violent Conflicts' (European Council 2001b) adopted in June by the European Council in Gothenburg, and its follow-up report adopted at the Seville summit the following year, together constitute important steps forward in the discussion on developing a more co-ordinated European external security policy better adapted to the current security context.

While attention has generally been on the external dimension of security, the internal aspects have also received increased interest. This has especially been the case after 11 September 2001, with international terrorism becoming strongly securitized (clearly presented as a security issue; see p. 8 for further explanation of the term) by all security actors, including the EU. In fact, the EC/EU has a long tradition of focusing on these aspects of security. The internal security dynamics of the integration process is linked primarily to the economic revival of the community, the internal market and the common policies. Further European economic integration and the creation of an internal market gradually created a greater demand for compensatory internal security measures (Furuseth 2003). Internal security is not limited to justice and home affairs, however. Other efforts to protect the individual against violations of human rights, unemployment and social exclusion, pollution, dangerous food, etc., are also seen as internal security mechanisms, and are frequently securitized in EU documents and speeches. In addition to the speeches of Delors and Prodi already referred to, the Commission statement on strategic objectives from 2000 to 2005 also emphasizes such areas. In this document, overall priority is given to employment and sustainable development, protection of the environment, food safety, consumer rights, and justice and security against crime (European Commission 2000: 5).

Since the EU is the only multilateral framework that covers all these policy areas, there has been growing interest in the Union's potential for providing a comprehensive security approach that can include both internal and external tools. Javier Solana emphasized the need for such a comprehensive security in a speech at the Stockholm International Peace Research Institute (SIPRI) in Stockholm in June 2001:

> I am convinced that security in Europe in the twenty-first century is increasingly multi-layered. It will require a wide range of instruments, and it will need closer cooperation both within the European Union itself, but also with the rest of the world. Security is achieved by tackling all those issues which threaten our stability and prosperity. [. . .] Taken together they constitute a formidable protection against the threats which we are likely to face over the coming years.
>
> (Solana 2001)

Although the discourse was clear, it proved to be difficult to implement such a comprehensive external security policy, not least for institutional reasons and the lack of co-ordination between different policy areas. In an independent contribution from the High Representative on 'Procedures for Comprehensive, Coherent Crisis Management: Reference Framework' (see Missiroli 2001b: Annexe D.2), however, a solution to the institutional problem was put forward in relation to the external dimension. This report proposed that the Political and Security Committee (PSC) in the Council should be given a co-ordinating role in such a *comprehensive security approach*:

> [. . .] in order to ensure consistency between the instruments available to the Union, it is essential that a single body should have access to all the information, proposals and initiatives relating to the crisis involved in order to make global assessment; following the conclusions of the Helsinki Council, this role would fall to the Political and Security Committee. This is without prejudice either to the institutional prerogatives or to the decision-making mechanisms peculiar to each pillar [. . .] military and non-military actions [. . .] need to be closely co-ordinated in the service of a single strategy.
>
> (Missiroli 2001b: Annexe D.2)

With the tragedy of 11 September 2001, the emphasis on comprehensive security has ideed been stronger. In fact, this has become the main content of the European Security Strategy, which was adopted in December 2003. It emphasizes, for instance, that:

> The post Cold War environment is one of increasingly open borders in which the internal and external aspects of security are indissolubly linked. Flows of trade and investment, the development of technology and the spread of democracy have brought freedom and prosperity to many people. Others have perceived globalization as a cause of frustration and injustice. These developments have also increased

the scope for non-state groups to play a part in international affairs. And they have increased European dependence – and so vulnerability – on an interconnected infrastructure in transport, energy, information and other fields.

(European Council 2003: 2)

In contrast to the massive visible threat in the Cold War, none of the new threats is purely military; nor can any be tackled by purely military means. Each requires a mixture of instruments. Proliferation may be contained through export controls and attacked through political, economic and other pressures while the underlying political causes are also tackled. Dealing with terrorism may require a mixture of intelligence, police, judicial, military and other means. In failed states, military instruments may be needed to restore order, humanitarian means to tackle the immediate crisis. Regional conflicts need political solutions but military assets and effective policing may be needed in the post conflict phase. Economic instruments serve reconstruction, and civilian crisis management helps restore civil government. The European Union is particularly well equipped to respond to such multi-faceted situations.

(Ibid.: 7)

With this major document favouring a comprehensive security discourse it is possible to argue that a comprehensive approach to security has become EU's dominant security discourse.

Didier Bigo has argued, for some time, that internal and external security have largely merged in Europe (Bigo 1996: 16), and Jacek Saryusz-Wolski has recently claimed that:

the distinction between different kinds of security – national and regional, military and economic, internal and external – [has] been progressively blurred for quite some time, but there is now a chance that this reality is mirrored in the functioning of the EU.

(Saryusz-Wolski 2002: 60)

In the remaining part of this chapter I will try to determine to what extent this discourse, covering both external and internal security aspects, has materialized in the form of a functioning comprehensive security policy.

The Union's capacity to act

To what extent has the comprehensive security discourse presented above materialized in the form of a comprehensive security policy? I will start by studying external and internal security separately, and later take a closer look at specific efforts to move beyond the internal/external divide. Many initiatives have been taken to render the EU capable of performing as a comprehensive security actor, even though not all decisions have been fully implemented yet. The EU's capacity to move beyond both the internal/ external and the civilian/military divide also makes it more appropriate to refer to the EU as a 'comprehensive security actor' rather than a 'civilian actor' or a 'civilian power'.

Towards a comprehensive internal security policy

After both the terrorist incidents of 11 September 2001 in the US and 11 March 2004 in Spain, the fight against terrorism became a priority for all member states and thus also for the EU. The Union emphasizes that:

> The European Union is committed to jointly combating terrorism and to providing for the best possible protection for its citizens. The EU's strategy is comprehensive, covering a wide range of measures. These aim at increasing co-operation in fields ranging from intelligence sharing to law enforcement and the control of financial assets in order to make it easier to find, detain and bring to justice terror suspects. Furthermore, the criminal law of the 25 Member States is being aligned so that terrorism is prosecuted and punished in the same manner throughout the EU.[15]

The European Council Declaration of 25 March 2004 set out the following seven strategic objectives for the EU's Plan of Action against terrorism:

> 1. To deepen the international consensus and enhance international efforts to combat terrorism; 2. To reduce the access of terrorists to financial and economic resources; 3. To maximize the capacity within EU bodies and Member States to detect, investigate and prosecute terrorists and to prevent terrorist attacks; 4. To protect the security of international transport and ensure effective systems of border control; 5. To enhance the capability of the European Union and of member States to deal with the consequences of a terrorist attack; 6. To address the factors which contribute to support for, and recruitment into, terrorism; 7. To target actions under EU external relations towards priority Third Countries where counter-terrorist capacity or commitment to combating terrorism needs to be enhanced.[16]

Still, it is possible to argue that it was a decision made at the Amsterdam European Council (June 1997) that marked the first step towards including these aspects in the Union's overall security approach. The heads of state then decided to incorporate the Schengen *acquis* into the EU and to create 'an area of movement of citizens and non-EU nationals throughout the Union within the following five years, while guaranteeing public security by combating all forms of organized crime and terrorism' (later referred to 'an area of freedom, security and justice'). Once fully in place, this area will cover issues like fundamental rights, EU citizenship, personal mobility, asylum and immigration, visa policy, managing the EU's external frontiers and close co-operation between national police, judicial and customs authorities. This package will ensure that the policies which apply to EU nationals, visitors and immigrants from other parts of the world – as well as to criminals and terrorists – are uniformly implemented across the Union. An extraordinary European Council meeting in Tampere, Finland, in October 1999 was entirely devoted to the development of this aspect of security.

Thus we can see that enhancing internal security in the EU was a process initiated several years before the tragic events of 11 September terrorist attacks on the United States. Then, when the fight against terrorism became the main security threat, this process was accelerated, and many proposals which had long been under discussion were now finally decided upon (a framework decision of the fight against terrorism and a European arrest warrant). In addition, the member states agreed on the establishment of EUROJUST – a co-ordination body composed of magistrates, prosecutors and police officers; the adoption of mutual recognition among the judicial authorities of EU member states on orders for the freezing of assets and the preservation of evidence., and the strengthening of EUROPOL's role in counter-terrorism. The 11 September 2001 attack has also led to a more co-ordinated EU response. At that time, only seven of the then fifteen EU countries had specific legislation on terrorism. Today, all twenty-five member states are bringing in such legislation, ensuring consistency on the definition of a terrorist act and the penalties and sentences which apply. The EU leaders have recently reaffirmed their priorities linked to the implementation of 'an area of security, freedom and justice'. In November 2004 they adopted the so-called Hague Programme which states that freedom, justice, control at the EU's external borders, internal security and the prevention of terrorism should henceforth be considered indivisible within the Union as a whole.[17] The so-called solidarity clause in the Draft Constitution further emphasizes the importance of internal security and emphasizes that the Union shall mobilize all instruments in order to:

> (a) prevent the terrorist threat in the territory of the Member States; protect democratic institutions and the civilian population from any terrorist attack; assist a Member State in its territory, at the request of its political authorities, in the event of a terrorist attack;

(b) assist a Member State in its territory, at the request of its political authorities, in the event of a natural or man-made disaster.
(European Constitution 2004: Title V, ch. II, art. I-43: 1)

Towards a comprehensive external security policy

The Maastricht Treaty defined the Union's external security policy in terms of the second pillar, the Common Foreign and Security Policy:

Common foreign and security policy shall include all questions related to the security of the Union, including the eventual framing of a common defence policy, which might in time lead to a common defence.
(Treaty of Maastricht 1992: art. J.4)

While the long-term goal was a common defence, the main focus at that time was the development of a common foreign and security policy. At the Lisbon European Council in June 1992, the member states identified two priority areas for the EU's foreign policy. The first was Central and Eastern Europe with Russia, the former Soviet Republics, and other countries in Central and Eastern Europe, including the Balkans and former Yugoslavia. The second involved the Maghreb countries and the Middle East. In this first period, the most visible policies were the beginning of the enlargement process (with the establishment of the accession criteria) and the establishment of a European Mediterranean Partnership (EMP). These were long-term, comprehensive civilian strategies aimed at creating stability along the borders of the Union. Working together with other organizations, the EU later initiated a similar comprehensive strategy towards the Balkans – the Stability Pact for South Eastern Europe.

The wars in ex-Yugoslavia throughout the 1990s, however, made it clear that the EU needed to develop a crisis management capacity to complement these broader approaches. The European Council in Amsterdam therefore initiated a process towards the development of a framework for the EU's future crisis management operations. The resultant Amsterdam Treaty established several new bodies, such as a High Representative for CFSP and a policy and planning unit in the Council, and opened up the possibility of future integration of the WEU into the Union. It also dealt with the problems related to the Maastricht Treaty and its formulation regarding the long-term goal of a common defence (Treaty of Maastricht 1992: V.J.4). This formulation was particularly problematic to some member countries. In fact, it was largely because of this aspect that the Danish people had rejected the Maastricht Treaty in a referendum; and when the new neutral members were admitted in 1995, it became important to reassure them that these plans would not enter into force. The Swedish–Finnish initiative, taken during the

1996 intergovernmental conference (IGC), to include the 'Petersberg tasks'[18] in the Treaty (Treaty of Amsterdam 1997: V.J.7), must be understood as such an attempt. These tasks were included in order to provide reassurance that the 'European security dimension' would be limited to crisis management, and would not include the collective defence dimension that had been stipulated as a long-term goal in the Maastricht Treaty.

Even though the Amsterdam Treaty clarified the EU's role and the overall institutional framework for external security policy, it was not until 1998 that the Union seriously started addressing its defence or military complement. This was largely a result of the Kosovo conflict, which had made even clearer than the previous Balkan wars that Europe was militarily dependent on the USA. This led to a Franco–British summit in St Malo in December 1998, followed up by concrete decisions at the EU summit in Cologne in June 1999. This laid the foundations for what is now referred to as the European Security and Defence Policy (ESDP). The member states agreed that:

> the Union must have the capacity for autonomous action, backed by credible military forces, the means to decide to use them, and the readiness to do so, in order to respond to international crisis without prejudice to actions by NATO.
>
> (European Council 1999)

At the subsequent summits in Helsinki and Feira, EU leaders established several 'headline goals' for military and civilian crisis-management capabilities designed to carry out the Petersberg tasks[19] introduced in the Amsterdam Treaty. While the ESDP was made operational by the European Council meeting at Laeken, it was not until 2003 – and in spite of the quarrel over Iraq – that the EU managed to undertake its first joint operations.

The development in EU security and defence policy since January 2003 clearly shows that the ESDP has moved beyond declaration. Since that time the EU has taken over UN's police mission in Bosnia; NATO's peacekeeping mission in Macedonia; and it undertook its first peace enforcement operation outside of Europe, in Congo. Finally, in December 2004, the EU also took over NATO's Stabilization Force in Bosnia. In addition the member states have agreed on several issues that will further strengthen the EU's security policy, the most important being the adoption of an EU Security Strategy (ESS) that defines threats, objectives and policy implications for the EU; the adoption of a Constitutional Treaty that opens up for important institutional changes; and finally, the adoption of a revised Headline Goal for military crisis management. A more concrete conceptualization and institutionalization of a common security policy at the EU level indicates that, in spite of its intergovernmental character, this policy is more than just the sum of its member states.

As already shown, it is a comprehensive security approach that has been emphasized by the EU through its official documents and speeches since the early 1990s. Since the middle of the 1990s, the EU has also managed to start to transform the ideas inherent in this discourse into concrete policy. Such a development has been the case in the shaping of a comprehensive ESDP, first with the incorporation of the Petersberg tasks in the Amsterdam Treaty, which shifted the focus from the development of a 'common defence' towards 'international crisis management', and then with the establishment of a civilian crisis management component in parallel to the military one. Other obvious examples of comprehensive security are of course the enlargement process as such and the programme for Conflict Prevention together with the Stability Pact for the Balkans, the Euro-Mediterranean Partnership. In addition to this comes the various efforts in both the justice and home affairs (JHA) and the Community areas (EC) in order to combat terrorism This shows that the EU, despite the lack of a coherent and clearly defined CFSP, as the dispute over the Iraq crisis clearly demonstrated, does have a distinct security approach, which is implemented both by the Commission and the Council, and which in addition to CFSP includes parts of both the Economic Community and justice and home affairs.

But in order to become an efficient comprehensive security actor the EU still has some important improvements to make. It has been argued, for instance, that a bridge between the different policy areas is still lacking (den Boer and Monar 2002: 11). However, the issue of coherence is not purely confined to the integration of the security policy tools, but it is also about the relations between the community pillar and the intergovernmental pillar within the EU, between the EU and its member states, and the EU and other organizations (Gourlay 2004; Keane 2004). However, both the members and the EU as such have expressed their wish to further strengthen this potential. The adoption of a European Security Strategy indicates, for instance, a clear will to have this further reflected in the functioning of the EU:

> The European Union has made progress towards a coherent foreign policy and effective crisis management. We have instruments in place that can be used effectively, as we have demonstrated in the Balkans and beyond. But if we are to make a contribution that matches our potential, we need to be more active, more coherent and more capable. And we need to work with others.
>
> (European Council 2003: 11)

A potential structural solution might be found in the Constitutional Treaty. Several of the proposals in the Treaty, such as a 'double-hatted' Foreign Minister (supposed to represent the Council and the Commission), supported by a Joint External Service, a solidarity clause, and structured co-operation in the area of security and defence (with the creation of multi-national battle groups), also indicate a clear will to improve the EU's capacity to act (European Constitution 2004). Two important policy analyses done for the EU, the proposed Human Security Doctrine for Europe (Study Group on Europe's Security Capabilities 2004) and the proposed European Defence Strategy (Lindley-French and Algieri 2004), provide concrete proposals on how to implement EU ambitions in the security field. Both documents emphasize the need for a comprehensive security approach that goes beyond the traditional distinction between external and internal security and between civilian and military instruments.

Beyond the internal–external divide

The EU has tended to separate its policies on internal and external security issues. By contrast, thinking in geopolitical terms would mean developing a coherent holistic approach that could combine considerations of internal and external security. As threats and sources of instability have become globalized, the only answer is to 'globalize' the response – to treat security in an indivisible and integrated manner (Saryusz-Wolski 2002). While the EU would appear to have a greater potential than other security actors to move beyond this traditional divide, the pillar structure seems to have made it more difficult to take full advantage of this potential. In addition to the CFSP, both JHA and parts of the Community policies are being referred to as integrated parts of the EU's security approach. Thus, we need to understand the interplay between these policy areas if we are to grasp how the EU functions as a security actor. The EU's police operation in Bosnia, for instance, clearly shows that the EU's area for security, freedom and justice (pillar III) in reality includes everything from fighting against terrorism within the EU to peace-keeping in the Balkans (pillar II) (Furuseth 2003: 112). We can also see a general tendency to combine economic and police activities in combating terrorism: the actions aimed at freezing terrorist assets and at fighting money-laundering, as well as approval of the Commission's proposal on air transport security, make direct use of first-pillar instruments. On the other hand, the extension of judicial and police co-operation with third countries and an initiative aimed at improving intelligence and exchange of information on terrorist incidents open up a direct link between the second and the third pillars (Saryusz-Wolski 2002: 53). Thus, the fight against terrorism seems to be an important cross-pillar test for the EU as a security actor (Gregory 2003).

The appointment of a co-ordinator for the Union's fight against terrorism, Gijs de Vries, under the High Representative for CFSP, Javier Solana, is one example of the Union moving beyond the internal–external divide. His main tasks are precisely to co-ordinate the Council's work in combating terrorism, to maintain an overview of all the instruments at the Union's disposal, to closely monitor the implementation of the EU Action Plan on Combating Terrorism, and to secure the visibility of the Union's policies in the fight

against terrorism. In the Constitutional Treaty there are also several proposals that aim at facilitate co-ordination between policy areas and institutions. The proposal concerning the appointment of a Union Minister for
Foreign Affairs, responsible for CFSP and for co-ordinating other aspects
of the Union's external action must be seen as a way of facilitating the
implementation of a comprehensive security approach.

'Comprehensive' rather than 'civilian'

Considering the EU as a *comprehensive security actor* is not the same as
treating it as a civilian power. Because of certain features and its surround-
ings, François Duchêne considered the EC as a civilian power as long ago as
in the 1970s (Duchêne 1972, 1973). The concept of 'civilian power' can be
understood in many ways. In its original form, it described an actor that did
not have access to or did not use military means, but it also implied a particular approach to international relations that favoured positive rather than
negative conditionality. With the EC's history of several (albeit unsuccessful)
attempts to add some sort of a defence dimension to the integration process,
the community was in fact a civilian power 'by default'. Nearly a decade
later, Hedley Bull (1982) criticized the concept by arguing that it was a contradiction in terms. More recently Christopher Hill has followed this line,
arguing that the EC 'could conceivably reach the position of being able to act
purposefully and as one while eschewing a military capability' (Hill 1993:
318). Others have put forward a normative argument: 'that a civilian power
does not have to rule out the use of military force as a means to defend
certain principles, if that option is unavoidable' (Ehrhart 2001: 13). Instead
of focusing on the distinction between civilian and military means, or between civilian, military or normative powers, the aim of this chapter has been
to show that the EU to a large extent has managed to develop a comprehensive approach – an approach that emphasizes a holistic approach to security,
exemplified by conflict prevention and civil military crisis management.

Concluding remarks

The chapter has sought to provide a better understanding of how the EU
functions as a security actor. Our analysis has presented the EU as a tightly
coupled security community with a comprehensive security approach. While
the development of such a comprehensive security approach at the European
level has taken place gradually and in parallel with changes in the security
context, the security policy approaches of the individual member states and
of the various frameworks for security co-operation established during
the Cold War seem to have had greater difficulties in adapting to the new
security environment.

During the Cold War, the principal concern of European Community was integration in the economic sphere. The organization did not have a clearly defined security identity at the end of the Cold War – which may explain why it has proved easier for the EU to adapt to a complex post-Cold War security context. Paradoxically enough, the member states' long-term reluctance to relinquish sovereignty in the area of defence seems to have contributed to the Union's innovative security approach – a security policy characterized by comprehensive security. This particular European security approach has not been the result of a clearly defined goal, but is rather a consequence of the character of the integration process. Improvements remain to be made, especially in relation to the external–internal divide. Many of the proposals made in the Constitution, however, indicate the EU's will to proceed in this direction.

With the EU becoming an increasingly important security provider, as well as being more tightly coupled than other multilateral frameworks, there is good reason to believe that its security approach will also have an impact on how security is defined at the national level, both in member states and in other states closely linked to this community. While a pluralistic security community does not erode the legitimacy of the state or replace the state, the more tightly coupled it is, the more the state's role or identity is transformed. In the following chapter I present a five-phase socialization model that sets out how this Europeanization can be expected to unfold.

3

EUROPEANIZATION AS SOCIALIZATION

The analysis in this book is based on the assumption that the national security identities of the Nordic states are being Europeanized, or that the major phases/changes in the development of a EU security identity presented in the previous chapter can be expected to lead to similar changes in the security approaches and identities of these countries. The aim of this chapter is to provide a theoretical framework for studying this process of Europeanization. We start with a general discussion about the relationship between community norms and identity change. Then we see how a process of Europeanization can be understood as a process of socialization. Finally, the chapter ends with a presentation of a five-phase model through which Europeanization is expected to happen. In the following, this model is discussed in relation to the main findings of each case study.

Community norms and identity change

Beyond integration theory

It has been argued that a 'neo-positivistic' approach often precludes from the start a study of whether and how the European Union transforms the identity of actors (Christiansen 1997: 26). However, it is also important to emphasize that social constructivist approaches are not totally new and that they build heavily on the work done by earlier integration theorists. Some of them have even assigned an important role to transformations of identity and interests (Deutsch 1957; Haas 1958, 1964). According to Ernst B. Haas, for instance, initially power-oriented governmental pursuits evolve into welfare-oriented action through the process of *learning* (Haas 1964: 47). He claims, in the words of Charles Osgood, that 'when people are made to keep on behaving in ways that are inconsistent with their actual attitudes, their attitudes tend to shift into line with their behaviour' (ibid.: 112). What is lacking in Haas' analysis, however, is a systematic theory of *how* such changes occur.

Social theories based on the Grotian tradition have also provided important contributions to social constructivism. Hedley Bull (1977) and the

English School are representative of this approach. From this perspective the international system is a 'society' in which states, as a condition for their participation in the system, adhere to shared norms and rules in a range of issue areas. But not even the scholars in this tradition have focused explicitly on how norms construct states with specific identities and interests. On the other hand, the sociological imagery is strong in their work, and it is not a great leap from arguing that adherence to norms is *a condition* for participation in a society to arguing that states are *constructed*, partly or substantially, by following these norms.

While all these approaches have provided social constructivism with important insights, they do not go far enough in imparting 'causality' to social structure. A constructivist analysis of the European security arrangements will suggest that four decades of co-operation have transformed positive interdependence into a collective 'European identity' in terms of which states increasingly define their self-interests. This means that even if egoistic reasons may have been the starting point, the process of co-operating has worked to redefine those reasons by reconstituting identities and interests in terms of new intersubjective understandings (Wendt 1994: 384). In the previous chapter, we identified a European comprehensive security identity, noting, however, that the security identity of the EU is not necessarily identical to the current security identities of its member states. Still, we may assume that, over time, these national identities will gradually change in accordance with the one held by the community.

It is important to be able to identify national security identities, since these are constitutive of a nation-state's security policy orientation. This means that a long-term change in policy orientation is dependent on a shift in a state's identity. Nation-state identities, however, are difficult to identify; they cannot be stipulated deductively, but must be investigated empirically in concrete historical settings. When such identities are analysed in specific historical contexts, it is possible to trace the effects that changing identities have on political interests and hence on the national policies.

Two mechanisms of institutional change frequently referred to in the literature may be useful for identifying changes in security identities as well. The first, often termed Rational Institutionalism, sees domestic change as a process of redistribution of sources; it embodies the 'logic of consequentialism' treating actors as rational, goal-oriented and purposeful. This means that actors engage in strategic interactions using their resources to maximize their utilities on the basis of given, fixed and ordered preferences. The second, often referred to as Sociological Institutionalism, draws on the 'logic of appropriateness', which means that actors are guided by collectively shared understandings of what is proper in a given rule structure. Such normative rationality implies that social norms and institutions have formative effects, i.e., that these rules not only regulate behaviour but also constitute identities and interests (March and Olsen 1989, 1998).

To return to the focus of this book: that *the Europeanization of nation-state security identities is assumed to take place through a process of socialization and learning*. This does not mean that strategically based changes are not expected, but that such changes tend to be less stable than those that are a result of a process of learning. In order to distinguish between the two it may be useful to employ the terms *adaptation* and *learning*. While the first refers to changes which occur when actors merely adjust their behaviour to external factors, the second refers to changes in their preferences or identities. This difference is similar to Argyris and Schön's concepts of 'single' and 'double-loop' (or complex) learning (Argyris and Schön 1978: 2–3). As in the study on Europeanization by Cowles, Caporaso and Risse, 'learning' is used in this book only to refer to the latter form (Cowles *et al.* 2001: 12). This makes it easier to distinguish between strategic adjustments (adaptation) and identity change (learning).

The distinction between adaptation and learning has been important in foreign policy analysis. However, while most researchers within this discipline have focused on continuity and stability rather than change, Kjell Goldmann (1988) argued that foreign policy change may occur in three distinct ways: by adaptation to changes in the external environment; by learning (revision of policies in the wake of negative feedback); and through changes in the domestic balance of power (when a new group with different ideas comes to power). This framework has been criticized by Walter Carlsnaes (1993a) for not leaving enough scope for actors and their capacity for innovative thinking. In this book, we address this problem by including a conceptual framework based on the notions of communicative action and deliberation (see pp. 57–8 below).

Europeanization of the security identities of nation-states

The natural and necessary starting condition of a socialization process is, as Börzel and Risse argue, a 'misfit' between the European and the national level (Börzel and Risse 2000: 11). The European level, or the tightly coupled European security community, is characterized by specific norms and a specific culture. While 'norms' are collective expectations about proper behaviour for a given identity (here: comprehensive security approach), 'culture' means the cultural context in which the actor operates. Thus, a tightly coupled European security community consists of norms, values and rules, implicitly or explicitly set by the EU in a post-Cold War European security context. In turn, these community norms establish expectations about the national security approaches which are operating in the same cultural context, but which are constrained by national security traditions. This means that there is a gap between the security identity of the EU and those of its member states.

National security identities are often referred to as the images these states have of themselves and their distinctiveness *vis-à-vis* 'others' (Neumann 1999). As argued in Chapter 1, a state's security identity can be identified by focusing on its dominant national security discourse. Thus, 'security interests' do not refer to basic interests such as survival and minimal well-being, which exist independently of a specific identity, but instead depend on a particular construction of self-identity. This means that states develop interests as a consequence of having a particular identity. Furthermore, constancy in an underlying identity helps us to identify underlying regularities in national security interests and policy. Correspondingly, changes in identity will precipitate changes in interests (Jepperson *et al.* 1996: 52–65), leading to policy changes. Since it is the process of change that is of interest here, we can now develop a more sophisticated model than the one presented in the introduction. This model also takes into account the difference between adaptation and learning:

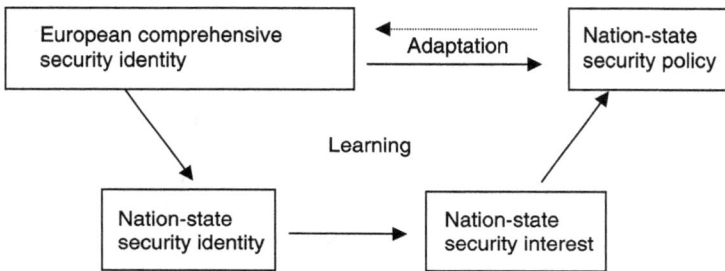

Figure 3.1 Europeanization as a socialization process.

The goal of this analysis is not to provide a comprehensive explanation for all the changes in national security policies. Working on the assumption that the EU influences national security approaches, we wish to see how such a Europeanization of national security happens – whether it occurs through a process of adaptation or a process of learning, and why it varies across nation-states.

It is ill-advised to have a preconceived notion of the way in which constitutive mechanisms work in practice. Rather, the link between the two levels (European and national) should be understood as relational – as a two-way process. It is difficult to establish unequivocally whether community norms lead to changes in nation-state identities, interests and policies, or whether it is the changes in nation-states, policies, provoked by various domestic factors, that lead to a change in norms, which in turn leads to a change in identities and interests. However, the choice of approach is not only a meta-theoretical question, but also depends on what we are interested in.

Whether research focuses on the influence of international community norms[1] or national (or societal) norms[2] depends primarily on whether the aim of the research is to investigate *similarities of foreign policies, given*

54

different national expectations of behaviour, or *differences in state behaviour, given identical international expectations of behaviour* (Boekle *et al.* 1999: 11–18). The aim of this book is a combination of the two, although the emphasis is on the latter. We want to investigate how identical international expectations (EU) influence national approaches and identities. Our point of departure is an assumption that this process will increase similarities despite very different starting points. This is why the focus is on the impact of community norms. However, some 'national norms' (i.e. different security policy traditions and type of relationships to the EU) may contribute to a better understanding of the differences when determining the degree of Europeanization.

Our next step is therefore to clarify under what conditions these community norms, defined as the dominant European security discourse, is internalized at the domestic level.

Norm compliance through socialization

While scholars of international relations are increasingly interested in studying norms and ideas (Finnemore 1996; Jepperson *et al.* 1996; Katzenstein 1996b; Kowert and Legro 1996; Finnemore and Sikkink 1998), few have yet demonstrated the actual impact of these norms. This means that the literature is under-specified with regard to the causal or constitutive mechanisms through which these ideas spread. However, as we shall see below, the existing socialization literature may provide a good starting point for developing a framework for studying the processes of Europeanization.

Level of analysis

Since the assumption here is that socialization in the first instance pertains to the behaviour of security policy decision-makers, this is principally seen as an elite and not a mass phenomenon. This is consistent with Ikenberry and Kupchan's (1990) argument that norms must take root within the elite community in order to affect state behaviour:

> [. . .] although normative claims articulated by the international or regional community may take root in the public at large, it is the ruling elites that must embrace these claims if they are to have a long-term and consequential impact on the behaviour of secondary states. While public opinion can influence elite restructuring, it is through the dynamics of elite politics and coalition-building that socialization takes place.
>
> (Ikenberry and Kupchan 1990: 293)

In its original, sociological meaning, socialization is a 'process in which a person grows into the society and culture surrounding him/her and, by learning social norms and roles, becomes an independent, competent social being' (Boekle *et al.* 1999: 8). In general, the socialization process of *foreign policy decision-makers* involves two analytically distinct socialization processes, running simultaneously. Political decision-makers are often at the interface between the international and the national (societal) system; they face two different groups of socializing agents and, consequently, undergo two different socialization processes. Although focusing on either international or societal norms runs the risk of being blind to the reinforcing or counteracting influence of the other level, it may be useful to separate these two levels analytically in order to analyse the differences between the two. As already argued, it makes sense to focus on international norms, given the aim of this analysis. There is also little pressure from social movements in the area of security policy – a policy area largely dominated by political elites.

A tightly coupled European security community may socialize the political elites in both member state and states closely related to the EU through association agreements. The speed and the character of the socialization process will vary, depending on their relationship to the security community. Socialization is a process of great complexity, and in order to understand how even states which are not an integrated part of the community become socialized, Ikenberry and Kupchan's conception of socialization may be useful. They see socialization as a process of learning in which norms and ideals are transmitted from one party to another through the influence of a 'hegemon'. They conceptualize this as:

> the process through which national leaders internalize the norms and value orientations espoused by the hegemon and, as a consequence, become socialized into the community formed by the hegemon and other nations accepting its leadership position.
>
> (Ikenberry and Kupchan 1990: 289)

The EU may be characterized as a hegemon in its relations to *potential* member states. The process or socializing these countries may occur through what Ikenberry and Kupchan call 'normative persuasion'. This means that the hegemon is able to secure the compliance of secondary states by ideological persuasion and transnational learning through various forms of direct contact with elites in these states (ibid.: 290). Also, it may be assumed that certain non-members with a particularly close relationship to the integration process are more or less open to a similar socialization process as are actual member states.

The analysis presented here indicates a structural approach. When the aim is to study the EU's impact on nation-states, such an approach is difficult to avoid. However, this structural dominance can be reduced by providing a role also for agency in the socialization process. While most constructivists insist on the mutual constitutiveness of structures and agents, most of the literature on socialization is based on a structural perspective (see Finnemore 1996: 24). The explanation for this is that it has prove difficult to operational-ize in empirical research the mutual constitution of structures and agencies. As a result, social constructivists have tended to leave unexplained the microprocesses of the socialization process, and thus also the variation in the degree of socialization across units.[3] They tend to assume that, once actors are interacting within institutions, the diffusion and homogenization of values is automatic and even predictable. This also explains why most con-structivist approaches are closely associated with the 'logic of appropriate-ness' (Sending 2002). While the logic of appropriateness is based on a structural approach, March and Olsen also focus on agency, and talk about rule-guided behaviour as a conscious process. They claim that actors have to figure out the situation in which they act, apply the appropriate norm, or choose among conflicting rules (March and Olsen 1989: 21–6). Thus Socio-logical Institutionalism, in fact, offers two potential explanations for change – one structuralist and one more agency-based. The first suggests that institutions (formal or informal) that interact frequently and are exposed to each other, or that are located in the same environment, develop similarities over time. The second focuses on the socialization processes through which actors learn to internalize new norms and rules in order to become members of a specific international society.

However, March and Olsen are unclear as to the mechanisms through which this socialization is supposed to happen. Thomas Risse has attempted to develop a model that puts more emphasis on agency. In order to present it as an alternative to both the logic of appropriateness and the logic of con-sequence, he calls it a 'logic of truth seeking or arguing'. According to such a logic of action, actors, when arguing about the truth, try to figure out in a collective communicative process whether their assumptions about the world and about cause-and-effect relationships in the world are correct, or whether norms of appropriate behaviour can be justified, and which norms apply under given circumstances (Risse 2000).

Socialization as a process

According to Risse, arguing implies that actors try to challenge the validity claims inherent in any causal or normative statement, and to seek a com-municative consensus about their understanding of a situation as well as justifications for the principles and norms guiding their action. Based on Habermas' 'theory of communicative action', argumentative rationality also implies that the participants in a discourse are open to being persuaded by the better argument, and hence that relationships of power and social hier-archies recede into the background.[4] This means that the goal of the dis-cursive interaction is to achieve argumentative consensus with the other, not to impose one's own world-view and moral values. Since the validity claims of identities and interests are at stake, an argumentative consensus has constitutive effects on an actor.

This logic helps to clarify the mutual constitutiveness of agents and social structure that social constructivism emphasizes. According to this logic, agents are not mere puppets of social structures, since they can actively challenge the validity claims inherent in any communicative action. At the same time, they are social agents that produce the intersubjective structures of meanings through their communicative practices (ibid.: 10).

Our conclusion must be that the various modes of social action (the logics, respectively of appropriateness, of consequences and of arguing) represent ideal types that rarely occur in pure form in reality. Actors often act both strategically and discursively, and by doing so they follow norms enabling this interaction in the first place. The logic of consequentialism is present to the extent that actors use rhetoric to convince others to change their interests, identities or views of the world. The logic of appropriateness prescribes what is considered a legitimate truth-claim in a given public discourse, thereby circumscribing the boundaries of this discourse. Finally, the logic of argumentative rationality and truth-seeking behaviour is likely to take over if actors are uncertain about their own identities, interests and world-views, and/or if rhetorical arguments are subject to scrutiny and counter-challenges leading to a process of 'argumentative self-entrapment' (ibid.: 23). Thus, it can be argued that all three types of social action or causal mechanisms discussed above are necessary for the enduring internalization of norms.

In line with this argument Risse, together with Kathryn Sikkink, has argued that the socialization process is characterized by three different processes: adaptation and strategic bargaining; moral consciousness-raising, argumentation, dialogue and persuasion; and institutionalization and habitualization.

A five-phase socialization model

Risse and Sikkink argue that the significance of each mechanism varies with different stages of the socialization process. To identify the dominant mode of social interaction in each phase of the socialization process, they develop a five-phase 'spiral model', specifying the causal mechanisms and the prevailing logic of action in each phase (Risse and Sikkink 1999: 22–35). In their view, instrumental adaptation usually prevails in the early stages of the socialization process. Argumentation, persuasion, and dialogue then become more significant at a later stage; and institutionalization and habitualization mark the final steps in the socialization process. The model also contains assumptions about the conditions under which progress toward the implementation of norms can be expected.

This model was originally developed in order to understand the process through which states go to comply with human rights norms, and builds upon previous work on transnational networks in the human rights area. In a study by Margaret Keck and Kathryn Sikkink, this process is referred to as the 'boomerang effect' (Keck and Sikkink 1998). A boomerang pattern of influence exists when domestic groups in a repressive state bypass their state and directly search out international allies in order to bring pressure on their states from the outside.

The process through which states go to comply with human rights norms may be rather different from the process involved in complying with security policy norms set up by a security community. Although Risse and Sikkink argue that their model is 'generalizable across cases irrespective of cultural, political, or economic differences among countries' (Risse and Sikkink 1999: 6), they say nothing about the generalizability of the model across policy areas. In my view, this framework is useful also in helping to explain the role of a security community and its impact on nation-state security identities.

According to this model, a socialization process starts when actors, for instrumental reasons, adapt their behaviour in accordance with the norm. In the beginning, they use arguments in order to further their instrumentally defined interests – they engage in rhetoric as Schimmelfenning defines it (1999a). The more they justify their interests, however, the more others will start challenging these arguments and the validity claims inherent in them. At this point, governments need to respond by providing further arguments. They become entangled in arguments, and the logic of argumentative rationality slowly but surely takes over. Processes of argumentation and persuasion rather than instrumental bargaining prevail when actors develop collective understandings that form part of their identities and lead them to determine their interests (Risse and Sikkink 1999: 16).

As mentioned above, social constructivists have been criticized for not being able to 'unpack' the socialization process (Schimmelfenning 1999a: 234). They have been criticized for being unable to explain how, and under what conditions, the socialization process takes place. The five-phase model applied here is an attempt to meet this challenge. This model shows how community norms may influence political change through a socialization process that combines instrumental interests, material pressures, argumentation, persuasion, institutionalization and habitualization.

On the basis of the logic of this model, five working assumptions or assumptions for the expected changes in the security approaches in Nordic states are presented in response to community norms. These are investigated in the four case studies presented in the following four chapters.

Phase 1: Traditional security concerns prevail.
The starting point in the socialization process of national security approaches is a situation where traditional security concerns remain dominant. The focus is on military threats against the territory of the nation-states. In this

phase, the traditional security rhetoric is still being used by the political leadership, even though the international context has changed. Our first assumption is therefore that:

> *The governments in the Nordic states continue to securitize the threat of military invasion (primarily from the East) after the end of the Cold War.*

Phase 2: A new security discourse and defence of traditional policy.
In the second phase a new political discourse starts to be heard. Some groups at the domestic level adopt this discourse, and try to lobby this view with the authorities. The initial reaction by the political leadership is a defence of the traditional policy. However, this might be seen as simply a demonstration that a process of socialization is already under way. In fact, if socialization were not under way, the political leadership would feel no need to defend the traditional policy. Our second assumption may therefore be formulated as follows:

> *Even though the national security discourse remained traditional for a longer time in the Nordic countries than in the rest of Europe (or the transatlantic community), changes start to be promoted by some domestic 'security experts' and politicians.*

Phase 3: Instrumental change.
In the third phase of the socialization process, the domestic political leadership realizes that it is important to adopt the new way of thinking and change policy, in order to obtain influence and to safeguard (traditional) national interests in a changed international context. Governments now start to adopt the new security discourse. Initially, the arguments resemble the logic of rhetorical action whereby justifications are used to further one's interests without being prepared to really challenge the validity claims inherent in these interests. This means that what dominates is instrumental adaptation to both domestic and international pressure. Domestically this means that certain groups will press for compliance with international norms because this is perceived to be in the state's interests. Internationally, the community itself will try to convince states to comply with community norms. This gives us the third assumption:

> *A new security approach can be identified in the Nordic countries, but the changes are instrumental adjustments (adaptations) to the EU rather than identity change (learning).*

Phase 4: Persuasion.
Slowly but surely, governments become entrapped in their own rhetoric, and the logic of arguing takes over. By the fourth phase, governments are

being convinced/persuaded that norm compliance is the 'right thing'. What is involved here is not only an instrumental adaptation to a changed international context. The transfer to this phase is dependent on the knowledge available about the new situation. As Haas has argued, this happens when political objectives and 'technical' knowledge are combined to reach the conception of what constitutes one's interest (Haas 1990: 9). In this phase national governments might then change their rhetoric, gradually accept the validity of international norms and start engaging in an argumentative process with their opponents, both domestically and abroad.

A second type of social action dominates the socialization process at this stage. While adaptation refers to an instrumental adjustment to community norms irrespective of discursive practices, learning or socialization happens through processes of communication, argumentation, and persuasion. Our fourth assumption is the following:

> *Instrumental adaptation is gradually being replaced by a change in the national security identities of the Nordic states. This happens as a result of persuasion by the representative of the community that comprehensive security is the best policy option.*

Phase 5: Institutionalization.
In the fifth, and last, phase of the socialization process, the international norms are institutionalized in domestic discourse and we see the emergence of rule-consistent behaviour (logic of appropriateness). Technical knowledge is becoming common knowledge, and we are now talking about learning and not only adaptation to external changes. Learning involves the penetration of political objectives and programmes by new knowledge-mediated understandings of connections (ibid.: 36). The more the political elites accept the validity of norms and the more they engage in a dialogue about norm implementation, the more likely are they to institutionalize these norms in domestic practices. The final stage of this socialization process is reached when these norms are 'taken for granted' (Finnemore and Sikkink 1998: 904). Our final assumption is therefore:

> *If the comprehensive security approach is also institutionalized in the national security policies of the Nordic countries, then socialization is achieved.*

Seen together with the perspective on security presented in Chapter 1, this means that the more a state becomes socialized or Europeanized, the more traditional security issues like territorial defence get desecuritized, while new issues get securitized and thus integrated into the national dominant security discourse.

Concluding remarks

The five-phase model presented above characterizes an *ideal* process. In practice, not all countries are expected to be fully socialized at the same time, and some countries might never reach the final phase. Different national factors may either accelerate or restrain Europeanization. Still, the socialization process is expected to follow a similar pattern, which means that instrumental adaptation is expected to precede identity change.

In order to structure the following case studies and make them comparable, I will study changes in the national discourse of each Nordic state between 1990 and 2003 with reference to the following aspects. In each case, the first task is to determine the Cold War security identity, which constitutes the starting point for analysis. Second, the establishment of the European Union and its impact on this identity is analysed. After this the focus is on the process towards a European Security and Defence Policy and its impact on the security discourse of each state. Subsequently, the analysis will address the impact of the comprehensive European security approach on each Nordic state. Each chapter will end with a discussion of the degree and character of Europeanization, by applying the five-phase socialization model presented above.

4

SWEDEN

Teacher and pupil

This chapter investigates the influence of the EU on the Swedish security identity. Some have argued that it is impossible to single out the role played by the EU when studying the Swedish security approach (see Hallenberg 2000: 20). As argued in the Introduction, I show that this is possible when one carefully examines the political discourse and the temporal order of the various changes. The analysis in this chapter, as well as in the following three, will apply such an approach.

The main argument here is therefore that it is possible to identify a change in the Swedish security identity, and the European integration process has contributed to this change. In the Swedish discourse there has been a move away from neutrality and total defence and towards European integration and a comprehensive security discourse. These changes have taken place in parallel to the gradual development of an EU security identity. While Sweden, through its Ministry of Foreign Affairs, has been particularly active in shaping the EU's security identity since it became a member in 1995, it is argued here that the change in the dominant Swedish discourse on security actually came about as a consequence of this development in the EU.

This chapter is divided into five main parts, beginning with a brief presentation of the historical background for Sweden's neutral identity as it was expressed in the dominant discourse on security towards the end of 1980s. The second part focuses on the establishment of the EU and how this has challenged Swedish neutrality. The third part examines Swedish EU membership and how the ESDP process has influenced the country's defence discourse. The fourth part investigates the impact of the Union's comprehensive security approach on the Swedish security discourse. The chapter concludes with a summary of the main findings and a discussion on the degree and character of Sweden's Europeanization, to determine whether the changes referred to represent instrumental adaptations or identity change.

Towards a neutral identity

While Sweden's neutrality had been established in the early nineteenth century, it was not until the Cold War era that this became an important part of the country's national identity. As we shall see, the changes in the international security context towards the end of the 1980s did not immediately challenge this approach.

An ambivalent neutral (1818–1948)

Neutrality as a policy in time of war was first established in Sweden early in the nineteenth century. At that time the newly crowned king, Karl XVI Johan, a former marshal in the Napoleonic armies, aimed at establishing the Kingdom of Sweden and Norway as a balanced unity between the major European powers. The background for this policy may be found in Sweden's drastically changed geopolitical and strategic position. During the eighteenth century, Sweden lost most of its possessions on the eastern and southern shores of the Baltic, finally surrendering Finland to Russia in 1809. The fact that Sweden, as part of the brief Napoleonic war, could annex Norway in 1814, and thereby form the union of Sweden/Norway, did not affect the overall view that Sweden had become a less significant state. The new Swedish situation was reflected in the declaration by King Karl Johan in 1818:

> Separated as we are from the rest of Europe, our policy and our interests will always lead us to refrain from involving ourselves in any dispute which does not concern the two Scandinavian peoples.
>
> (Quoted in Wahlbäck 1986: 10)

During the first years, neutrality was foremost perceived as an *ad hoc* strategy. In 1834, however, the king elaborated his system of 'strict and independent neutrality', which indicates that he, at least, considered this option as a strategy for the long term (quoted in Ojanen *et al.* 2000: 157). But despite this declaration, King Karl Johan and his two successors nevertheless had difficulties in accepting the restraints linked to the policy of neutrality.[1] Hence this policy was not well established in Swedish discourse prior to the turn of the century. Certain attempts were made at that time by the peace movement to give it a formally more permanent character, but these proposals were defeated by the Swedish Parliament. The argument was that there was no need to abandon Swedish freedom of action (Cramér 1998: 176–7).

When the union with Norway was dissolved in 1905, a programme was initiated for the modernization and consolidation of the armed forces. Nevertheless, there was widespread pessimism as to whether Sweden could preserve its neutrality in the event of a major war. The fear that Russia was planning an attack on Sweden in order to acquire access to ports on the Atlantic contributed to this view, enticing Sweden to look to Germany for support (Cronenberg 1986: 57–81). But while influential circles in Sweden had developed considerable sympathy for Germany, which also had become a major trading partner, the policy of neutrality remained.

Despite this ambivalence with respect to neutrality, Sweden's neutral position was not questioned officially during the First World War (Wahlbäck 1986: 20–2; Cramér 1998: 182–3). The result of this war – a defeated Germany, a weakened Russia and a sovereign state of Finland – put Sweden in a rather favourable position for retaining neutrality. The establishment of the League of Nations, however, caused a re-evaluation of Sweden's future foreign and security policy. It was obvious that the policy of neutrality could no longer be pursued to the same degree if Sweden decided to join the League of Nations; however, a policy of *neutrality in case of war* was not excluded (Cramér 1998: 193). While some argued that League membership might drag Sweden into war, those who advocated membership emphasized that Sweden should act in solidarity with the majority of European countries and contribute to the new system for collective security. In 1920 the Swedish Parliament (the Riksdag) decided to approve Swedish membership in the League of Nations, and the concept of neutrality fell out of use.

By the early 1930s it had become clear to Sweden that the League of Nations had failed to become the powerful international actor that many had expected. In June 1936 the policy of neutrality was re-established and a period of rearmament was initiated (Huldt 1986: 190–4). In the late 1930s, as the signs of impending war became more frequent, the idea of a Nordic neutral bloc was considered, but it was soon realized that the geostrategic differences among the Nordic countries were too great for this to succeed. When war broke out in September 1939, the Swedish government declared that Sweden would observe strict neutrality – a choice based on the belief that the belligerents would be tied to continental European battlegrounds and have very little interest in the Nordic area.

Soviet threats against Finland and the military attack of 30 November 1939 led to intensive political discussions in Sweden as well as discussions between the two governments. Although many in Sweden favoured military intervention, the result was that Sweden became a 'non-belligerent'. This status, in contrast to that of being 'neutral', permitted the country to send extensive amounts of weapons and materiel from the Swedish defence forces' own supplies. In addition, some 8,000 Swedish volunteers and an air unit fought on the Finnish side (Ojanen *et al.* 2000: 160).

Between April 1940, when Denmark and Norway were invaded, and the end of the war in Europe in May 1945, Sweden was practically surrounded by German forces or forces allied to Germany. The space for political manoeuvring was therefore very narrow when the Germans demanded concessions, and in June 1940 they were granted the right to transport troops to and from Norway on Swedish railroads. This was widely criticized, being perceived as a break with Swedish neutrality. As a result, Sweden cancelled the railroad agreements with Germany in August 1943 (Wahlbäck 1986: 62–6; Andrén and Möller 1990: 39–40). In addition, towards the end of the war several breaches of neutrality were committed, but this time favouring the Allied countries (Andolf 1995: 22–5).

Despite these breaches, the Second World War had a far greater impact on the Swedish political debate on neutrality than any earlier war. Experiences were mixed, but an important factor in the post-war analysis was that not only the government but also the Riksdag as a whole was responsible for the decisions taken during the war. In a way, all parties had to share the burden of the past (Ojanen *et al.* 2000: 160–1).

After the end of the war two major issues with consequences for Swedish neutrality were debated. The first concerned the plan to create a new world security organization – the United Nations. The second was the formation of a Scandinavian defence alliance. On the issue of UN membership, all political parties proved to be positive. The parliamentary decision enabled Sweden to join the UN, while staying out of any alliances that meant joining either of the two military, political and economic blocs (Wahlbäck 1986: 76–7). It is important to note that priority was given to collective security over neutrality; and, as concluded by Cramér (1998: 268), the policy of neutrality was perceived as an alternative in case collective security failed to work.

Neutrality and collective security (1948–1990)

Against the background of rising international tensions, Sweden took the initiative in early 1948 for negotiations on a defence alliance between Denmark, Norway and Sweden. Due to Finland's recently concluded treaty with the Soviet Union on friendship, co-operation and mutual assistance (FCMA), it was clear that the latter could not be included. Such a defence alliance was not seen as incompatible with Sweden's long-standing policy of neutrality, since it was conceived as being independent of the two power blocs. However, the negotiations failed, because the Swedish view could not be reconciled with Norway's perceived need for strong military assistance for the defence of its northern borders. Norway and Denmark preferred joining the North Atlantic Alliance, whereas Sweden declared that it would pursue a policy of non-alignment backed by a strong national military defence (Huldt 1990: 12). Sweden chose to formulate its policy as a policy of *non-alignment in peace, aiming at neutrality in the event of war*. Such a policy option would have to be accompanied by a credible defence policy combined with a national defence industry that could supply this force with materiel in case of war.

While Swedish security policy aimed at being credible and independent, it was at the same time based on an unofficial assumption that the other

Western countries would assist Sweden militarily, if necessary.[2] Unofficial contacts with NATO also show that the difference between Norwegian and the Swedish security identities was less important than is often believed. One important difference, however, is to be found in the two countries' relationship to the European integration process. While Norway considered potential EC membership in the early 1970s, this was regarded as impossible for Sweden due to the policy of non-alignment and neutrality. It was felt that Sweden could not play an active part in this process without relinquishing this policy, since the Soviet Union regarded NATO and EEC as essentially two sides of the same coin. Still, Sweden was a founding member of the European Free Trade Area (EFTA), which was created in order to provide a free-trade zone, and later became a force in the establishment of an expanded market (EEC + EFTA).

When Great Britain applied for EEC membership in 1961, the Swedish non-alignment policy was put to a test. In view of the tense political situation at that time, Sweden decided not to apply for membership, citing concern for the credibility of Swedish non-alignment. Instead Sweden, together with Austria and Switzerland, submitted an application for associated membership (Andrén and Möller 1990: 163–6). Throughout the Cold War period there were groups in Sweden who urged EEC membership. During the late 1960s, for instance, Swedish industry worked energetically for a closer relationship to the EEC. This effort led to some results, and when Great Britain (followed by Denmark, Ireland and Norway) again submitted its application in 1967, Sweden followed suit, delivering an 'open application' without specifying whether membership or association was sought. For Sweden, the policy of non-alignment was still crucial, but the government now showed a willingness to consider whether EC membership and continued non-alignment were compatible or not (Lindahl 1995). However, the French veto blocked these negotiations.[3] Negotiations were resumed in November 1970, but were aborted at the initiative of Sweden in March 1971. In explanation the Prime Minister, Olof Palme, referred to the European Economic and Monetary Union, proposed in the Werner Report, and to European Political Co-operation, proposed in the Davignon Report, both of which the EEC had accepted two months earlier. Palme declared that he saw little chance of the EEC granting Sweden the necessary exemptions to these policies (Gustavsson 1998).

In the early 1980s a new debate concerning a Swedish application for membership was initiated, fuelled by a combination of a general political interest in the integration process and the economic situation at that time. However, several submarine intrusions, including the famous 'Whisky on the rocks' incident in 1981 (when a Soviet 'Whisky'-class submarine ran aground inside a military restricted area on the southern coast of Sweden), pushed this question temporarily into the background. While these intrusions strengthened the anti-Soviet attitudes among Swedish citizens, they did not promote more favourable attitudes towards abandoning the policy of non-alignment (Lindahl 1995: 167).

The EC issue again came to the fore in the mid-1980s with the establishment of a Single European Market. This project, which involved removing all internal barriers to trade among the EC states, left Swedish export industries at a disadvantage compared to their competitors within the EC area. A new initiative was thus deemed necessary, and Swedish industry once again favoured full membership. However, there remained the problem of the compatibility between membership and neutrality, and the government reiterated old arguments that Swedish neutrality excluded the possibility of membership.

The government's ambition was instead to deepen and widen co-operation within the EEC. In fact, this represented an important change in Swedish policy. With the goal that Sweden should enjoy the same economic benefits as current EC members, an overhaul of legislation was initiated, aimed at making it compatible with that of the EC. Sweden thus supported the European Economic Area (EEA) agreement, which was then under negotiation.

In summary, Sweden's policies towards the EC during this period were shaped by three considerations: the security situation; the economic factors associated with the conditions for Swedish trade; and perceived EC developments towards integration (Ojanen *et al.* 2000: 171).

While the EEA agreement was seen as compatible with Swedish neutrality, full EC membership was still deemed impossible by the political elites. As late as in May 1990 the Swedish Prime Minister, Ingvar Carlsson, declared in a newspaper article that Sweden could not apply for membership in the EC because of the country's policy of neutrality (Strömvik 1999: 248).

Neutrality and the question of EU membership (1990–1991)

For Sweden, the end of the Cold War, with the collapse of the Soviet Union, meant above all a vast improvement in the security situation. The dualistic bloc system, which had constituted the rationale for a policy aiming at neutrality in wartime, had suddenly disappeared. This also had an impact on Sweden's role in the world. There was no longer a need for a mediator or a bridge-builder between states from different sides of the bloc. Sweden suddenly found itself with few possibilities to have an impact on other countries, since it was not a member of the organizations that were now actively shaping the new Europe.

This situation, combined with the economic crisis in Sweden at that time, goes a long way towards explaining why the Swedish government, only five months after having rejected the idea of applying for membership, changed its policy and instead – in a press release – expressed Sweden's ambition to join the EC. In a subsequent message to the Swedish Parliament, the government clarified its position by noting that, as a consequence of positive developments on the continent, 'Swedish membership in the European Community is in the national interest, provided that her policy of neutrality is retained' (quoted in Carlsnaes 1993b: 82).

This change, however, is not reflected in the Swedish security discourse. EC membership was understood to be compatible with the policy of neutrality insofar as the Swedish government chose to downplay the issue of a future foreign and security policy, focusing instead on the socio-economic challenges of the time (Agrell 2000: 270). Membership was seen as a potential means to increase international confidence in the Swedish economy, then under acute pressure from currency speculation (Miles 1997: 182–3). In an article in *The Economist* 8 November 1990, Carlsson stressed that the main reasons for the change in the government's policy were economic – high inflation, big budget deficits and low growth (ibid.: 193). After a series of deliberations in the Parliament, the decision was made, on 12 December 1990, to recommend that Sweden, while maintaining its policy of neutrality, should seek membership. On 1 July 1991, Ingvar Carlsson formally presented Sweden's application for membership in what had then become the EU.

Swedish neutrality continued to be dominated by a strong emphasis on territorial defence. Thus, the end of the Cold War did not immediately lead to a change in Swedish security identity, which was still characterized by neutrality and military defence against a potential invasion. As we shall see below, EU membership was to put heavier pressure on this identity in the years to come.

The EU challenges Swedish neutrality

Even though it was made clear that Sweden's policy of neutrality remained valid, the Maastricht Treaty would put this policy under great pressure. In fact, while it was not its national security identity that prevented Norway from joining the EU, Sweden found that it had to change its security doctrine in order to make membership possible. Although the first changes occurred shortly after the membership application was submitted in 1991, the increased political importance of the EU throughout the 1990s raised the question of the need for a more important change that would jettison the neutrality concept and only keep the reference to 'non-alignment'. Membership in a political union aiming at a common defence contributed to such a debate.

Effects of the Maastricht Treaty

While the Maastricht Treaty and the acceleration of the European integration process led to a slight change in the Norwegian security discourse, producing a stronger emphasis on the European dimension in European security, it also paved the way for the first reconsiderations of Sweden's security policy doctrine. The Maastricht Treaty made it increasingly difficult to retain neutrality, since it had to be compatible with the EU's CFSP.

The new centre-rightist coalition government, which came into power in September 1991, recognized this implication. In his first major post-election statement on this topic, Prime Minister Carl Bildt claimed that:

> whereas strategic realities in Northern Europe and North Atlantic are such that Sweden's prime security principle, summarized in the expression 'non-alignment in peace aiming at neutrality during war' retains its fundamental importance, Sweden's foreign and security policies are nevertheless changing in tune with European developments, creating new possibilities for security cooperation with other European states.
>
> (Quoted in Carlsnaes 1993b: 83)

A month later, the Prime Minister gave a speech in Bonn in which he went a bit further:

> it is obvious that the term 'neutrality' no longer can be utilized as an adequate general designation for the foreign and security policies which we wish to pursue within a European framework. Sweden must pursue a policy with a clear European identity
>
> (Ibid.: 83)

After an extensive debate, the Parliamentary Committee for Foreign Affairs then presented a new view on security, and concluded that Sweden should be more active on the international scene, while maintaining the foundations of non-alignment. In its statements the Committee also included a passage declaring that the Swedish policy of military non-alignment in peacetime remained valid in order to enable Sweden to maintain neutrality in the event of war in its vicinity. This was done by amending the formulation from 'non-alignment in peacetime aiming at neutrality in wartime' to 'non-alignment in peacetime, in order to enable Sweden to remain neutral in the case of war in its vicinity' (quoted in Ojanen *et al.* 2000: 178). The result of this change was that the term neutrality was phased out in official usage, replaced by the notion of military non-alignment – referring strictly to defence issues in military terms, and to Sweden's continued intention of not being part of any form of military alliance system.

While this specification of non-alignment in military terms was a reconfirmation of a policy that had been a reality for many decades, it now paved the way for Swedish membership in a multilateral framework not classified as a military alliance – the European Union. But the formulation in the Maastricht Treaty that emphasized the long-term goal of eventually achieving a common defence remained problematic for Sweden. The Swedish political leadership found itself faced with the challenge of convincing both public opinion at home and the other EU countries that Swedish EU membership could be combined with a policy of non-alignment. During the formal negotiations that started on 1 February 1993, the Minister for European Affairs and Foreign Trade, Ulf Dinkelspiel, declared:

> [A]s recently stated by the Swedish parliament, Sweden's policy of non-alignment in military alliances remains unchanged. At the same time, we recognize that the eventual framing of a common defence policy, which in time might lead to a common defence, is one of the CFSP goals which is to be further discussed in the context of the 1996 review conference. We will not hamper the development of the European Union as it moves forward towards this goal.
>
> (Quoted in Ojanen *et al.* 2000: 180)

One year later, in a report written for the Ministry of Foreign Affairs, in which the foreign and security consequences of both joining and remaining outside the EU (SOU 1994) were discussed, it was argued that there was no barrier to full Swedish participation in the CFSP (Archer 1996: 24). This means that there was a move towards acceptance of the compatibility of non-alignment and EU membership.

It is interesting to note that participation in NATO's Partnership for Peace (PfP) programme[4] caused no controversy in Sweden.[5] The explanation may be that the PfP programme was closely identified with Sweden's tradition of participating in collective security through the CSCE and the UN. The role of PfP was fairly clear, whereas there was more uncertainty attached to what the security and defence dimension of the EU really meant.

The fact that the scepticism towards the EU as a political actor decreased in Sweden in this period must be seen in connection with the implementation of the EEA agreement. The EEA agreement, which entered into force a year before Sweden joined the EU, can be viewed as a stepping-stone for obtaining experience of what it actually meant to be a full member.[6] A certain Europeanization of Swedish foreign policy can be identified during this period. UN voting records of the time, for instance, indicate that Sweden had begun to adjust its policy to the West European political mainstream (Lindström 1997: 6). As in Norway, explicit recognition of the need for EU involvement in the newly established Council on Baltic Sea States and the Barents Euro-Arctic Council also shows that the EU was beginning to be perceived as an important political actor (Herolf 2000: 153).

On 1 March 1994, the European Union managed to secure a final agreement with Sweden, Finland and Austria on the details of their accession packages. This led to an intensive debate within the Swedish electorate, and as a result of a referendum on 13 November 1994,[7] Sweden joined the EU on 1 January 1995 (Miles 1997: 248). The Swedish security identity was to experience even heavier pressure after Sweden became a member; but as we shall see below, this also opened up the possibility of influencing the development of the EU's security approach.

Effects of EU membership

Sweden changed its security doctrine slightly in 1992 in order to enable EU membership. Despite this change, the new formulation – 'non-alignment in peacetime, in order to enable Sweden to remain neutral in the case of war in its vicinity' – remained problematic for Sweden as a EU member. The difficulties were especially related to the WEU and to the Maastricht Treaty formulation concerning a potential future common defence.

With regard to Sweden's relationship with the WEU, the Swedish government found a solution: the status of observer was considered to be consistent with Sweden's non-alignment policy:

> the government regards it as valuable that Sweden, while keeping military non-alignment, is given the opportunity to gain insight and participate in the security policy discussion which is maintained within the WEU; especially humanitarian and peace-keeping missions as well as crisis management . . . Observer status also provides the opportunity to participate in the discussion of EU decisions whose implementation has been given to the WEU.
>
> (Quoted in Lindström 1997: 13)

However, the Swedish political leadership continued to be sceptical about the formulation in the Maastricht Treaty. Once inside the EU, it therefore became important for Sweden to use its influence to avoid such a development. Since Finland shared this concern, the two countries decided to take a joint initiative in this regard.

This explains why the foreign ministers of Sweden and Finland, Lena Hjelm-Wallén and Tarja Halonen, published a joint article in the morning newspapers *Dagens Nyheter* and *Helsingin Sanomat* on 21 April 1996, in which they suggested that the EU should enhance its role and capabilities within the area of conflict management. This was the beginning of a Swedish–Finnish initiative that led to the incorporation of the Petersberg tasks[8] into the Amsterdam Treaty (Dagens Nyheter and Helsingin Sanomat 1996). This 'demilitarization' of EU's security dimension was perceived both in Finland and in Sweden as a major diplomatic success. It meant that development towards collective defence was avoided, and that participation in the European security dimension was compatible with the policy of non-alignment.

Despite this success, the development towards a common European security policy continued to make it difficult for Sweden to retain its security policy formulation of 1992. Although 'non-alignment' was the most accurate term for the Swedish security approach, the concept of 'neutrality' was still being referred to, and Sweden continued to be perceived as a neutral country, both by the electorate itself and internationally. Indeed, together with other important Swedish keywords such as the 'welfare state' and 'internationalism' through the UN, 'neutrality' was considered by many to be an integral part of the Swedish national identity. The fact that neutrality was still referred to in the security doctrine made it difficult for the Swedish electorate, and even for some parliamentarians, to understand what the changed formulation in 1992 really meant (Miles 1997: 200; af Malmborg 2000). The same goes for foreign political leaders. As late as in April 2000, Jacques Chirac, in a speech given in Stockholm, claimed that 'I know how important neutrality is to the Swedish people' (Dagens Nyheter 2000).

Due to this confusion or ambiguity, several Swedish researchers and journalists argued that the time had come to erase the term 'neutrality' (Wahlbäck 1986; Åström 2000; Dagens Nyheter 2001). Some even wanted to let go of non-alignment now that Sweden was an EU member. In their opinion it had become difficult to understand how non-alignment could be consistent with Swedish participation in the ESDP (Aftonbladet 2000; Dagsavisen 2001; Landerholm 2001).

While there has been no real tendency towards abolishing the policy of non-alignment, the Swedish political leadership started to question the relevance of the concept of neutrality. On several occasions the Swedish government declared that Sweden could not remain indifferent in the case of an EU member being attacked. Deputy Minister at that time, Lena Hjelm-Wallén, claimed in an article in *Dagens Nyheter* on 8 February 2000 that:

> there are no military commitments in the EU but we have a political duty to help each other. I cannot see Sweden as being passive in the case of a war in our neighbourhood.
>
> (Quoted in Ojanen *et al.* 2000: 188)

But, recognizing the important role occupied by the concept of neutrality in the Swedish identity, she also argued for the need for informed debate before the concept could actually be erased from the formulation of Swedish security policy. One year later, in the annual declaration on foreign policy, the government invited the Riksdag to reconsider the security formulation from 1992 (Utrikesdepartementet 2001). The terrorist attacks on the USA on 11 September 2001 and the subsequent war on terrorism gave new dynamics to the debate. The Swedish government used the opportunity to make clear that the threat posed by terrorists and the risk that they could obtain weapons of mass destruction radically changed Sweden's security needs. The former Minister of Foreign Affairs, Anna Lindh, even suggested that Sweden would be 'unlikely' to stay neutral if an armed conflict should break out in her vicinity (*The Economist* 2001).

In parliamentary debate on the Swedish security doctrine and the use of the word 'neutral', the government proposed that, in the event of a crisis in neighbouring areas, militarily non-aligned Sweden would have three options: to act (military intervention), to remain neutral, or to be a non-belligerent (Ojanen 2002: 162). In February 2002, an assessment on the past benefits of the policy was added to the Swedish doctrine, which now is officially formulated as follows:

> The aims of Sweden's security policy are to preserve our country's peace and independence, contribute to stability and security in our vicinity and strengthen international peace and security. Sweden pursues a policy of non-participation in military alliances. This security policy, making it possible for our country to remain neutral in the event of conflicts in our vicinity, has served us well.
>
> (Utrikesdepartementet 2002)

While the concept of neutrality was still referred to in 2002, it seems to be fading from the formulation of Swedish security policy. The 2003 foreign policy statement makes no mention of it whatsoever (Utrikesdepartementet 2003).

Still, the government insists on the continued validity of non-alignment. On several occasions it has been argued that this policy is consistent with Swedish participation in the ESDP. The argument is that the European security dimension is not about collective defence but about international crisis management. Anna Lindh and Björn von Sydow (the latter at that time Defence Minister) emphasized this in an article in *Dagens Nyheter* on 12 November 2000:

> The EU's military capability is about international crisis management, and not about collective defence. Sweden may therefore be militarily non-aligned and participate in peace-keeping and peace enforcement operations together with other EU and UN countries.
>
> (Lindh and von Sydow 2000, my translation)

This section has shown how the establishment of the EU and EU membership have influenced Swedish security doctrine, and that this represents a change in the Swedish security identity. Since neutrality also served as a 'unifying element of a fairly effective national coordination mechanism aimed at defining the parameters for permissible external engagements' (Ekengren and Sundelius 1998: 143), EU membership led to various institutional adjustments. First, the creation of a co-ordinating group for EU relations (EU beredningen), composed of the state secretaries of the cabinet office, the Ministry of Justice and Finance and chaired by the state secretary on European Affairs in the Ministry of Foreign Affairs. Secondly, it led to increased co-ordination within the Ministry of Foreign Affairs itself – while CFSP was the responsibility of this ministry, its broad scope meant that it involved almost all departments in the ministry, so also here it became necessary to increase co-ordination (ibid.: 138). As Ekengren and Sundelius have argued:

> One of the most significant consequences of abandoning the neutrality doctrine as a guiding dogma for Swedish security policy has been erosion of this core of the domestic decision regime for foreign policy.
>
> (Ibid.: 143)

They also emphasize that, while a new decision regime for foreign and security policy has been established, there is a prevailing gap between the political elites and the population. The Swedish state has been Europeanized, while Swedish society has not (ibid.: 145).

EU membership has clearly influenced Swedish neutrality, but it is also important to note that Sweden has had a certain influence on the development of the EU's security dimension as well. In relation to the ESDP, for instance, Sweden has showed greater interest in the non-military aspects than most other EU members. At the Helsinki summit, Sweden proposed the establishment of a Civilian Crisis Management Committee in parallel with the military institutions; and during the Swedish EU Presidency, an action programme for the prevention of violent conflicts was proposed and adopted by the Gothenburg European Council in June 2001 (European Council 2001b). While Sweden has changed its security policy doctrine in order to make it compatible with EU membership, the Swedish government has also promoted several initiatives concerning the further development of European security. For instance, it has been particularly important for Sweden to fight any tendencies towards a collective defence system.

Despite this eagerness to 'demilitarize' the EU, and to emphasize non-military dimensions of European security policy, the Swedish discourse on national security and defence long continued to give priority to a traditional security approach focused on the military. Despite force reductions, qualitative changes have until recently been few. Until the end of the decade, the national security and defence discourse remained dominated by territorial defence against a potential military invasion. However, as we shall see in the next section, the development towards a European Security and Defence Policy has led to changes also in Swedish defence policy.

Impact of the ESDP

At the same time as Sweden joined the EU, a change can be identified in the Swedish security discourse towards more emphasis on the country's international commitments in security questions. While these changes must be seen in relation to EU membership, the increased Swedish participation in NATO as of 1994 is also important here. But despite some changes in the discourse in 1995, it was not until 1998 that the Swedish government proposed to undertake a major qualitative reform of its national defence forces. While NATO also pushed for such changes, the political leadership in Sweden explicitly referred to the ESDP process as the main reason for the changes. Territorial defence had remained the main task of the defence forces until late 1990s, and as Ricard Bengtsson has argued, the recent changes towards greater emphasis on international crisis management must be understood in relation to the European integration process and the development towards an ESDP (Bengtsson and Ericson 2001). This was a continuation of an increased acceptance of the EU as a security actor, an acceptance that has developed gradually since Sweden joined the Union.

Towards international crisis management

Since both neutrality and a credible independent national defence have been the defining elements of Sweden's security identity, it was important to obtain a national consensus before proposing any radical changes in Swedish defence policies. In order to obtain such a consensus, the government decided to establish a permanent commission, consisting of representatives of the government and representatives of the political parties of Parliament, for consultations concerning the long-range development of Swedish defence and security policy. Thus the Swedish Defence Commission was established in 1994, with the task of preparing major defence resolutions on defence programmes by publishing a series of reports. These have been used as a basis for government bills to the Riksdag.

In 1995, the same year that Sweden became an EU member and one year after Sweden had joined NATO's North Atlantic Co-operation Council (NACC) and Partnership for Peace (PfP), the Defence Commission presented a report which emphasized the importance of enhancing co-operation among the European states, and stated that Sweden should give high priority to 'conflict prevention', 'crisis management' and 'humanitarian efforts'. Continued European integration was seen as an important part of Swedish security, especially with the EU being expanded to include Central and Eastern Europe and the Baltic states (Försvarsdepartementet 1995: 125–6). This report represented the first change in the Swedish post-Cold War defence discourse, recognizing, at least in principle, the need for more emphasis on Swedish international commitments than on the tradition of national territorial defence. While important elements of the latter were retained, Sweden was now starting to take a greater responsibility for European security, rather than seeing itself as dependent on a security situation determined by the great powers (Archer 1996).

The parliamentary decisions of 6 December 1995 and 14 February 1996, on the formulation of Swedish security policy, also reflect this shift. In reference to Sweden's first year within the EU, it was stated that:

> membership in the EU and participation in the CFSP framework gives Sweden an improved security policy position as well as increased opportunities to engage in foreign and security policy issues in our vicinity.
>
> (Quoted in Lindström 1997: 14)

Similarly, the February 1996 Declaration continued along the same line, adding a call for greater interaction with the outside world:

> we shall all depend on our common understanding and can in the long run only evolve in cooperation with the outside world.
>
> (Ibid.: 14)

These decisions made Swedish participation in peace-support operations possible. It was underlined that taking part in such operations should be considered a major task of Swedish defence policy. The same year the Swedish government decided to establish SWERAP (Swedish Rapid Reaction Unit), a 500-strong rapid reaction force that was declared operational on 1 July 1998.

More emphasis on the European dimension and a move towards a greater European commitment has also become increasingly evident in the annual declarations on foreign policy since 1997. In the declaration presented in February 1997, four months before the Amsterdam Treaty was signed, the Swedish government for the first time discussed the European dimension in international co-operation alongside co-operation with the other Nordic countries and with the UN. This was further emphasized in the next declaration (Utrikesdepartementet 1998). The 1999 declaration, presented shortly after the St Malo summit, explicitly stated that 'Sweden has a European identity and a European responsibility'. Emphasizing the continued Swedish policy of non-alignment, the government also expressed its intention to 'strengthen Europe's crisis management capability'. It was argued that 'with its breadth and community of values, the EU has great potential in this area' (Utrikesdepartementet 1999). At the European Council in Feira, the Swedish Prime Minister had also explicitly supported the Portuguese proposal concerning the constitution of a European force before the end of 2003, and that this force should have close relations with NATO (Bengtsson and Ericson 2001).

But how is it possible to claim that it is the EU, and not Sweden's participation in NATO, that has been the main driving force behind this increased interest in participating in international crisis management? With regard to Swedish participation in NATO-led operations in the 1990s, this started when the UN's UNPROFOR force became a NATO force, IFOR, in 1995 (later SFOR). It was then natural for the Swedish contingent, which had participated in UNPROFOR, to remain in Bosnia. This was also a result of the establishment of the formal relationship between Sweden and NATO that had developed since 1994, when Sweden joined the NACC (which was succeeded by the Euro-Atlantic Partnership Council, EAPC, in 1997) and the PfP. As already mentioned, participation in PfP was not controversial in Sweden. It was seen as a wide form of co-operation, very similar to the type of international engagement Sweden had had through the UN and CSCE. In addition, the PfP was also seen as strengthening Sweden's capacity to participate in international peace-promoting and humanitarian operations. Moreover, since 1995 Sweden has also participated in the Planning and Review Process (PARP), the purpose of which is to increase the interoperability of the participating countries' armed forces so that they can better co-operate in joint operations. This process within NATO has of course had an impact on the Swedish security discourse.

Nevertheless, when looking at the discourse, it is the EU that is highlighted as the main reason for these changes. This argument becomes even stronger when one includes developments within the Swedish defence industry. In fact, this industry started to be Europeanized before the Swedish security policy changed. Traditionally, the national defence industry has been strong in Sweden, and has been seen as essential to the credibility of neutrality. For a long time, it was important to uphold the independence of this industry. The need to be technologically advanced and also to compensate for the overall force reductions in Europe, however, has contributed to changing this view. Increasingly, the defence industry is viewed as one industry among others, and a field where European co-operation can increase competitiveness.

Defence industrial co-operation has also had consequences for the national security discourse in Sweden, since it implies a choice between European and transatlantic frameworks. Sweden, with the fifth largest defence industry sector in Europe, has participated in the Western European Armament Group, as observers since 1997 and as a full member since November 2000 (Mörth 2000: 135–6). In 1998 a Letter of Intent was signed with the other defence industry great powers – Germany, France, the United Kingdom and Italy – with the aim of creating a European Aerospace and Defence Company (EADC). In light of the report from the Ministry of Defence presented in 2001, this indicates that the country is drawing closer to European co-operation in this section:

> Sweden is dependent on a close co-operation and exchange with the US in this area. However, this has to be compatible with an active participation in the European defence industrial co-operation to avoid creating dependency on one part.
>
> (Försvarsberedningen 2001: 204, my translation)

Adapting the national defence forces

The decision to undertake the first major and qualitative reorientation of the Swedish defence forces was made by the Riksdag as recently as in 1999. While this decision must be seen as a logical result of a process which had started back in 1995, the timing of the parliamentary decision indicates that it was more directly related to the ESDP process.

Increased recognition of the development of a European military capacity, and the Swedish contribution to this dimension, led to the initial reforms in national defence policy. The 1996 Parliamentary defence decision establishes that Sweden's capacity for participation in peace-promoting activities must be enhanced, and that participation in such operations is to be regarded as one of the main tasks of the total defence authorities. On 1 July 1997, the Swedish International Command (SWEDINT) was established. SWEDINT organizes, trains and supports the peace-promoting operations in which Sweden takes part, and includes an international force sizeable enough to take part as an independent unit – a battalion – within a larger international force. Special units for command and control and field operations (e.g. de-mining, transport and medical services) can also be organized by the International Command, and can also take part in civilian humanitarian operations.[9]

More radical changes were proposed later by the 'review report for security and defence policy', undertaken by the Defence Commission during the spring of 1999 (Försvarsberedningen 1999). The Commission's report emphasized the need for higher priority to be given to developing a crisis management capability. On the basis of advice from the Commission and the defence establishment, the Swedish government presented a proposal for major defence reform in November 1999 (Försvarsdepartementet 1999–2000), approved by the Riksdag in March 2000. This marked the beginning of the biggest transformation of Swedish military defence in the post-Cold War period. It represents a clear move away from territorial defence towards smaller and more flexible forces ready to meet a broad spectrum of challenges.

The relationship between the development of an ESDP in the EU and these changes was also emphasized by the Minister of Defence:

> Similar reforms have been implemented in other European countries . . . The events of recent years in the Balkans have strengthened the European countries' will to develop a capability for crisis management and conflict prevention. Important steps in that direction were taken by the European Council in Cologne, where the EU's Member States decided to develop an effective European capacity for crisis management. This decision is followed up by the European Council in Helsinki with a decision concerning concrete headline goals for

the European crisis management capability and institutional framework for commanding the future capabilities . . . We are going to
reform our national defence forces, giving priority to a new defence.
This is a reform that follows the development in Europe and which
will give Sweden a modern defence for the future.

(von Sydow 1999, my translation)

In the 2000 declaration on foreign policy the government also affirmed
that 'Sweden is part of Europe and its foreign policy is characterized by a
triple identity . . . at the same time Nordic, global and European'. It also
emphasized 'that the Swedish government fully supports the recent progress
towards a strengthened European capability in both military and civilian
crisis management'. The policy of non-alignment is still referred to, but at
the same time it is underlined that 'Sweden's security has a clear European
dimension' (Utrikesdepartementet 2000).

The ESDP process forced Sweden to produce specific force commitments
to future EU crisis management operations. At the Capability Conference in
November 2000, Sweden committed in all about 1,900 troops.[10] While this
commitment may seem rather generous, it was not automatic, and was to be
based on a case-by-case decision made by the Riksdag (Ojanen 2002: 164).
When the EU's Ministers of Defence declared, at a similar conference four
years later, their intention to commit up to thirteen battle groups, Sweden
and Finland declared the intention (together with Norway) to establish such
a group with Sweden assuming the responsibility as Framework Nation.

Sweden's continued attachment to collective security has been particularly
evident in its emphasis on the need for a UN mandate for future EU operations. However, in the March 2001 report from the Ministry of Defence, the
government suggested a change of this practice (Försvarsberedningen 2001:
192). Such a change would make participation in operations possible even in
the absence of a mandate from the UN (or the OSCE), and, furthermore,
without consulting Parliament. This shows that the Swedish security discourse, throughout the second half of the 1990s, has moved away from its
traditional security approach. Gradually the Swedish security identity has
changed from being characterized by neutrality and territorial defence, to
increased Europeanism and international crisis management.

Impact of the EU's comprehensive security approach

All the Nordic countries are well known for their interest in non-military
aspects of security and for being active promoters of these aspects in multilateral frameworks like the UN and the OSCE. While allied countries
had the opportunity to discuss questions related to 'hard' security in a
multilateral framework with their allies in NATO, for neutral countries the
international arena has been limited to 'soft' security issues. This has, as

Ann-Sofie Dahl argues, 'helped put Sweden on the map as a country with disproportional wide-ranging internationalist ambitions, given its size and location, and with strong moralist and ideological convictions to match' (Dahl 2002: 143). Traditionally this kind of activism took place within CSCE (later OSCE), and the UN, but more recently also in NATO (PfP) and the EU.

As the discussion in the previous sections concerning Sweden's traditional security approach has shown, there has been an important difference between the Swedish discourse at home, and that expressed on the international level. While Sweden presented a rather progressive line of security thinking in various international frameworks, at home, the security discourse remained far more traditional and military-focused. As we have seen, the EU has contributed to a change from territorial defence being seen as the central task of the Swedish defence forces to a greater emphasis on international military crisis management. In addition, this section will show that EU membership has led to a more profound recognition of the complexity of the security context in the Swedish discourse. In fact, a decision was made to incorporate the widened concept of security into the Swedish security doctrine in 1995, the year when Sweden joined the EU. While many states introduced the wider security concept only at the rhetorical level, Sweden managed to operationalize it, by redefining the traditional concept of 'total defence' (Holmen and Ulriksen 2000).

It is interesting to note that the Ministry of Defence actually defines a comprehensive security approach as a guide for its security and defence policy as well as co-operation within the EU.[11] Accordingly, the current Minister of Defence, Leni Björklund argues that:

> Developments in society have made us increasingly dependent on modern technology and an efficient infrastructure. Society has become more susceptible to disruption and attack. Climate change has increased the risk of natural disasters. Man-made environmental disasters continue to afflict us. Terrorist attacks are a genuine threat. In the search for a more secure society, the various players in public life must work together towards common goals.[12]

This indicates that Sweden has in fact managed to 'institutionalize' a comprehensive security approach in relation to external and internal security as well. In the following two sections we will look at this development, asking what role the EU has played in this process.

Internal security

The major defence reforms of 1999 have been followed by initiatives to increase the emphasis on civilian security and on 'the vulnerability of civil society'. Two recent reports are important in this context.

The first is a report from the Swedish Defence Commission, which must be seen as a contribution to the ongoing discussions concerning the national security doctrine. It emphasizes 'the need to define more clearly the capabilities required to deal with threats that are not armed attacks in the strict sense of the term, but rather threats coming from attacks where advanced methods and weapons, including non-conventional weapons, that are implemented by other actors than states' (Försvarsberedningen 2001: English summary). The report focuses on various forms of terrorist attacks, but has been criticized for being too preoccupied with cyber-terrorism while ignoring other, more likely, threats (Eriksson *et al.* 2001).

The second is a report from an independent commission established by the Ministry of Defence to analyse and to submit proposals for a more integrated approach to civil defence and emergency planning. The Commission has proposed the establishment of an institution for co-ordination of the various national security mechanisms (SOU 2001b). Such a co-ordinated security approach has received increased attention, and in an article written for the Swedish Defence Commission, Bengt Sundelius argues that Sweden needs to replace the traditional total defence, which was built upon the conception that civil society would need to assist the military in the case of war, by what he calls a 'societal defence' system in which priority is given to the protection of an increasingly vulnerable civilian society (Sundelius 2001: 8).

In most countries, greater attention has been given to these aspects of national security in the wake of 11 September 2001, and Sweden is no exception. Acting on a recommendation by the Commission mentioned above, the government decided to replace the Swedish Agency for Emergency Planning (ÖCB) with a new co-ordinating authority for national crisis management (Försvarsdepartementet 2001–2). This new authority for national crisis management, the Swedish Emergency Management Agency (KBM), became operational on 1 July 2002, taking over some of the tasks of now defunct ÖCB and the National Board for Psychological Defence (SPF). The main task of the KBM is to create a national crisis management capacity better adapted to the new security context by improving co-ordination between the relevant authorities. The KBM is also intended to operate internationally in emergency co-operation ventures pursued within the EU.

At the government level, it is the Swedish Ministry of Defence that has the co-ordination responsibility for civil defence. This has its origins in Sweden's tradition of neutrality and the total defence tradition, which aimed to preserve peace and freedom in the event of war, and has facilitated Swedish adaptation to the new security context. Director of KBM, Ann-Louise Eksborg, argues in favour of a profound change in the Swedish national security approach:

Now that the Cold War is over, we can see other threats that could jeopardize national security. This is why we must now broaden our threat perspective and think along new lines. The threats are different, and our resources must be organized differently.

(Eksborg 2002)

She argues that 'total defence is now just one part of a larger concept, namely the collective efforts to enhance our national security' (ibid.). This indicates that there is an ongoing development in the Swedish security discourse towards improving comprehensiveness also within the internal security dimension.

The need to fight international crime and terrorism has been defined as a security issue both in the EU and in Sweden. While the fight against international crime is the responsibility of the Ministry of Justice in Sweden, the Ministry of Defence is involved with the Coast Guard, which takes an active part in crime prevention and border control. The events of 11 September have undoubtedly increased the need for strengthening police co-operation and border control. On the other hand, this was a development that had already occurred in Sweden in line with the EU's heightened focus on internal security. This process started with the Schengen agreement and the Maastricht Treaty; then the Amsterdam Treaty, followed up by the Tampere European Council, initiated a more focused process with the creation of an area of freedom, security and justice. The introduction of European police co-operation and the focus on fighting international crime in the dominant Swedish security discourse seem to be products of this development within the EU.

Referring to Swedish efforts to get the civilian aspects of external crisis management included in the EU's external security dimension, Bengt Sundelius has recommended that Sweden follow up these initiatives by emphasizing the need for the establishment of an internal crisis management capacity within the EU (Sundelius 2001: 14). As a result of the terrorist attacks of 11 September 2001, this proposal has indeed been put on the EU agenda – but without a Swedish initiative, which indicates that the recent emphasis on comprehensive security rather is a result of a Europeanization process. At least, it seems as if EU membership has made it more difficult for Sweden to have two different discourses on security – one military-oriented at the national level, and a broader one at the European level. Defending a civilian or comprehensive approach to security on the EU level makes it more difficult to uphold an internal security approach that is dominated by the military dimension and the concept of total defence.

This is why Sweden's political leaders can be said to have adapted their security discourse on the national arena to their own discourse on within the EU. In other words, Swedish membership in the EU and the Swedish Ministry of Foreign Affairs' promotion of comprehensive security within the EU may in turn have contributed to an increased awareness of the need to adapt to the new security context at home, and especially within the Ministry of Defence.

External security

In fact, Sweden has been a major promoter of a comprehensive external security identity for the EU (Björkdahl 2002). After the establishment of the Petersberg tasks, which made planned military co-operation part of a collective security arrangement, the country's political leaders have strongly emphasized the need to develop further the non-military aspects of the Union's security approach as well.

This was rapidly emphasized in the Ministry of Defence. CIMIC became part of the new doctrine, and the army's newly established reaction force (SWERAP) was provided with a CIMIC section. Since then there has been a major focus on improving the Swedish training activities both on the military side (SWEDINT) and on the civilian side (SOU 1999).

For Sweden, military crisis management within the EU is acceptable only if combined with civilian crisis management and conflict prevention. Thus, in yet another joint newspaper article, the Swedish and the Finnish foreign ministers explained that civilian and military crisis management complement each other; and, since the most serious shortcomings are still on the civilian side, they plead for its further development. In their view, the EU should concentrate on the areas in which it works best, complementing other international actors (Lindh and Tuomioja 2000).

During the Swedish EU Presidency in 2001, the Swedish government was particularly active in this area. The Committee for Civilian Aspects of Crisis Management was established to complement the new crisis management institutions on the military side (the Political and Security Committee (PSC), the Military Committee (MC) and the Military Staff), and a programme for conflict prevention, drafted by the Presidency, was adopted at the European Council in Gothenburg (European Council 2001b). The Swedish presidency also sought to ensure that the EU would take the initiative to a regional meeting between the various organizations involved in crisis prevention in Europe.

While Sweden has, as Annika Björkdahl argues, contributed to the establishment of a culture of conflict prevention in multilateral frameworks such as the UN and the EU (Björkdahl 2002: 87, 103, 111), this is mainly a result of efforts made by the Swedish Ministry of Foreign Affairs. The Ministry of Defence, which expresses the dominant Swedish discourse on security, was, until recently, far more military focused. Recently, however aspects of comprehensive security have also been incorporated into this discourse. Thus, it is also possible to claim that the increased emphasis on comprehensive security in the EU (in which conflict prevention is an important element) has gradually influenced Sweden's dominant security discourse as well. As we have seen, this discourse has been far more traditional and military-focused than the one which Sweden has promoted internationally. As the former Minister of Foreign Affairs Anna Lindh recognized, it is not an easy task to change a state's security policy:

> The rapid and far-reaching political upheavals of recent years have not only given rise to a totally new security policy situation in both Sweden and in Europe; they have also had repercussions on other continents . . . But agreement on the existence and nature of a new reality does not mean that the ability to deal with new security policy challenges has developed accordingly. Many debates still cling to views and notions dating back to the Cold War era.
>
> (Lindh 2001, my translation)

However, in parallel with the changes in the EU towards a more comprehensive security approach, some specific decisions have been taken also in Sweden to improve the country's contributions to the development of a comprehensive European crisis management capacity. Following an initiative from the Ministry of Foreign Affairs, the Swedish government established several commissions to prepare proposals on how to improve civilian–military co-operation in crisis management and conflict prevention (SOU 1999, 2000, 2001a). On the basis of their conclusions, the government decided in May 2002 to establish a civilian military co-operation centre for recruitment and training of personnel for international operations. The centre (the 'Folke Bernadotte Academy') was opened 1 September 2002, and as the Ministry of Foreign Affairs emphasized, 'the academy is a Swedish response to the EU decision to improve its capacity for crisis management'. The academy has been established under the authority of the Ministry of Foreign Affairs, but the intention, at least, is to have a close co-operation with Swedish Armed Forces International Centre (SWEDINT) in the armed forces.[13] The fact that the Ministry of Defence has also shown increasing interest in a broader security approach should facilitate a close co-operation. For instance, a CIMIC handbook was published in 2002, and steps have been taken towards strengthening civil–military co-ordination, by the institutionalization of weekly meetings of the Ministry of Foreign Affairs, the Ministry of Defence and the Ministry of Justice (Jakobsen, forthcoming: ch. 6).

Beyond the concept of CIMIC, the current Minister of Defence, Leni Björklund, also focused on the broader security concept at the annual conference on Swedish defence in Sälen in 22 January 2003:

> There is today no threat against our sovereignty. In addition we cannot see that there is one in the near future. At the same time we may argue that security is far more than the lack of military threats.

We are talking today about a broader security concept and a broader threat picture.

(Leni Björklund 2003, my translation)

The general interest in comprehensive external security is also evident in a speech she gave in Switzerland, explaining the main content of the Swedish defence reforms:

If I were to describe in a few words the very essence of the reform I would say that we abandon a defence based on the threat of invasion and instead we aim for a modern defence that can quickly adapt to new situations. The emphasis is on efficiency, flexibility and output with a higher capacity for international interventions. Against the new security threats we can cut the spending on defence. Instead we strengthen other means and instruments that are also essential and even more so for security. This is why we for example will increase the financial resources for the police and the judicial system.

(Björklund 2004, my translation)

In addition, the introduction of EU battle groups can be seen as an initiative to strengthen the Union's comprehensive security approach. Referring to Swedish participation in this arrangement, Leni Björklund recently argued that:

In this context it is necessary to emphasize the importance of developing methods and procedures that can bring civilian and military processes closer together at all levels. By doing so I believe that the European Union will ensure coherent and effectively coordinated crisis management operations. In this work we should also draw on the experiences of the UN in this field.[14]

Europeanization and socialization

Main findings

The relationship between the EU and Sweden is one of great complexity. Many would argue that it is Swedish policy-makers that influence the European discourse, rather than the other way around. As we have seen, Sweden has taken several initiatives aimed at making the European security dimension compatible with non-alignment, and these initiatives have been adopted by the EU as well. Together with Finland, Sweden proposed that the Petersberg tasks be incorporated in the Treaty; more recently, Sweden has been promoting the development of a comprehensive European security approach, in the area of external security. While this activism can be understood as a continuation of the discourse that Sweden promoted in other multilateral frameworks throughout the Cold War period, there is one important difference, linked to the fact that the EU is not merely another international organization. The high level of political integration within the EU makes it more difficult for Sweden to maintain two different security discourses – one at the international (here: European) level, and a different one at the domestic level. The analysis in this chapter shows that the EU has had an important impact on the development of Sweden's national security discourse throughout the 1990s. This Europeanization has come about gradually and in accordance with the different phases in the development towards an EU security identity.

The first change happened as a reaction to the Maastricht Treaty and the establishment of a *political union*. This led to increased interest in EU membership, which in turn required a change in Sweden's national security doctrine. Discussions about whether to abandon the concept of neutrality have gradually resulted in a toning-down of this concept, while retaining the reference to non-alignment. The first change in the Swedish security formulation was made in 1992, in order to enable membership; when Sweden had become an EU member and the Petersberg tasks were included, the EU was increasingly accepted as a security actor, and a new debate concerning the security formulation began to emerge.

Second, the development towards a *European Security and Defence Policy*, which started with the Amsterdam Treaty, has also accelerated the process away from a security discourse dominated by territorial defence, and towards one with greater emphasis on international crisis management. This has led to a gradual internationalization of the Swedish defence forces. While discursively this process was started in 1995, it went further after the ESDP was launched. The first major change in the national defence forces started in 1999. While Sweden's participation in NATO's PfP since 1994 is also relevant here, official statements refer to developments within the EU as the main reason for these changes.

Third, and parallel to the ongoing changes towards a *European comprehensive security approach*, we can see a move towards greater comprehensiveness also in the dominant Swedish discourse on security. This seems to be the case both when it comes to the external dimension, where CIMIC (civilian–military co-operation) and conflict prevention have been given far more attention than purely military crisis management; and in relation to the internal dimension, where the traditional 'total defence' concept gradually is being replaced by something that, in Bengt Sundelius' term, may more accurately be defined as 'societal defence'. In relation to this aspect, there are few explicit references to the EU. Indirectly, however, these changes may also be understood in relation to Swedish EU membership. In fact, it can be argued that the Swedish emphasis on developing a comprehensive external security approach in the EU, with conflict prevention and civilian crisis management as its cornerstones, has made it difficult to uphold at the national level a discourse focused on military aspects.

Does then this process of Europeanization represent a radical change in national security identity? Or should it be characterized as an instrumental and necessary adaptation to external changes? Let us approach these questions by using five-phase socialization model presented in Chapter 3.

Instrumental adaptation or identity change?

As noted, a traditional security discourse dominated by territorial defence prevailed in Sweden throughout the 1990s. This traditionalism was expressed through an attachment to neutrality and a strong military defence. While this seems to indicate that Sweden had not moved beyond the first phase of a socialization process, characterized by status quo and the continuation of a traditional security approach before the end of the 1990s, a new political discourse did start to emerge in the early 1990s (phase 2). These voices, influenced by the processes in the EU, began to challenge the traditional security discourse.

As we have seen, the Maastricht Treaty and the establishment of a political union led to a debate concerning possible EU membership for Sweden, and questioned the value of continued Swedish neutrality. Then, the development towards an ESDP opened up for questions concerning the need to transform the national defence forces. And finally, the development towards a comprehensive European security approach led to greater interest in these issues and the possibilities of a similar development at home. All this shows that there has been a move into the second phase – a phase characterized by exchange of views, and one in which arguments both for change and continuity are expressed.

In the third phase of the socialization process, the security discourse of domestic political leaders undergoes instrumental adaptation in response to external and internal pressures. In relation to all three dimensions, the new ideas were gradually adopted by the Swedish political elite – initially for instrumental reasons and without a change in the national security identity. In the fourth phase of the socialization process, governments are convinced and/or persuaded that norm compliance is the 'right thing', not merely a necessary instrumental adaptation to a changed external context. Little by little Sweden's security discourse has undergone such changes, which also indicates a change in identity. The fact that these ideas are also largely institutionalized indicates a move into the fifth and final phase.

With the Maastricht Treaty and the creation of a Common Foreign and Security Policy, the membership question was put on the agenda. A change in the country's security doctrine was considered necessary in order to make membership possible, and membership was increasingly perceived as a way to safeguard against Sweden's becoming marginalized in European affairs in general and European security in particular. A first change in the Swedish security doctrine was adopted in 1992 in order to enable Sweden to join the EU, which means an instrumental adaptation to the EU. Slowly, pressure was put on this revised security formulation as well, which in the end led to a gradual fading of the neutrality concept. Since neutrality had long been an important part of the national security identity, the decision to eradicate almost any references to it must indicate that the political leadership had become convinced or persuaded that this was the 'right thing' to do. Thus, this change had evolved into an example of identity change.

After Sweden had joined the EU, Swedish political leaders became engaged in a process of careful argument within the EU concerning the character of the Union's identity. While the Swedish security identity has been clearly Europeanized, Sweden has also managed to exert influence at the European level. This has resulted in a certain Swedish process aimed at making the EU compatible with non-alignment – first with the incorporation of the Petersberg tasks into the treaty, and later with the introduction of the concept of conflict prevention. It is interesting to note that, in turn, this new European security discourse can also be shown to have influenced the domestic Swedish discourse. A similar development can be found at the national level.

This means that there has gradually been increased interest in international crisis management and a comprehensive external security approach in the Ministry of Defence. Previously, comprehensive security and soft security were the competences of the Ministry of Foreign Affairs. In relation to national or internal security there has also been a move away from a military-oriented concept of total defence to a more civilian-oriented approach. The fact that such a comprehensive security approach is referred to in the official documents produced by the Ministry of Defence, and has thus become an integral part of the dominant national discourse on security, indicates that this represents an example of identity change. The broad spectre of the areas of responsibility for the Ministry of Defence also shows that a comprehensive security approach has even become institutionalized (phase 5).[15] While the influence seems to go both ways, it is possible to argue that the European integration process has influenced the Swedish security identity and has contributed to making comprehensive security an integral part of the dominant national security discourse.

5

FINLAND

Pragmatic adapter

After a study of the Union's impact on Sweden's security identity we continue with a similar analysis of Finland's security approach. According to Teija Tiilikainen, there is no necessity for small states to adapt to the dominant conceptions behind European integration. 'Newcomers like Finland could, on the contrary, use their virginal position for the introduction of solutions to the age-long conflicts burdening European government building', she argues (Tiilikainen 1998: 175). Without overlooking Finland's contributions to the integration process, I will argue that the country's security approach has been largely influenced by the EU since the early 1990s. Painful historical experiences combined with a fragile geopolitical position, however, have made it difficult for Finland to move beyond a security identity dominated by territorial defence against a potential attack from Russia. While this has not prevented changes in the Finnish security approach, these are, as we shall see, characterized by instrumental adaptation rather than identity change.

The structure of this chapter follows that of the previous one. We begin with a short historical background to the Finnish security identity as presented in the country's dominant security discourse in the late 1980s. The second part studies the first changes in the security discourse after the end of the Cold War and the establishment of a political union. The third part takes a closer look at changes in the Finnish discourse on security in the period after the process towards a European Security and Defence Policy was initiated. The fourth part investigates the impact of the Union's comprehensive security approach. The chapter concludes with a discussion of the degree and character of the Europeanization of the Finnish security discourse.

A pragmatic neutral

After 700 years under Swedish and Russian rule, Finland gained its independence in 1917. It was some years later, in 1935, that the government declared that Finland was a neutral country.[1] Because of its geopolitical position and painful historical experiences, this choice was perceived as the

only viable option at the time. Ever since then, Finland has retained a pragmatic attitude to neutrality – in sharp contrast to Swedish neutrality, which is
based on an ideological conviction. If 'neutrality' is the codeword that long
defined the dominant security discourse of Sweden, then 'territorial defence'
has had such a function in the Finnish discourse.

Three historical periods have been important for the consolidation of the
Finnish security identity that took place in the late 1980s and early 1990s.
The first period, lasting until the end of the Second World War, was characterized by a series of struggles for national survival, ultimately with the
choice of neutrality as the sole possible option. The second period, from
1945 until the mid-1970s, was characterized by a policy of concessions to the
neighbouring Soviet Union. The third, which started in the 1970s, might be
characterized as a policy of 'active neutrality' – involving neutrality and
bridge-building between the two superpowers.

Fighting for survival (1808–1945)

Finland was separated from Sweden in 1808 – a separation that came about
as a by-product of a deal struck between Napoleon and the Russian czar,
Alexander I. The deal implied that the Russian czar should persuade Sweden
to join Napoleon's blockade against Britain. When Sweden refused, however,
Russian forces occupied Finland, and the country became annexed to the
Russian empire as a Grand Duchy of the czar. Its borders were not drawn up
along any ethnic or linguistic principles, and dialects of Finnish were spoken
on both the Swedish and the Russian side of the Grand Duchy. This was,
in essence, a geopolitical entity or a buffer state for the protection of the
Russian capital, St Petersburg.

The switch of allegiance was rewarded with enhanced political status. In
reality this meant the birth of a separate Finnish state with an independent
administrative structure – a central administration headed by a Senate[2] and a
Diet.[3] In addition, Finland retained such previous attributes as Lutheran
religion, constitutional monarchy, Swedish civil and criminal law, and the
freedom of the peasantry. Thus, while Finland became part of the Russian
empire in geopolitical terms, it remained part of the Western world in
cultural terms (Jakobson 1998: 12).

It soon became important for Finland to develop a national identity of its
own, and the Finnish elite set about constructing a national identity within
the framework of imperial Russia. As Max Jakobson argues, 'Finnish
nationalism echoed the slogan of Italian nationalists in the 1860s: "We have
made Italy – now we must make Italians"' (ibid.: 14). An important part of
this nation-building was the publication of the national epic, *Kalevala*.[4] This
infused the Finnish people with pride in their cultural heritage, and made
Finnish claims to nationhood widely known abroad (Joenniemi 2002: 193).
From the 1860s the Finnish language was by law granted equal status to

Swedish, the Diet was convened regularly and the Grand Duchy got its own central bank and introduced its own currency.

After almost a century of relative harmony, the relationship between Russia and Finland found itself transformed into a classical confrontation between a great power bent upon safeguarding its imperial interests and a small people fighting for its own way of life. Unrest in Russia during the first decade of the twentieth century (Russian defeat in the War against Japan in 1905, and revolutionary tendencies at home) also spread to Finland, and forced on the czar the demand for constitutional rule. In Finland, the old Diet of four estates was replaced by a single-chamber Parliament elected by universal suffrage in 1906.[5] The Russian Revolution and the overthrow of the czarist regime in 1917 subsequently provided Finland with the opportunity to declare full independence on 6 December of that year.

But formal independence did not lead to immediate stability. Once the external threat receded, the social unrest that had brewing since the beginning of the century exploded in a violent conflict between the 'Red guards' supported by the Bolsheviks and the 'White army' supported by the Germans. In the civil war that raged from January until May 1918, a total of 30,000 Finns were killed.[6] After the war Finland was perceived, both in Moscow and in Western Europe, as a German satellite. Finland's primary goals were therefore to ensure that it would not be drawn into a new conflict between Germany and the Soviet Union, and to improve the country's international image. Finland joined the League of Nations in 1920. Then, in December 1935, the Finnish government declared that it wished to adhere to a 'Scandinavian orientation' – the neutrality of Finland, the government stated, could best be preserved in association with other Scandinavian nations whose loyalty to the concept of neutrality was universally acknowledged (Jakobson 1998: 24).

However, this avowed neutrality did not succeed in avoiding a new conflict, and in 1939 Finland was once again attacked by its neighbour to the East. The non-aggression pact signed between Germany and the Soviet Union on 24 August 1939 (the Molotov–Ribbentrop Pact) shattered the very foundations of the international order that had emerged in the Baltic region following the collapse of the Russian empire. The secret protocol attached to the treaty was not known, but it was easy to guess that Moscow must have obtained from Hitler what it had failed to extract from the Western powers: a free hand in the Baltic area. In the course of only a month, the German war machine crushed Poland, dividing it up as had been agreed between the two dictators. It took another two weeks for the Soviets to bully the governments of the three Baltic states into accepting 'mutual assisting treaties' granting Soviet forces access to all military bases south of the Gulf of Finland that Russia had lost in the First World War. On 5 October 1939, the Finnish government received an invitation to send a delegation to Moscow to discuss 'concrete political issues'.

Stalin informed the Finns that he needed more depth for his defence of Leningrad, so the Finnish borders would have to be moved farther north from city (ceding parts of Karelia to the Soviet Union), and that the Soviet Navy had to have a base on the southern coast of Finland, close to Helsinki (at Hanko). The Finnish government first made a desperate search for international support. But with the realization that no such assistance would be forthcoming, the Finnish government felt forced to agree to give up some territory. The Finnish authorities refused, however, to yield the base that Stalin had asked for, fearing that it could be used to subvert Finnish independence. It was on this very issue that the talks with Moscow broke down, which led Stalin to launch his attack on Finland in November 1939. Unexpectedly, the Finnish army managed to defend the country, and this stand against overwhelming odds led to a flood of international sympathy for Finland and its Winter War (ibid.: 28–9). However, Stalin launched a second attack some months later (in March 1940); this time he got both the base he wanted as well as a great deal more territory than he had originally asked for (all of Karelia).

While this war is an important factor in Finland's history, it was not the last one between Finland and the Soviet Union. The fate of the Baltic states, annexed to the Soviet Union in the summer of 1940, sharpened Finnish anxieties. That Finland was next on the list was confirmed in November 1940 when Molotov told Hitler in Berlin that his government 'intended to resolve the Finnish question' in the manner he had applied to Barbarossa and the Baltic states (ibid.: 35). Molotov's strategy, however, did not fit into Hitler's greater war strategy. The latter's own plans for an invasion of the Soviet Union and his intentions to make Finland part of these plans led him to give Finland the chance to buy German arms as long as Finland allowed German troops to pass through the country to and from occupied Norway – an agreement similar to the one already reached with Sweden. Finland agreed, hoping that this could restore the balance of power between Germany and the Soviet Union, and enable Finland to restore its own neutrality. In reality, however, Germany considered Finland as an ally, and the Western countries saw Finland as a friend of the enemy. The widespread international sympathy and admiration which had arisen after the Winter War had now largely dissipated.

On June 1944, as the Allies were landing in Normandy, Finland was once again attacked by the Soviet Union. This time too, Finland accepted military assistance from Germany on the condition that it did not make a separate peace. This agreement, however, was reached informally between Hitler and the Finnish President at the time. This meant that it was no longer valid when President Risto Ryti resigned in August 1944. With Marshal Mannerheim as the new President, an armistice agreement was thus made possible and was signed in Moscow on 19 September 1944. The peace terms restored the borders of March 1940, except in the far north where the Soviet

Union annexed Petsamo with its valuable nickel mines and its ice-free port on the Arctic. A Soviet naval base was again established on the southern coast of Finland (even closer to Helsinki than Hanko). In addition, Finland had to undertake to pay war indemnity to the Soviet Union in the form of industrial goods, and to hand over all former German assets. While some argue that Finland had lost the war, Max Jakobson argues the opposite: 'Finland did not fight for Karelia or Hanko, but for national survival. When the fight was over, Finland was a nation crippled and exhausted. But Finland survived' (ibid.: 39).

These historical experiences explain why geopolitics and the struggle for independence have a central place in the Finnish national security identity. Even today, the primary goal of Finland's foreign and security policy is to ensure that the country will not once again be used as small change in a deal between leaders of the big powers.

A policy of concessions (1945–1975)

In April 1946 the 79-year-old Marshal was in poor health. He retired, and Juho Kusti Paasikivi was virtually unanimously elected President for the remainder of Mannerheim's term. Paasikivi was subsequently re-elected, at the age of 80, for a full term of six years. Thus, at this rather dark moment in the history of their country, the Finnish people turned for leadership to two elderly men who appeared to personify the past: Mannerheim, a former czarist officer and Paasikivi, a retired banker who had been the chairman of the Conservatives. Paasikivi brought to his office a lifetime's experience of addressing the problem of reconciling Finnish and Russian national interests. He offered a concept of Finnish–Soviet relations that was not only tailored to fit the prevailing strategic realities but also designed to restore the faith of the Finnish people in an independent future. In the years after the Second World War, the most dominant characteristic of Finnish foreign policy was therefore to maintain the country's policy of concessions to the Soviet Union.

This started with the Finnish decision in 1947 to decline the invitation to join the Marshall Plan – a decision made in order to avoid arousing Soviet suspicions, while at the same time forcing Finland to accomplish the post-war reconstruction without foreign assistance. Then, on 23 February 1948, President Paasikivi received a personal letter from Stalin, asking whether Finland was prepared to conclude a treaty of mutual assistance with the Soviet Union, similar to the treaties that the Soviet Union already had concluded with Hungary and Romania. To President Paasikivi, the idea of a treaty with the Soviet Union was not in itself unacceptable, but he had difficulties with the models offered by Stalin. These imposed on the parties the unlimited obligation to political consultations in time of peace, and automatic mutual assistance in the event of a war. If there was one dominant theme in Finland's foreign policy at that time, it was the desire to avoid being drawn into conflicts and controversies with more powerful nations.

After important diplomatic efforts from the Finnish side, a treaty was finally signed on 6 April 1948. This document was unique among the scores of security arrangements made between big powers and smaller states in the period after the Second World War. It took into account Finland's desire to stay outside great power conflicts – in other words, Finland's desire to remain neutral. Its first article states:

> In the eventuality of Finland, or the Soviet Union through Finnish territory, becoming the object of an armed attack by Germany or any State allied with the latter, Finland will, true to its obligations as an independent State, fight to repel the attack. Finland will in such cases use all its available forces for defending its territorial integrity by land, sea and air, and will do so within the frontiers of Finland in accordance with obligations defined in the present Treaty and, if necessary, with the assistance of, or jointly with, the Soviet Union.[7]

While there were no identical twins among the neutral countries in Europe, the position of Finland differed fundamentally from that of the others because of this security treaty with the Soviet Union. No other neutral state had such treaty commitments. This shows that Finnish neutrality was a *pragmatic choice*, aimed at sending a clear signal to the rest of the world. As Max Jakobson argues:

> To the West the message was: we are neutral, that means we are an independent democracy, not a Soviet satellite. But we have to be careful, so don't make our life more difficult than it already is. And to the East: We are neutral; that means we will not join your enemies, and if they try to attack you through Finland, we will defend ourselves, and we do it – or have you forgotten?
>
> (Ibid.: 74)

Although the Finnish policy of concessions to the Soviet Union did not mean that there was no orientation towards the West in Finnish foreign policy during the Cold War, Finland also had to ensure that its integration with Western Europe was acceptable to the Soviet Union.[8] This explains why, during the Cold War, the Finnish orientation to the West was represented as being based on purely economic considerations.[9] When Finland joined the Nordic Council in 1955 it therefore insisted on not making security policy matters a part of the Nordic co-operation. In 1956, Finland finally joined the United Nations – after several attempts had been vetoed by the Soviet Union in the Security Council. In 1961, Finland became an associated member in EFTA (FINEFTA), and it joined the OECD in 1968. In 1972, it concluded a Free Trade Agreement with the EC (Tiilikainen 1996: 118).

Despite its economic ties to the West, Finland continued to be perceived by most West Europeans as a country closer to the East than to the West. In West Germany, for instance, the Bavarian leader, Franz-Joseph Strauss, launched a new political slogan, *Finlandization*, in his campaign against Willy Brandt's *Ostpolitik*. The term has been defined as a 'process by which a democratic nation living in the shadow of a militarily powerful totalitarian state gradually submits to the political domination of its neighbour and finally loses its internal freedom' (quoted in Jakobson 1998: 85). It was probably meant as a warning of what might happen if the nations of Western Europe trusted the Soviet Union and lowered their guard, but it also indicates how Finland was perceived in the West. While the policy of concessions to the Soviet Union was believed to reveal a limitation of sovereignty, the intention was, according to Max Jakobson, the very opposite:

> By refraining from open criticism of Soviet violations of international law or human rights, the Finnish government ought to protect human rights of Finnish citizens and defend the integrity of the Finnish state.
>
> (Ibid.: 85)

A policy of 'active neutrality' (1975–1990)

The improvement in East–West relations that set in after the 1962 Cuban missile crisis also opened the way for Finland to move from its evasive line of neutrality to a more active role on the international scene. As we have seen above, this led not only to a stronger integration in the existing structures of European economic co-operation, but also to a stronger commitment to collective security arrangements. With the European security conference in Helsinki in 1975, the signing of the Helsinki Final Act and the establishment of the Conference for Security and Co-operation in Europe (CSCE), Finnish policy became very closely linked to détente and bridge-building (Ojanen *et al.* 2000: 91). For Finland, this policy was designed to overcome Western scepticism as to Finland's ability to maintain a genuinely neutral position between East and West, without at the same time arousing suspicions in Moscow. In addition to the CSCE the UN also offered a natural arena for this delicate diplomatic exercise. Finland achieved global recognition for this policy, which has been referred to as a policy of 'active neutrality' (Arter 1995: 364). According to Tomas Ries, Finland's Cold War activism can best be summed up in the country's declaration that it 'wishes to be the doctor not the judge', and that this is better described as an *anti-activist* policy. Ries argues: 'in contrast to most notions of activism Finland avoided moral judgements and sought solutions through a consensus and compromise rather than condemnation and pressure' (Ries 2002: 75).

With the acceleration of the European integration process in the 1980s, and the process towards a deepening of relations between EFTA and the EC, it was important for Finland to establish closer ties to the EC in order to avoid becoming increasingly sidelined. The first move was for Finland to become a full member of EFTA, which it did in 1986. Such membership was perceived as compatible with neutrality since it was limited to economic co-operation. However, with the signing of the Single European Act (SEA) in 1985, foreign and security political co-operation had become an integral part of the Community. In order to clarify Finland's position, the Finnish government presented a declaration to the Parliament in November 1988, in which it underlined that no significant change had taken place in Finnish policies and that it continued to endorse the traditional elements of Finnish neutrality policy.

Several government reports submitted between 1988 and 1992 show how Finnish policies changed in tune with those of the other EFTA countries that were developing their relations with the EC (Ojanen *et al.* 2000: 92). These changes started with a wish to join the EEA and ended with the question of possible Finnish membership in the EU. While the proposal made by Jacques Delors, in January 1989, to create the EEA had been viewed as an attractive alternative to full membership, Swedish and Austrian membership applications to the EU soon demonstrated that the European Economic Area had lost much of its importance even before the EEA agreement was signed (ibid.: 92–3).

This development shows the flexibility of the neutrality concept in Finland. It has been argued that Finland wanted to change what it saw as the incorrect international perception of Finland as a Soviet satellite, and that this explains why the Finnish government was eager to strengthen its ties with the European integration process in the early 1990s – in other words, that the decision to seek EU membership was a strategy for strengthening Finland's Western identity (Arter 1995; Browning 1999: 21).

The failure of the attempted coup in the Soviet Union in August 1991, followed by the dissolution of the Soviet Union in December, paved the way for a new security policy doctrine in Finland. With the replacement of the FCMA treaty with the Soviet Union by a treaty of good neighbourly relations with Russia, the primary framework in terms of which neutrality had been practised had disappeared. But even though this new context made increased international co-operation possible, it does not mean that traditional national security issues became unimportant. These issues continued to top the Finnish agenda. By the early 1990s, Russia was no longer regarded as threatening Finland's sovereignty, but the traumas of the past had left traces in foreign policy thinking that were not easy to erase. Russia's behaviour towards the Baltic republics also led to some uncertainty in a country like Finland. Its long joint border with a Russia that was, at that time, socially and economically deprived but still fully armed meant that there remained some potential for instability (Archer 1996; Vaahtoranta and Forsberg 1998: 193).

In many ways, Finland continued its traditional way of coping with security concerns. This strategy has been described as one that combines three different strategies: power-balancing, non-provocative behaviour, and strengthening of common norms (Vaahtoranta and Forsberg 1998; Heikka 2003). Heikka argues that:

> The Finnish security approach can be characterized by non-offensiveness, a strong will to defend republicanism when needed, and a commitment to the idea of international society.
>
> (Heikka 2003: 2)

According to him, Finland seems to have been a part of a larger normative project in Northern Europe, which was able to flourish in Finland partly because of the realist practices that were followed by Finnish leaders when needed. During the Cold War such considerations led to a policy of neutrality. With the end of the Cold War, however, the room for manoeuvre increased and the establishment of a closer relationship with the European integration process now became the new priority in Finnish security policy. According to Tuomas Forsberg and Tapani Vaahtoranta, a strengthened role for the EU fits well with the Finnish security identity because the EU balances Russian power in the area, without provoking Moscow. Along with the OSCE framework the EU could be viewed as an appropriate organization for strengthening common norms (Vaahtoranta and Forsberg 1998: 209).

Replacing neutrality by EU membership

Despite some important changes, traditionalism continued to dominate Finnish security approach in the early 1990s. The country's geographical location and history, combined with uncertainty concerning developments in Russia, have made it difficult to formulate a foreign policy free from traditionally oriented security policy considerations. The decision to seek membership in the EU (but not in NATO) made it possible for Finland to avoid being isolated in a potential future international crisis without upsetting Russia. Thus, reduced emphasis on neutrality and moves towards EU membership represented a change of tools and policy options, rather than a profound change in the national security identity. Territorial defence continues to be the main 'code' that defines the dominant Finnish security discourse.

From neutrality to non-alignment

The fact that traditional neutrality was incompatible with EU membership was widely recognized. In 1990, Finnish Prime Minister Harri Holkeri had compared the task of combining neutrality and EC membership to that of squaring the circle (Ojanen *et al.* 2000: 95). In November 1990 he argued that:

> Finland's neutrality constitutes the corner stone in the protection of our living, our independence, our sovereignty and our national existence . . . submitting to the EU's foreign policy and giving in to the demands of a joint defence would imply that Finland voluntarily abandons its independence and becomes part of a major power.
>
> (Quoted in Joenniemi 2002: 183)

Little by little the government's discourse changed. Instead of focusing on the incompatibility between EU membership and neutrality, it began to argue that changes such as the disappearance of the bloc division and the EU's willingness to accept new members required a reaction also from the Finnish side. Considerable efforts were therefore made to reassure the domestic audience that membership would not imply any dramatic changes for Finland's security orientation. Even the most sensitive field, the CFSP with its provisions for a common security and defence policy and eventually a common defence, was in the final analysis rendered compatible with traditional Finnish policies. This was achieved by arguing that Finland actually shared the goals and values behind these policies, that an independent decision-making capacity still was possible, that the CFSP did not imply a need to alter bilateral relations, and that the responsibility for defence could remain national (Ojanen *et al.* 2000: 97–8).

The main political elites seemed to be almost unanimously in favour of EU membership, with the notable exception of the Centre Party. However, opposition to membership soon began to increase both within the party structures and among the general public (Tiilikainen 1996). Nonetheless, once the party elites had almost unanimously decided to advocate membership, the revised integration policy was recommended to the Finnish people, and little by little a majority became convinced. Sweden's membership application and the crisis in the Finnish national economy due to the collapse of trade with the Soviet Union were used as arguments for joining the EU. The government submitted its application to Brussels in March 1992.

A formula was found to combine EU membership with basically unaltered Finnish policies. The 'terms' of the deal that made Finnish policies compatible with neutrality were twofold. First, the Finnish policy of neutrality was reduced to its essence, becoming equivalent to non-alignment. Second, the consequences of membership were interpreted in rather vague terms.

The new definition of neutrality was first referred to in the governmental report on integration of 1992, in which only the 'core of neutrality' was retained (Ojanen *et al.* 2000: 104). This implied that neutrality now came to be reduced to the military field and narrowly defined in security policy terms. Neutrality was no longer a value in itself, nor did it have the instrumental value it had had in the past. On the contrary, neutrality was perceived as harmful, since it could hinder Finnish participation in European co-operation (ibid.: 105).

How could it be that only a few months were sufficient to reorient Finnish security orientation? This was because Finland's neutrality was not deeply rooted in the national security identity, but rather based on a pragmatic choice in a given historical setting (Antola 1999). Thus, the change was a pragmatic adaptation rather than a change in security identity. While this change was necessary to make EU membership possible, the Finnish government emphasized that membership would not change the essential goals of the country's foreign and security policy, which would continue to be based on non-alignment and a credible national defence. The Finnish political leadership did not see any reason to abandon this policy, which was motivated by a concern for stability and was seen as a way of increasing Finland's room for manoeuvre.

While there are several reasons for Finland's applying to join the EU, former President Mauno Koivisto has argued that the decision was based primarily on considerations of national security. This, however, this was not made explicit at the time.[10] Referring to this debate, Pertti Joenniemi argues that 'themes of security and defence did not stand out in any distinct way'. He emphasizes that 'instead of arguing that Finland joined the Union due to reasons of security, one could claim that the move became possible with an increasing non-concern for traditional and territorial security' (Joenniemi 2002: 184). Gradually, however, EU membership was perceived as the best way to ensure friendly relations with Russia, and thus as a new avenue for maintaining Finnish security. The collapse of the Soviet Union and the uncertain economic and political situation in Russia made the Finns look for security guarantees – something that the EU could provide (Tiilikainen 1996, 1998: 173; Antola 1999; Ries 2001). In the governmental report from 1995 we can note an interest in soft security. Still, there is little doubt that membership was also seen as strengthening Finland's territorial security:

> A capable and unified European Union in which the interests of all member states are taken equally into account will strengthen Finnish security. Union membership will help Finland to repel any military threats and prevent attempts to exert political pressure.
>
> (Council of State 1995: 57–8)

Finland's neutrality policy no longer served any purpose – indeed, it was now perceived as an obstacle to Finland's efforts to be as deeply embedded in the EU as possible (Ries 2002: 72). This is why this governmental report, presented only six months after Finland joined the Union, announced that Finland was no longer neutral, since that was not compatible with the goals of the CFSP. However, the importance of non-alignment was emphasized, and it was argued that Finland's defence capability would strengthen the security of the Union:

> In today's changing world, Finland can best further stability in the northern Europe by remaining outside military alliances and by maintaining a credible independent defence. Finland's national defence capability also strengthens the common security of the European Union and its member states.
>
> (Council of State 1995: 2)

While non-alignment was upheld and NATO membership was not on the agenda, Finland also gradually intensified its relations with NATO in the early 1990s. In fact, Finland was the first neutral country to become an observer in the newly established North Atlantic Co-operation Council (NACC) in 1992.

Towards recognition of the EU's defence dimension

Despite the national debate concerning the compatibility between EU membership and non-alignment, the Finnish government did not take up this argument when dealing with the Union. In fact, Finland applied for membership without any particular emphasis on being neutral or non-aligned. The European Commission, however, was sceptical and asked neutral applicants to confirm their commitments. The Commission seemed particularly keen to ensure that these countries would accept the CFSP. This was important for the Union due to the vulnerability of this vaguely formulated policy. The Commission apparently feared that neutral members would constitute a hindrance to the full acceptance of the foreign policy of the Union, including a future development towards a common defence. The Commission argued that the CFSP necessitated a clear commitment, and recommended specific and binding assurances on political commitment. In Finland this resulted in a statement from the Minister of Foreign Trade, Pertti Salolainen, in February 1993, in which he emphasized that Finland not only supported but that was also ready to contribute *constructively* to the development of the defence dimension of the EU (Ojanen *et al.* 2000: 100).

The debate that preceded the referendum in 1994[11] was characterized by a mix between economic, image-related and security arguments. Just as in the period before the application for membership, the most common arguments invoked the economic benefits of membership. Still, security considerations were important. Security political considerations have traditionally been the cornerstone of Finnish foreign policy, and it was only natural that the EU had been approached in terms of security (Joenniemi 2002: 183). The first governmental report on security, presented six months after Finland joined the EU, confirmed that international co-operation had now replaced neutrality as a new tool in Finnish security policy:

> Since the end of the East–West division, the policy of neutrality that Finland followed in the Cold War is no longer a viable line of action. During the Cold War, Finland tried to avoid making political and especially military commitments that might have drawn it into conflicts between the great powers. In the new situation, Finland's strategy is an active participation in international political and security cooperation for prevention and resolution of security problems.
>
> (Council of State 1995: 56)

While references to neutrality were abandoned rather easily, Finland remained attached to its policy of non-alignment. This orientation was motivated by a concern for regional stability and was intended as a way of avoiding the formation of new dividing lines in Europe (ibid.: 19). While the CFSP was seen as being compatible with non-alignment, Finland's relationship to the WEU was less certain. The government's position in 1992 was that Finland's relations to the WEU would have to be decided on later. During the actual membership negotiations, however, the Commission insisted on a clarification of this point. Thereupon Finland settled the question and became a WEU observer in February 1995, only a month after having joined the EU (Ojanen *et al.* 2000: 107–8). This was argued as being compatible with military non-alignment since the WEU was not a full-scale military alliance:

> Despite the provisions of its founding character, the WEU is not a full-scale military alliance; the common defence of its members is managed in coordination with NATO and in practice relies on NATO's military structures and resources.
>
> (Council of State 1995: 57)

Prime Minister Esko Aho noted that observer status did not change Finland's position as a militarily non-aligned country with an independent and credible defence (Ojanen *et al.* 2000: 108). This shows that the traditional security discourse based on the concept of territorial defence was still very much alive in Finland at that time.

Impact of the ESDP

Even though the 1995 governmental report on security continued to emphasize territorial defence as the most important task of the national defence forces, it also included a more considered appreciation of the new international situation. The report called for a 'broad and comprehensive concept of security' that would include, in addition to political and military aspects, respect for human rights and consolidation of the rule of law, economic co-operation, and mutual solidarity in protecting the environment (Council of State 1995: 4).

Finland seemed to find the EU useful for such a soft security approach. In fact, the Finnish government seized the opportunity to contribute actively to the strengthening of these aspects of the Union's security dimension, as shown by Finland's initiatives on the Petersberg tasks and the Northern Dimension. However, even these initiatives were based on traditional security policy considerations. The fact that they helped to make Finland part of the EU core has also served to strengthen Finland's traditional and national security conceptions. While territorial defence still seems to have priority, a slight internationalization of the Finnish defence discourse can be identified in the period after 1998.

To the core: a 'good pupil' strategy

Since Finland joined the EU, the political leadership has worked hard to become accepted as a core member. Karvonen and Sundelius explain Finland's rather smooth transformation into a full-fledged European player within a relatively short period by referring to the skills of the Finnish foreign policy leadership and Finland's tradition of centralized decision-making (Karvonen and Sundelius 1996: 258). As Hanna Ojanen argues, 'Finland has made a national strategy out of being a good pupil, a strategy that is supposed to pay off sooner or later' (Ojanen *et al.* 2000: 117). This policy is based on two major assumptions. First, that a strong Union bolsters Finnish security. Second, that political participation and closer integration are necessary preconditions for a small member to gain influence in questions that would be otherwise decided without Finnish participation. Former Prime Minister Lipponen has often been seen as the personification of this policy, and he was strongly supported by former President Ahtisaari.[12]

The 1997 White Book on Defence emphasized that EU membership is seen as important for Finnish security. It observes that EU membership has 'increased Finland's opportunities to influence and broadened its responsibility in a stability policy encompassing the whole of Europe' (quoted in Ojanen *et al.* 2000: 110). It also emphasizes that membership has strengthened Finland's ability to work for security in Northern Europe and in the Baltic Sea region. It even gives a positive evaluation of WEU observer status, stating that this offers Finland the opportunity to follow and participate in European discussions and co-operation. This pragmatic attitude to Finland's security orientation is confirmed by the following statement:

> if the security constellation in Europe changes essentially, Finland will assess its security situation and arrangements in the light of these developments.
>
> (Ibid.: 114)

The two initiatives promoted by Finland (alone or together with Sweden) – the Petersberg tasks and the Northern Dimension – are both 'progressive' EU initiatives. While they promoted the EU as a strong policy actor, they can also be seen as efforts to make the CFSP compatible with non-alignment. Fearing a merger between the EU and the WEU, and also fearing that this might bring Finland into a military alliance 'through the backdoor', the Finnish government decided to present an alternative proposal. This proposal, submitted together with Sweden, involved including the Petersberg tasks. The proposal was important for Finland because it drew a line between crisis management and defence, thereby enabling the participation of non-aligned countries on an equal footing with allied EU members. This initiative, however, was not presented only in order to make the CFSP compatible with non-alignment: it also indicates that crisis management was seen as an important tool for handling the challenges in the current European security context. As President Ahtisaari put it in June 1998:

> the fact that the EU should become more effective in crisis management corresponds to today's security needs in Europe and is also a realistic step in the development of common defence the EU is the broadest actor in crisis management as it also has economic and political means at its disposal.
>
> (Ibid.: 129)

The other Finnish initiative related to the CFSP is the 'Northern Dimension' – aimed both at multilateralizing Finland's relations with Russia (Pursiainen 1999) and to demonstrate Finland's commitment to the integration process. The initiative was launched by Prime Minister Lipponen in September 1997. In his view, the EU needed a policy for its Northern regions comparable to the Mediterranean policies (the 'Barcelona process'). He urged the Union to define its interests in the region and develop strategies and actions in fields such as infrastructure, economic activities, environmental matters and nuclear safety. While the initiative excluded traditional security policy, it involved elements that would contribute to regional security in broad terms. In order to convince the EU of the importance of this initiative, its promoters stressed how it would facilitate the integration of Russia into the West. With regard to implementation, it was argued that the dimension would be made more concrete in fora such as the Council of Baltic Sea States and the Barents Council, financed through co-ordinated sources, using existing programmes such as TACIS, PHARE or INTERREG – thus obviating the need for new institutions or new funding (Ojanen *et al.* 2000: 137).

The Northern Dimension must be understood as a result of Finland's eagerness to develop the Union's wide strategies and policies aimed at supporting stability in Russia. Although the initiative does not deal specifically with traditional military security, the underlying idea has been the belief that security should be understood in a wider sense, and that hard security can best be achieved through soft means. In an opinion poll conducted in the autumn of 1998, Finns were asked what they felt Finland should emphasize when developing the Northern Dimension. The issues most often referred to were nuclear safety, cleaning up the Baltic Sea, security in Northern Europe and improving living conditions in Eastern and Northern Finland. Far less important were returning Karelia to Finland, or decreasing NATO's importance in the area and fostering Russian membership in the EU (Forsberg 2001).

The Northern Dimension initiative can also be understood as an expression of Finland's 'good pupil' behaviour. The fact that this initiative was developed along the same lines as the EU's Southern policy also shows Finland's commitment to the EU as a soft security actor. Since the initiative would not involve extra expenditure (no new institutions), and could be justified by pointing to the existence of a Southern dimension, it was also acceptable to all member states. On the other hand, it has been argued that the very vagueness of the initiative which contributed to its success in the first phase has later hampered its development (Ojanen 1999).

The rather rapid development of a European defence dimension seemed to take the Finnish political leadership by surprise – perhaps because they had been preoccupied with soft security and the Northern Dimension. This led to reluctance, despite the introduction of the Petersberg tasks. For instance, Finland expressed its scepticism about the appointment of the High Representative of the CFSP as the Secretary General of the WEU. This appointment meant that this position would be responsible for questions linked to common defence, thus bringing common defence into the EU willy-nilly. In addition, under-secretary of state Jaakko Blomberg noted as late as in September 1999 that the more difficult questions concerning crisis management capabilities would be left for later; and in November – only one month before the European Council was to decide on the 'headline goal' – the Minister for Foreign Affairs stated that a concrete decision on troops would not be made in Helsinki (Ojanen *et al.* 2000: 131).

However, this Finnish reluctance was not to last for long. When the decision concerning the establishment of a European Rapid Reaction force was taken in December 1999, it was strongly supported by Finland. Finnish political leaders now argued that this actually was in line with Finland's views, and that it was a continuation of the original Finnish–Swedish initiative on the Petersberg tasks (ibid.: 130). This change is another example of Finland's pragmatism and its willingness to be part of the core of the integration process. The decision was also easier to accept because the Helsinki documents emphasized the importance of UN principles and civilian crisis management, and that the goal was not the development of a European army.

From independent to credible defence

Despite Finland's 'good pupil' policy in the EU, the dominant national security discourse continued to give priority to an independent national defence. The 1995 governmental report, *Security in a Changing World*, emphasized the importance of non-alignment and the maintenance of a credible and independent defence. But it also stated that this would actually contribute to the common security of the EU (see quotation on p. 101).

The importance of territorial defence is strongly emphasized towards the end of the report, and it is made clear that the development of crisis management preparedness is first and foremost seen as an element in strengthening Finland's national defence capability:

> In the sphere of national defence, Finland's situation is stable. A defence capability that is credible in the view of the security environment must be further developed, based on an up-to-date and long-range security evaluation. This calls for consistent work to develop the defence forces' capabilities. A defence system based on territorial defence, universal military service and mobilization offers the best way for Finland to guarantee its own security and promote regional stability in northern Europe. . . . A distinction can be made between national defence and military crisis management at the level of commitment and practical collaboration. Military non-alignment does not prevent participation in international cooperation for crisis management in accordance with Finland's own will and ability.
>
> As well as fulfilling its national defence function, Finland must create and enhance its preparedness for international peacekeeping and crisis management operations, which are more demanding militarily and also more diversified. Crisis management preparedness must be seen as a growing component in defence policy overall, and as a new tool of security policy and also as an element in strengthening the country's defence capability.
>
> (Council of State 1995: 21)

Preparing Finland for increased participation in international crisis management operations was seen as a new way of achieving traditional security policy goals. In fact, Finland continued to argue for a national defence capability that could stand up against potential aggression from Russia. While general threat perceptions had not changed much, some adaptations to enable Finnish participation in international crisis management operations were made. This process should be seen in relation to Finland's participation in NACC and its preparation for Finnish participation in NATO crisis management operations in the Balkans through the PfP programme. At this point the EU had not yet begun to make concrete its security dimension.

In order to enable Finnish participation in NATO operations it was first necessary to remove some of the existing self-imposed national limitations to such involvement. The Finnish legislation on peace-keeping therefore became the subject of continuous debates throughout the 1990s. Two developments in particular contributed to this heated state of affairs. The first is that the nature of peace-keeping operations had changed – from traditional mandate-based missions, to missions involving the possibility of proactive use of force. The need for mutual agreement between both parties to such operations had also been partially abandoned. Second, the number of organizations involved in peace-keeping and conflict management had grown. As a result, the Finnish law on peace-making was perceived as too restrictive, as it permitted the use of force only in self-defence and allowed Finnish troops to be sent abroad only for UN missions.

In December 1995 the legislation was modified in order to enable Finnish participation in operations that were mandated by the UN and OSCE but executed by other organizations. It also permitted restricted use of coercive means if necessary for the safety of the operation. However, a further change, added on the initiative of Parliament, ensured that Finnish troops would not be allowed to participate in 'peace enforcement'[13] – defined as active first use of force or threat of using force. The new Finnish legislation made it possible for Finland to participate in the NATO-led IFOR/SFOR operation in Bosnia.[14] These changes demonstrated Finland's willingness and ability to play a role in increasingly demanding international operations. This willingness was further confirmed by the creation of a special Rapid Deployment Brigade in June 1996.

In 1997 the Finnish government presented a new report on security, *The European Security Development and Finnish Defence*, which went further than its predecessor. Importantly, the 'national' character of the Finnish defence was toned down. According to the 1995 report, Finland aimed at maintaining a *credible independent national defence*; the 1997 report stated that the cornerstone of Finland's security policy had become a *credible national defence capability* (Council of State 1997: 7). Omitting the criterion of independence put increased emphasis on Finnish participation in international crisis management. At the same time the government continued to argue that expanding international co-operation was primarily a way of strengthening national defence preparedness:

> International military cooperation is a growing part of Finnish security policy. Participation in international crisis management operations strengthens Finland's capacity for military co-operation and enhances its defence preparedness.
>
> (Ibid.: 6)

Towards the end of the report it was made clear that 'the foundation of Finland's security policy is a credible national defence' (ibid.: 51).

The need to establish rapid deployment ground-force brigades was emphasized. The main argument, however, was that these would 'heighten [the national] defence preparedness rapidly and credibly'. It is interesting to note that these changes were primarily aimed at increasing the capacity to react rapidly to potential national crises (ibid.: 66). The changes included strengthening the Finnish air force through investment in American F/A-18s, and redefining three land brigades into rapid reaction brigades. However, the defence structure from the Cold War period was largely retained and the total number of brigades was only reduced from 27 to 23.[15]

As indicated, the ESDP process took the Finnish leadership by surprise. But once it was institutionalized, Finland followed its 'good pupil' approach and strongly supported the process. It even came up with a candidate to head the newly established Military Committee – General Hägglund, who was also appointed only a few months after Finland had expressed scepticism regarding the ESDP process.

In the 2001 review report on security and defence – *The Finnish Security and Defence Policy* – the changes introduced in 1997 were followed up and strengthened. Procurement was limited almost solely to the three rapid deployment brigades, and for the first time 'participating in international co-operation to enhance security and stability' was defined as one of the three goals of Finnish security policy. The other two were 'maintaining a credible defence capability' and 'remaining militarily non-aligned' (Council of State 2001: 7).

However, despite these changes, a large-scale offensive with mobilized forces, aimed at seizing strategically important areas or making use of Finnish territory for action against a third party, will to be retained as one of the four possible types of crisis scenarios underlying Finland's defence planning.[16] The likelihood of such a crisis, however, is not deemed to be high. This conclusion was reflected in the 1997 White Paper, which proposed important cuts in the wartime strength of the Finnish defence forces.[17] The 2001 report reinforced this trend,[18] but it does not seem to have any major impact on the dominant Finnish security discourse. As argued by Pauli

Järvenpää, defence counsellor at the mission of Finland to NATO, size is 'quite irrelevant', since:

> what is important to note is that for years to come Finland will remain one country in Europe that will continue to maintain a large reserve army, based on universal conscription and continuous refresher training. That army is deployed according to a territorial defence system and equipped with relatively simple weapons, including anti-personnel land mines.
>
> (Järvenpää 2001: 14)

This means that even in 2001 a traditional security discourse remained dominant in Finland. The changes that have been initiated continued to be based on traditional considerations. Among the scenarios included in Finland's defence planning is a *strategic strike*. Since this is the most difficult type of outside action to defend, special efforts have been undertaken to create elements in the army that can be deployed quickly to counter such a strike. This is the reason why three brigades, one in each military command area (Western, Eastern and Northern), are being made into rapid deployment brigades (ibid.: 14). While these were not initially intended for use in international operations, their existence makes the Finnish defence forces better prepared for such operations. This means that while participation in international crisis management operations is gradually being defined as a force multiplier in Finnish security discourse, such participation is primarily viewed as important for creating a better national defence (Council of State 2001: 69). In fact, participation in international co-operation is understood as a way to raise professional skills within the Finnish defence forces, which in turn increases the credibility of the Finnish defence effort (Järvenpää 2001: 15):

> Finland is also developing its own defence capability, making use of the experience gained in peacekeeping and crisis management within international organization In international crisis management Finland mainly uses the resources which are reserved for its own national duties.
>
> (Council of State 2001: 11)

Despite this traditionalism, further confirmed by Finland's reluctance to sign the Ottawa Convention on landmines, there have been – as we have seen above – some important changes in the Finnish security discourse since Finland joined the EU. While international crisis management was barely mentioned in the 1995 report, this aspect was given greater emphasis in 1997, and the 2001 report devoted an entire chapter to the topic. In the 2004 report Finland finally also announced that it was going to 'accede to the Ottawa

Convention in 2012, and destroy its land mines by the end of 2016' (Prime Minister's Office 2004: 8).

While it is clear that Finland's military crisis management capacity initially was developed to meet the crisis management objectives of NATO, later it came to include those of the European Union and the ESDP process as well. In November 2004, Finland announced that it would participate in two of EU's battle groups: in the German-Dutch-Finnish battle group, intended to be in readiness for the first time in early 2007, and in the Swedish-Finnish-Norwegian battle group, intended to be in readiness for the first time in early 2008. It is also clear that the changes are made in response to the development at the EU level. In the 2004 report from the Finnish Ministry of Defence, it is argued that:

> Finland is developing its capability and readiness to participate in the EU's civilian crisis management activities and military crisis management operations, including rapid response forces, currently being developed. Finland contributes to the forming of permanent structured cooperation and takes part in the Union's capabilities cooperation and the activities of the European Defence Agency. The obligation to provide assistance included in the Constitutional Treaty will strengthen the Union's mutual solidarity.
>
> (Ibid.: 6)

Impact of the EU's comprehensive security approach

Since Finland's security discourse continues to be based on traditional security considerations, one should assume that Finland would also be more reluctant to introduce notions of comprehensive security. Still, soft and hard security are traditionally viewed as two parts of a whole, and the former has been actively promoted by the Finnish political leadership within the UN and the CSCE/OSCE framework. While this was an important part of the country's policy of 'active neutrality' during the Cold War, this aspect of Finnish security approach gradually attracted increased attention throughout the 1990s. In addition to the UN and OSCE, the role of the EU has been increasingly emphasized. While civilian crisis management was given greater emphasis in the general Finnish foreign policy, CIMIC and comprehensive external and internal security have also received increased attention in the security discourse. In the 2001 governmental report on Finnish security and defence policy, aspects such as civilian crisis management, civil–military co-operation, vulnerability questions and the need for better co-ordination between different institutions responsible for national security are for the first time provided with separate chapters. Such a comprehensive approach was further emphasized in the 2004 report. However, a certain traditionalism is still evident and comprehensive security is first of all legitimized by referring to how it strengthens Finland's national security:

> Finland's line of action is based on a credible national defence, the functioning of society, a consistent foreign policy as well as a strong international position and an active participation as a member of the EU. The key challenge for Finland's security and defence policy is retaining and strengthening the nation's capability in a changing environment, where global developments, regional conflicts and new threats have become of increasing significance to Finland's security.
>
> (Prime Minister's Office 2004: 5)

Internal security

The 2001 report on Finnish security and defence contains, for the first time, a whole section on how to handle threats to society, or societal security. This means that it also stresses the importance of developing a comprehensive national approach to handling various societal threats and vulnerability issues – aspects that were missing in earlier reports. In the 2001 report, it is argued that:

> European and international security requires not only cooperation to prevent conflicts but also efforts to combat international political, economic, ecological and information system threats. Finland is improving its ability to deal with such security risks especially international crime and environmental and health risks, as well as the risk of disasters, including problems of nuclear safety. Finland is also seeking more effective means to manage the effects of globalization and non-military security risks. Information gathering and analyses concerning globalization issues are being further developed. To manage the new security challenges, the activities of the different branches of government and their coordination is made more effective and is based on common views subject to regular revision. Cooperation will also be strengthened with the business sector, research and educational institutions and non-governmental organizations.
>
> (Council of State 2001: 7)

While this is here viewed as a continuation of the traditional concept of *total defence*, the report also recognizes that 'new' threats have made it increasingly important to put emphasis on countering the vulnerability of modern societies. Instead of looking at civilian defence as support functions for the defence forces in a military crisis, civilian tools are now understood to have an independent value. The need for a better co-ordinated security approach is thus emphasized:

> Finland's precautionary measures, based on the concept of total defence have proved to be both effective and appropriate. The increasing interdependence between the various sectors of society makes it essential that precautionary measures are based on extensive collaboration.
>
> (Ibid.: 82)

> Total national defence includes military defence, economic defence, civilian defence, social welfare and health care, functioning of technical systems in society, public order and security, and defence information activity. Total national defence is supported by a wide arrange of voluntary non-governmental, cultural and educational work. The needs of various sectors and the actions to be taken in exceptional coordinated under the planning principles of total defence.
>
> (Ibid.: 83)

The importance of the EU is also explicitly referred to:

> Finland's membership of the European Union and its increasing interaction with the world at large have improved the capacity of Finnish society to tolerate a crisis.
>
> (Ibid.: 82)

The section on these issues is divided into two parts, the first focusing on *internal security* and the second on *security of supplies*. With respect to both, the importance of the European integration process is strongly emphasized. Concerning internal security, the report especially notes the need to fight terrorism and international crime by strengthening the national police force and border controls, but it also focuses on civil protection. The importance of the European integration process and the progress made at the Tampere summit in relation to the concretization of an 'area of freedom, security and justice' is also clearly recognized:

> Cooperation between the internal and justice authorities of EU member states will deepen and will become more concrete, based on the decision taken at the Tampere European Council in 1999. Certain practical projects related to the EU's Europol police cooperation, and cooperation between authorities based on the Schengen Agreement is also aimed at improving crime prevention. Key areas include common threat assessments, planning of operations, making

information systems compatible and exchanging information ...
The EU aims at more visible and integrated action in combating
terrorism and includes anti-terrorism on the agenda in its cooperation with other countries.

(Ibid.: 84–5)

The Finnish Frontier Guard will continue to monitor all Finland's
borders and participate in the defence of the nation ... In order to
maintain Finland's internal security, external borders must be
controlled credibly and in keeping with the requirements of the
European Union ... Finnish border policy takes into account the
evolving EU legislation on justice and internal affairs.

(Ibid.: 86–7)

On the question of security of supplies, most attention is given to food
and energy issues, in addition to transport, information systems, and social
and health care. Throughout this part of the report, the need for improving
the EU's role is emphasized:

The European Union has not developed any joint arrangements to
ensure security of supplies in a major crisis ... At Finland's initiative, the Nice European Council decided to request the European
Commission to undertake a fundamental review of the EU's security
of supplies, together with the Council secretariat, and to determine
the scope for cooperation in this area.

(Ibid.: 89)

Reference is also made to the importance of the Union's role in relation to
transport and social and health care:

The main priority is to secure maritime transport. Finland has begun
to develop measures for supporting shipping in accordance with the
guidelines of the EU.

(Ibid.: 93)

The European Union's early warning and response system for infectious diseases is now well established. The system can be used to
prevent and control the outbreak and spread of infectious diseases
within or outside the Union.

(Ibid.: 95)

While increased interest in comprehensive security predates the terrorist
attacks of 11 September 2001, these tragic events have further accentuated
the importance of such change. With reference to the terrorist attacks, the
Finnish Minister of Foreign Affairs, Erkki Tuomioja, stated:

the September attacks . . . have dramatically underlined the fact that security and the threats against it in today's world are different from what we and the entire international system of cooperation have traditionally prepared us for . . . The new security challenges include long-term, continuing deterioration of the environment and sudden environmental crises, the spread of HIV/AIDS and other contagious diseases, international crime, drugs, human rights violations, internal conflicts, disintegration of organized societies, terrorism and uncontrollable population movements and refugeeism that are linked to all these phenomena . . . The Union's strength lies in its ability to use tools and resources from the entire domain of security policy and thus promote the creation of sustainable solutions. This is Finland's point of departure and opinion. Determined development and operationalization of civilian crisis management capabilities play a major role here, and Finland is pro-active in promoting them. We are developing cooperation between various authorities and our readiness to participate in the EU's and other international civilian operations.

(Tuomioja 2002)

The 2004 report further confirm this change. In this report a comprehensive approach to internal security is to a larger extent integrated into the overall national security and defence policy. It is argued that:

Internal security in Finnish society will be maintained in all situations. To this end, the Government has prepared an internal security programme. This will also cover threat factors inside Finland that affect security and the necessary measures to respond to them. A long-term approach will be taken in promoting internal security. The functions vital to society will be protected against threats and crises with the aid of effective and comprehensive internal precautionary measures and associated external capabilities. The strategy drawn up for securing these functions will be effectively implemented and will be subject to continuous development. Existing executive assistance arrangements will be developed and refined as part of the precautionary measures against new threats. Joint action and shared responsibility within the EU will also serve to strengthen Finland's internal security.

(Prime Minister's Office 2004: 85–6)

This shows that there has been a rapid development of a comprehensive national security discourse in Finland since 2001. It was introduced somewhat later than in Sweden, but the focus is broader and it has been more closely integrated into the security discourse. As in Sweden, this development has been facilitated by long traditions of co-ordination between civilian and military defence components through the concept of total defence. The fact that both dimensions are under the authority of the Ministry of Defence facilitates such an approach. In addition, Finland has a rather unique tradition of close coordination across different ministries, which also makes the development of a comprehensive internal security approach easier (Jakobsen, forthcoming: ch. 4). The importance of the EU in this context is also more evident than in Sweden.

External security

Concerning the external dimension, the security report from 1995 already pointed out that 'Finland is pursuing a security policy founded on a broad and comprehensive view of security and expanding and deepening international co-operation' (Council of State 1995: ch. 1). Traditionally, Finland has seen the framework of the OSCE and the UN as based on a value community which enjoys broad legitimacy and domestic support, and is thus seen as a suitable forum for conflict prevention and conflict management. The 1995 report also emphasized the EU as an appropriate framework for developing such a comprehensive security approach:

> the EU must be able to act as a buttress for change and an anchor for stability, and also promote cooperative security. Thanks to their political, economic and social capabilities, the European Union and its Member States have exceptional potential for supporting reforming countries, working to prevent disputes and encouraging their peaceful settlement. . . . Europe's security problems call for common tools in conflict prevention and management and in dispute settlement. Better conflict management means sufficiently early warning and prevention, and rapid action. In its management of conflicts and crises, the international community must be able to integrate its use of the political and military tools and mechanisms with those related to the human dimension and economic support.
>
> (Ibid.: ch. 4)

While this report strongly emphasized the importance of comprehensive security, it was rather vague concerning Finland's actual contribution – on how this comprehensive security approach was to be implemented.

> Resolving the new security problems calls for a broad and comprehensive concept of security, and awareness among citizens and states of the action that this demands. As well as its political and military aspects, security means respecting human rights and

consolidating the rule of law, together with economic cooperation and mutual solidarity in protecting the environment.

(Ibid.: ch. 4)

Throughout the report the distinction between military and non-military security was maintained; it stated that 'Finland's military security remains its own responsibility'. The primacy of territorial defence was heavily emphasized (ibid.: chs 5 and 6).

As we have seen, the first qualitative reforms of the national defence forces were introduced in 1997, leading to greater emphasis on international crisis management. Even though it is argued that 'no significant changes have occurred in Finland's military situation', 'international military cooperation was seen as a growing part of Finnish security policy' (Council of State 1997: 6–7), and the comprehensive approach that was outlined in the 1995 report was emphasized somewhat further. In the 1997 report Finland's security policy is divided into three functional categories:

1   *Stability policy* (promoting democratic political and economic changes and preventing threats to security by strengthening peaceful structures);
2   *Conflict management* (early warning, conflict prevention and military crisis management and rehabilitation and reconstruction);
3   *Defence* (to create a deterrent to military threats and to protect the independence and security of the nation through force if necessary).

While the 1997 report aimed to set forth the lines to be followed in the development of the defence policy and the defence forces, Finland's attachment to a broad security concept was emphasized:

> Since the concentration in the report is on military security, other challenges are deliberated only if they are of significance from the perspective of developing defence policy or the military defence system. Nonetheless a broad concept of security has retained its status as the foundation of Finnish security policy.

(Ibid.: 10)

All the same, there was little evidence of any concretization of this comprehensive security concept. Military crisis management received the most attention, with very little emphasis on civil–military co-ordination; only a short paragraph was reserved for the 'development of civil alternative services' (ibid.: 71).

The 1997 report was the first real attempt to reorganize the defence forces, which may explain why it paid so little attention to comprehensive security. However, in the review report from 2001,[19] we can note some important progress in that direction. Traditional territorial defence is still referred to as the most important part of the Finnish security approach (Council of State 2001: 7), but civilian crisis management and conflict prevention are now emphasized. In fact, for the first time, there is a whole section on international crisis management, both military and civilian (ibid.: 69–82). Civil–military co-operation and the need for better co-ordination between different institutions are also emphasized, and the importance of the EU is highlighted:

> The range of means available for crisis management is extensive . . . Finland's participation in international crisis management requires close cooperation between various authorities. . . . Participation in crisis management requires quick decisions and actions at the national level. In Finland, the development of decision-making processes pays particular attention to EU crisis management.
>
> (Ibid.: 69)

Despite a rather recent focus on CIMIC and conflict prevention in the official documents produced by the Ministry of Defence, an official publication on Finland's development co-operation emphasized that 'Finland is one of the leading countries in the EU and OSCE in the training of civilian crisis management experts' (quoted in Jakobsen, forthcoming: ch. 4). This is true in the sense that Finland, together with Sweden, actually is one of the countries involved in developing EU's civilian training programme. However, it is interesting to note that when these aspects are introduced in the dominant security discourse, these are also legitimized by reference to their usefulness for bolstering the Finnish national security:

> Finland's capability to security cooperation is further developed in view of contributing in international crisis management. . . . This will also serve to improve Finland's ability to manage crises and threats affecting its own territory.
>
> (Council of State 2001: 7)

> Conflict prevention and crisis management will continue to be key elements in improving international security. This is also significant to Finland's security environment.
>
> (Ibid.: 19)

> Most of Finland's resources available for international crisis management operations are resources reserved for national defence. Participation in international crisis management also serves to strengthen Finland's national resources.
>
> (Ibid.: 69)

While this indicates a continued 'traditionalism', it also demonstrates that comprehensive external security has become an integral part of the dominant Finnish security discourse. The many references to recent developments in the EU also indicate that this is a result of a Europeanization. First, the EU's comprehensive security approach is widely recognized:

> The EU's ability to pursue a comprehensive range of political and economic and military means will now allow it the opportunity to prevent crisis and to participate in crisis management.
>
> (Ibid.: 11)

> The EU is increasing its influence not only as an economic actor but in the sphere of foreign and security policy too, by acquiring new means for crisis management. The Union is also improving its capability to prevent security problems and to strengthen comprehensive security.
>
> (Ibid.: 15)

Second, it is explicitly stated that the Finnish government aims at developing its security approach along the same lines as in the EU:

> The various means for crisis management cover both military and civilian tasks. In international crisis management Finland mainly uses the resources, which are reserved for its own national duties. The ability to make preparations, take decisions and implement actions rapidly, essential for crisis management, is further developed, particularly with a view to the EU's crisis management activities.
>
> (Ibid.: 11)

> Finland is playing an active role in developing the civilian crisis management capacity of the EU. Finland is also developing its national capability in line with EU's objectives, especially in four policy areas: police, strengthening the rule of law, and civil administration and civil protection.
>
> (Ibid.: 11)

Finland's commitment to the Union's comprehensive security approach was also further emphasized in a joint article by the Foreign Ministers of Sweden and Finland. In this article they clearly show their shared intention to improve the Union's comprehensive external security approach. They also emphasize the Nordic experience in civilian–military co-operation:

> The EU should also strengthen its preparedness to prevent conflicts. We need to be able to utilize all of our resources better than hitherto;

including political, diplomatic, military and civilian resources. To be credible and effective in conflict prevention we have to be able to deploy military units or observers to prevent the escalation of political crises into armed conflicts. In the important field of civilian–military cooperation the Nordic countries are exemplary.

(Lindh and Tuomioja 2002)

The 2004 governmental report on Finnish security and defence policy continues along the same lines, but with a somewhat increased emphasis on comprehensive security. It starts by stating that:

The report conducts a thorough examination of the change in Finland's international environment and its effects on Finland's capability as well as on comprehensive security into the 2010s. The assessment of the environment creates the basis for determining the line of action. Based on these, the report shows the development and resource needs that focus on the different dimensions of the capability, external capability, especially crisis management capability, defence, the maintaining of internal security and the safeguarding of society's central basic functions.

(Prime Minister's Office 2004: Abstract)

While the increased emphasis on comprehensive security must be seen as an adaptation to the processes in the EU, this development has also been facilitated by Finland's active engagement in peace-keeping operations, as well as the Finnish tradition of close co-ordination between the Ministry of Foreign Affairs and the Ministry of Defence (Jakobsen, forthcoming: ch. 4).

Europeanization and socialization

Main findings

As we have seen in this chapter, it is possible to identify changes in the Finnish security discourse in response to all three dimensions of the European security dimension: the Maastricht Treaty and the establishment of a political union, the gradual institutionalization of its ESDP and the recent emphasis on a comprehensive EU security approach.

Finland was eager to reaffirm its Western identity, so the end of the Cold War made possible EU membership immediately interesting to the country's political leaders. With the *establishment of a political union* with a Common Foreign and Security Policy, however, Finland found that it would have to change its security doctrine to make membership possible. But since Finland had a much more pragmatic approach to 'neutrality' than was the case in Sweden, it was also more easily replaced. The reference to 'the core of

119

neutrality', which in reality meant non-alignment, opened the way to EU membership. In fact, membership in the EU replaced neutrality as the main ingredient of the Finnish security policy orientation – joining the EU was primarily based on considerations of security policy, and the integration process was to become Finland's primary security policy tool. Finland saw the EU as an appropriate framework for multilateralizing its relations with Russia, and the Finnish initiative on the Northern Dimension must be seen as an example in this regard.

As an EU member Finland joined Sweden in an effort to make sure that the military dimension did not develop into a collective defence arrangement. However, the Union's military dimension was less problematic for Finland than for Sweden. While Finland's active line in relation to the CFSP/ESDP might be seen as an attempt to ensure that this dimension would remain compatible with its non-alignment, it can also be understood as an example of Finland's sincere dedication to the integration process and the fact that a stronger Union was viewed as a way of increasing Finnish national security. This argument is further strengthened by the fact that the Finnish government has stated that it would contribute constructively to the development of the defence dimension of the EU. It has also made an important change in the country's legislation by opening up for participation operations that allow a more extensive use of military force (peace enforcement operations). With a Finnish general appointed to head the Military Committee, the latter explanation seems the most likely. In parallel with the concretization of an EU crisis management capacity, the traditionally independent character of the Finnish defence discourse was gradually toned down. Several initiatives were taken in order to modernize the national defence forces, making them more oriented towards international crisis management. While these changes also were made in order to enable Finland to participate in the NATO operations, the development of the ESDP made such a development even more necessary for Finland. In Finland's 2001 government report, the many references to the EU in relation to the transformation of the national defence forces also provide a clear indication of Europeanization.

In response to the development of a *comprehensive security approach* in the EU, a similar process can be identified in the Finnish national discourse, with regard to both internal and external security. The 2001 report from the Ministry of Defence focuses particularly on a co-ordinated approach, and this was emphasized further in the report from 2004. In relations to the external dimension, the incorporation of a comprehensive approach may have been facilitated by the close co-ordination with the Ministry of Foreign Affairs, which has focused on this aspect for some time. The internal dimension may have been facilitated by the fact that the security policy tradition of neutrality and total defence has always involved close co-ordination between civilian and military aspects of national defence, and thus facilitated such an approach.

The many references to the EU in relations to both internal and external security are also a good indication that this is the result of a process of Europeanization. In contrast to the Swedish case, the impact of the EU is also more obvious here than in relation to the reorganization of the defence forces.

Instrumental adaptation or identity change?

As we have seen, the Finnish security discourse has become Europeanized, and the impact of the EU also seems more obvious than in Sweden. The changes, however, are not especially profound, and Finland's dominant security discourse is still very much based on a traditional conception of security. In fact, most of the changes referred to above seem to be legitimized by reference to how they in the end help to strengthen Finland's territorial defence capacity.

Since the Finnish security discourse has retained many traditional elements, it might be claimed that the Finnish discourse has not moved beyond the first phase in the socialization process. However, Finland's eagerness not only to join the EU, but also to show its commitment as a member state, does indicate a certain process of adaptation.

Shortly after the Maastricht Treaty and the establishment of a political union, Finland moved into the second phase. In fact, the EU process led to debate concerning EU membership as well as the continued relevance of neutrality (phase 2). While various opinions were expressed, the debate was less agitated than in Sweden, and EU membership was rapidly perceived as the best solution. Some scepticism prevailed towards the Maastricht Treaty, the CFSP and a possible future European defence, but as long as this dimension did not provoke Russia, the majority of the Finnish political leadership could accept also this part of the integration process.

In Finland the decision to abandon the concept of neutrality, and thereafter the application for EU membership, must be understood as a move into the third phase of the socialization process, which is characterized by instrumental adaptation. These decisions were taken mainly on the basis of traditional and interest-based security considerations, and EU membership was primarily seen as a substitute for the policy of neutrality. In order to make the European integration process move in accordance with the country's dominant national interests at that time, Finland aimed at becoming a central player within the EU. Its 'good pupil' behaviour, with initiatives such as the Petersberg tasks and the Northern Dimension, was Finland's way of showing its interest in and commitment to the process, and making the EU more relevant. In consequence, ever since Finland joined the EU, the country's security discourse has undergone a gradual internationalization. However, instead of radical alterations in the Finnish security identity, these changes seem to have been initiated primarily for instrumental reasons, strengthening the national defence.

After some years of membership in the European Union, most of the changes that have been introduced into the Finnish security and defence discourse also seem to be perceived as a 'good thing'. This should indicate a transition into the fourth phase – but these changes continue to be legitimized by reference to them as strengthening the national defence capacity. This is the case even for a comprehensive security approach, which, as in Sweden, builds heavily on the traditional concept of total defence. While this dimension seems less developed than in Sweden, it is far better integrated into the dominant national security discourse in Finland. This may be explained by Finland's continued eagerness to remain a 'good pupil' within the EU.

The fact that all changes in the Finnish security approach noted here are seen as a way of strengthening Finnish territorial defence makes it difficult to claim that they represent changes in the Finnish security identity. Hence, *instrumental adaptation* is the main characteristic of the Europeanization of the Finnish security discourse. Writing in 1996, Pertti Joenniemi argued that Finland had moved beyond traditional security thinking and had begun to recognize that the security context needed new answers (Joenniemi 1996: 127). The analysis in this chapter, however, has shown that even the arguments used to justify the greater focus on comprehensive security in the Finnish discourse are based on traditional security arguments. However, the recent decision to accede to the Ottawa Convention in 2012, and destroy its land mines by the end of 2016 is an indication of a more profound change.

6

DENMARK

Reluctant adapter

Compared to Sweden and Finland, Denmark has had a very different reaction to both the end of the Cold War and the establishment of a political union. In both Sweden and Finland, this period was characterized by moves towards the EU. In Denmark, however, it led instead to a demand for a looser membership arrangement. A member since 1973, the country experienced an increased scepticism towards the EU in the early 1990s. The fact that this led to a special arrangement in the EU meant that, despite many years as a Member State, Denmark's security discourse still seemed less Europeanized than that of Sweden or Finland. As we shall see, however, there have been some tendencies to instrumental adaptation to the European security approach in Denmark as well.

This chapter is structured as the previous two. The first part provides a short presentation of the historical background for the Danish security identity as it can be identified in the early 1990s, and which is referred to here as *Atlantic-oriented universalism*. The second part analyses the security and defence discourse in the first half of the 1990s – a period characterized by opt-outs from the Maastricht Treaty and by major defence reforms. The third part analyses the impact of the ESDP process on Danish perceptions of the EU as a security actor and Denmark's security discourse in general. The fourth part inquires whether there has been any influence of the EU's comprehensive security approach. The chapter concludes with a discussion on the degree and character of Europeanization, asking whether what has taken place is a change in identity or merely an instrumental adaptation to external changes.

Towards Atlantic-oriented universalism

The consolidation of the Danish security identity, as it can be identified in the early 1990s, seems to have happened gradually and through different phases. I highlight here three phases that appear to be particularly important. The first is Denmark's attachment to neutrality up until the end of the Second World War. The second is a period characterized by NATO membership and subsequently Denmark's ambivalent positioning in NATO. The third is the end of the Cold War, the transformation of NATO and a Danish security discourse characterized by an Atlantic-oriented universalism.

From neutrality to NATO membership (1720–1949)

While most historians would argue that maintaining neutrality was the paramount goal of Danish foreign policy from the end of the Napoleonic wars up until 1949, when Denmark joined NATO, the year 1720 is normally taken as a turning point in Danish history.[1] This was the year when a peace settlement was reached between the Nordic powers – Denmark and Sweden – after several years of war. From 1720 to 1807, the kingdom of Denmark enjoyed a hitherto unparalleled success. In the early nineteenth-century, however, Denmark-Norway overplayed its hand and ended up as an adversary of Britain in the Napoleonic wars. The battle of Copenhagen in 1801, the British bombardment in 1807, the subsequent loss of the navy and final defeat at the hands of the anti-Napoleon coalition led to bankruptcy of the state in 1813 and the loss of Norway to Sweden in 1814 (Østergaard 2000: 155).

The period after 1814 was characterized by relative solidarity among the great powers. Meeting at a series of congresses in the post-war years, their sovereigns and ministers attempted to direct European politics through a formal concert. For Denmark these years were characterized by relative security. After the breakdown of the congress system in early 1820s, however, this co-operation was increasingly disrupted by rivalry and conflicts. For Denmark the intensified rivalry between Prussia and Austria, within Germany in particular, seemed to offer new opportunities (linked to vital Danish interests along the southern border). However, pursuing them in two wars (1848 and 1864) proved disastrous.[2] Despite several attempts to find a diplomatic solution, Denmark lost the region of Schleswig-Holstein to Prussia in 1864. These wars had an important impact on the Danish security identity, and soon made a unified Germany the principal threat to Denmark's national security (ibid.: 158).

In the last few decades before 1914, tensions in the state system increased until all the great powers of Europe were split into hostile camps, with Germany and Austria-Hungary facing France, Russia, and Britain in preparation for a major war. Under such conditions, some of the lesser states in the system became objects of diplomatic rivalry between the great powers. For those able to exploit a stronger bargaining position than Denmark, this could have been an advantage. But Denmark, diplomatically isolated and geographically close to Germany, was too exposed to be able take advantage of the situation. When the war broke out, the government issued a series of declarations of neutrality (Holbraad 1991: 49).

After the defeat of Germany in the First World War, a concert of great powers was restored and the League of Nations established. The external situation of Denmark now seemed safer than it had been for centuries. Peter Munch, who became Foreign Minister in 1929, started out as a convinced internationalist in the early 1920s and was a stalwart believer in handing over power and possibly sovereignty to the League of Nations. However, he was not a doctrinaire pacifist, and supported the idea of enabling the League of Nations to use military force when acting with a mandate from the parties involved in international conflicts. Only when he realized the lack of necessary determination within the international community to implement the initial ideals of the international organization, did he and his coalition government, under the Social Democrat Thorvald Stauning, endorse a policy of unarmed neutralism towards Germany. However, with the outbreak of the Second World War and the German occupation of Denmark, Munch's policy of *de facto* pacifism regarding military means fell into disrepute (Østergaard 2000: 169–71).

When German forces, racing against the British to reach Norway, invaded Denmark on 9 April, they met only sporadic resistance. The Danish government capitulated immediately. Since the occupation took place in a peaceful manner and Germany presented it as an act of protection, promising not to use Danish territory as a base in the war with Britain and to respect the territorial integrity and political sovereignty of the country, the government was able to maintain that Denmark was still formally a 'neutral' state. The invasion and occupation in 1940 nevertheless became a turning point in the history of Denmark's foreign policy. The series of events denoted by 9 April could be seen as the final outcome of a long-standing inclination to seek to stay out of European power politics – and that proved an experience traumatic enough to provoke the nation to check, and to begin to reverse, what since the nineteenth century had been the base line of Danish foreign policy. Towards the end of the war the conflict with the occupying power thus intensified, and the military and diplomatic efforts of the Danish resistance movement in the final years of the war marked a big step back to active engagement in the conflicts of international politics (Holbraad 1991: 79–80).

Between 1945 and 1948 Denmark allowed its general security to be handled politically through the UN. However, when the Security Council could not function as anticipated due to the ensuing Cold War, it became important for Denmark to have the UN Treaty accept the legitimacy of collective defence organizations, as this would mean that Denmark could join such arrangements without weakening the UN. It is also clear that Denmark would have preferred a Scandinavian solution to an Atlantic one. However, plans for a Scandinavian Defence Association (SDA) did not work out, due to the incompatibility of Norway's and Sweden's objectives. The Norwegians wanted this arrangement to have a formal connection with the US-led North Atlantic Alliance, which Swedish neutrality could not accept. The collapse of SDA negotiations left Danish decision-makers with a dilemma: isolated neutrality could tempt the Soviet Union to attack Denmark, while full NATO membership together with Norway might be perceived as a provocation. In this situation, the choice fell on NATO membership (Villaume 1999: 30).

A reluctant NATO member (1949–1989)

As Hans Hedtoft's speech in the Danish Parliament (the Folketing) on 31 October 1951 indicates, the decision to join NATO was not an easy one:

> Nobody should deny – and I will not deny – that the cooperation under the Atlantic Treaty raises complicated problems for our country, problems that might be difficult for a people, with our neutrality tradition and scepticism towards all great powers, to understand.
>
> (Quoted in Nielsen 2001)

The main reason for membership, however, was that the United States was perceived to be the sole country that could guarantee Danish security against a potential attack from the East. Denmark was the only European country with possessions on the North American continent (Greenland) which could not be defended without American assistance. In addition, Denmark needed to promote security *vis-à-vis* Germany (Honkanen 2002: 39–40).

While Denmark's placing of bases in Greenland at the disposal of the US Air Force was an important contribution to the common NATO defence, Denmark, just like Norway, had two self-imposed restrictions: rejecting the US request for peacetime bases in Denmark proper, and refusing to follow the 1958 NATO doctrine of 'nuclearization' of the member states' defence forces (Villaume 1999: 32–7).

In the second half of the 1960s Denmark engaged in a rather remarkably proactive Ostpolitik, which at certain points led Danish détente policies somewhat away from – or perhaps rather ahead of – mainstream NATO views. A series of multilateral contacts were arranged, and the 'group of ten' – NATO members Belgium, Denmark and the Netherlands, Warsaw Pact countries Bulgaria, Hungary and Romania, and non-aligned Austria, Finland, Sweden and Yugoslavia – discussed proposals and initiatives to promote European security. Prominent among the proposals were a North European nuclear-free zone and an all-European collective security conference. The latter was originally a Soviet idea, first broached in 1954, which the Danish government had supported publicly in 1965 – earlier than any other NATO country (ibid.: 38). In the ensuing years Denmark also strongly supported the CSCE process, which aimed at making dividing lines in Europe less categorical through the establishment of political, cultural and military co-operative relations between East and West. This means that Denmark's Atlantic security identity was modified to some extent by the country's active engagement in the CSCE process.

126

In addition, there was also a Western European dimension to Denmark's Cold War security approach. But since Western Europe was not perceived as having the potential of developing into an independent security actor, this was primarily linked to a perception of the European integration process as an important peace project. This is why Denmark was reluctant to join the WEU, the ECSC and the EDC.

Together with the United Kingdom, Denmark joined the EC in 1973. While the Danish political leadership continued to seek its security primarily through NATO, it relied on the EC as a unit for integration with some broad security aspects – not least the involvement of Germany in a narrow European project (Heurlin 2001). Despite these security aspects, the EC was still seen as primarily an organization for economic co-operation. This meant that Denmark in reality relied on two institutions for its security (in addition to the UN) – NATO to provide basic security by deterring the Soviet threat, and the CSCE to soften Cold War tensions and underpin détente and contacts with Eastern Europe.

In the 1980s, however, the Atlantic priority in Danish security policy was toned down. The Danish government reacted negatively towards Washington's new confrontational security policy, which was based on nuclear rearmament, abandonment of arms control and heightened demands on the USSR concerning arms control negotiations (ibid.: 10). Danish security was now to be promoted by a policy based on the priority of co-operation rather than deterrence. Denmark therefore continued to be actively involved in the construction of the CSCE, but became a rather lukewarm member of NATO (Petersen 2000c: 106). Within NATO, this was often referred to as the 'footnote policy', and led to the appearance of the concept 'Denmarkization' – referring to a country that is a free-rider in an alliance and does not wish to share mutual burdens while continuing to enjoy both full protection and guarantees (Heurlin 2001: 10).[3]

According to Bertil Heurlin (2001), the complexity of Denmark's Cold War security approach can be illustrated by identifying five different security priorities in Danish security policy over the last fifty years:

1   Universalist (the UN);
2   Atlantic (NATO);
3   Western European (EC);
4   All-European (CSCE); and
5   Nordic.

Heurlin argues that, while these security priorities functioned more or less independently during the Cold War, today there is only one priority left in the post-Cold War security discourse – what he call an *all-European-Atlantic line with an emphasis on the universal dimension*. In fact, while Denmark has actively supported the transformation of the CSCE into a broad institutionalized framework for European security, the new NATO has largely replaced the important position held by the CSCE and the UN in the Danish security approach during the Cold War (ibid.: 20).

Atlantic-oriented universalism (1990–1991)

As we have seen, Denmark's footnote policy in NATO in the 1980s was combined with international activism in the UN and the CSCE, which was further strengthened after the end of the Cold War. The notion of 'active internationalism' was first employed by Foreign Minister Uffe Ellemann-Jensen and the Foreign Policy Commission of 1989 to describe the new foreign policy then under development (Olsen 2001). Denmark had pursued an active internationalist approach for some time; now that Denmark's immediate security environment had become more stable, it was possible to make this the main priority (Holm 1997, 2002).

From being a frontline state, situated close to the Iron Curtain and bordering on the Soviet-dominated Baltic region, Denmark suddenly found itself surrounded by friendly states. This meant that the security context changed more fundamentally for Denmark than for the other Nordic states, which helps in explaining why Denmark could more easily change its national security doctrine. In fact, Denmark was one of the first countries, not only in Norden but also in Europe as such, to move beyond a traditional security discourse dominated by the notion of territorial defence.

While the Defence Commission's report of 1989 was the first official analysis of the changing security environment, it still represented a rather traditional security discourse. One year later, however, a Foreign Office report indicated several new trends, such as a shift from a bipolar to a multipolar world and a change in superpower relations from confrontation to co-operation. The report also noted the need to take into consideration new threats and challenges, specifically in the fields of chemical weapons, missile technology, terrorism, drugs, pollution and human rights, as well as the need to integrate the Third World into the world economy. However, certain military spokesmen continued to refer to the Soviet Union's military capacity and uncertainties concerning political developments, warning against jumping to conclusions too quickly on the basis of the recent changes (Petersen 2000c: 101). By late 1991, however, the Danish security doctrine had changed – and this was several years before the other Nordic countries embraced similar changes.

With the end of the Cold War, Denmark's security concerns changed rapidly from a focus on direct military threats to a far broader threat conception focusing on political and economic disorder in Denmark's vicinity, on the implications of ethnic conflicts in Europe, and on a wide range of social and ecological challenges (ibid.: 102). The immediate effects of the end of the Cold War on Denmark's security environment combined with its traditional support for the UN also made the country one of the earliest and most dedicated participants in post-Cold War peacekeeping operations. When peacekeeping and other forms of intervention were stepped up in the early 1990s, Denmark responded accordingly. Most significantly, Denmark sent a corvette to the Persian Gulf in 1990 to police the embargo against Iraq – the first time a Danish armed unit had been sent out-of-area, and outside a clear UN peacekeeping context (Heurlin 2001).

Despite this change in threat conception, NATO continued to be at the core of Denmark's security policy. Indeed, its attitude towards NATO was now more positive than ever. While Denmark had been sceptical about NATO's deterrence strategy in its relations with the Soviet Union, it reacted very positively to the significant changes in NATO's strategy, force structures and organization in the early 1990s (Petersen 2000c: 103). Denmark's early post-Cold War security identity characterized by support for peace-keeping and the new NATO can therefore be referred to as an *Atlantic-oriented universalism*. The main element of this identity was NATO's perceived role as an 'entrepreneur' for legitimizing universalist authorities such as the UN or the CSCE/OSCE in peacekeeping and peace-enforcing operations (Villaume 1999: 50). Since NATO had changed, this active Danish participation represented no dramatic rupture with past Danish security policies or traditions. However, this changed when Denmark began to support US and/or NATO actions without the consent of the UN. In addition, Denmark initiated a rather active foreign policy towards the Baltic states, starting with economic aid, support for independence and continuing with support for the integration of these states into the Western structures and – more controversially – assistance in the building of national military forces (Holm 2002: 88–90).

From NATO 'footnote' to EU 'footnote'

With the end of the Cold War, Denmark's role in the Alliance shifted from a 'footnote' country to an active NATO member. In relations to the EU, however, there was a shift in the opposite direction. Here the Danish political leadership went from strongly supporting the establishment of a political union in the early 1990s, to 'opting out' from central parts of it once it was established. In a way, Denmark's footnote status in NATO in the 1980s was now, to some extent, replaced by a similar status in the EU.

With the opt-out from the Union's defence dimension, the integration process continued to be perceived primarily as a forum for economic co-operation. By implication, the new NATO became the main forum for Denmark's post-Cold War security approach. In order to contribute effect-ively to NATO, Denmark rapidly adapted its security approach, making international crisis management the most important part of its security approach.

EU 'opt-outs' and Atlanticism

In the early 1990s and before Denmark became a committed NATO ally, the EU was seen as the most important cornerstone of Danish foreign and security policy. In fact, the five security priorities that had constituted the Danish approach throughout the Cold War period – Atlanticist, universalist, all-European, Western European, and Nordic – seemed to become one in the newly proposed political union (the EU). The security role of this EU was seen as one of 'peace through integration'. In the memorandum presented by the Danish government in October 1990, the Union was understood as an anchor for European security. This meant that while there was general agreement that co-operation involving defence guarantees should not take place within the EU, the security dimension of the EU was increasingly recognized among the political elites (Larsen 2000b: 94–6). This 1990 memorandum, which was published with the consent of the opposition and as a basis for participation in the Intergovernmental Conference (IGC) leading up to Maastricht, was the most pro-European official document at the time. It provided the government with substantial room for manoeuvre at the conference, and led to specific Danish fingerprints in the final text (Nehring 2001: 156).

Despite this pro-European approach, the transatlantic dimension was still presented as a priority. A report from the Committee on Danish Security in 1991 emphasized that a European defence dimension was seen as a means rather than an end in itself – it would have to be functional for the Alliance, maintain transatlantic solidarity, and aim at solving necessary security tasks in Europe in situations where the USA did not want to participate. In other words, the EU as a security actor should be strengthened as long as it did not weaken American political engagement in Europe. In this context, Denmark's political leadership also seemed to reconsider its traditional opposition towards the WEU, which was now seen as a possible bridge between NATO and the EU or as a European pillar in NATO. At the WEU meeting in Paris on 21 August 1990, Denmark, together with Greece, was given observer status. In order to allow Denmark to follow EU's security developments, the Folketing accepted this invitation, but there was no support for actual participation in a WEU operation.[4]

Danish public opinion was more sceptical as to the establishment of a European political union. In the campaign prior to the referendum on ratifying the Maastricht Treaty in June 1992, the deeper implications of this project were discussed. Traditional Danish opposition to a federal type of European integration could be identified: in particular, the project of giving the European Community a future defence dimension provoked negative reactions. Opinion polls later showed that arguments warning against the Community as a would-be military superpower contributed significantly to the negative outcome. Although the majority of the political elites in

Denmark reacted positively to the new Treaty, they had no choice but to adapt to the tendencies within public opinion at that time.

The dilemma was solved by a national compromise negotiated among seven of the eight political parties in the Folketing in October 1992. The agreement proposed that Denmark should opt out from four areas of the integration process: European citizenship, the third phase of the EMU, the European defence dimension and the supranational parts of justice and home affairs. The government succeeded in getting its demands accepted by the European Council in Edinburgh in December 1992. In addition, the exemptions were further reinforced prior to the second referendum in May 1993 by an agreement, among the political parties taking part in the national compromise, that it was possible to abolish the exemptions only by holding new referenda (Petersen 2000c: 104–5).

Even though the political establishment adapted to the results of the referendum, the integration process continued to be referred to as having important direct and indirect security policy implications. As the 1993 official report of the Danish Ministry of Foreign Affairs states:

> The EC [has at its disposal] the main part of those means, which will secure stability and economic development in Europe after the end of the Cold War. This gives the EC a very central security policy role as the framework of a broadly conceived European cooperation. The EC thereby acquires a decisive stabilising function.
>
> (Quoted in Petersen 2000c: 107)

However, the report continues to refer to the *EC* instead of the *EU*, which indicates that it was the security effects of the economic integration process that was referred to, and to a lesser extent the effects of the newly established CFSP.

The Danish discourse on European security now reflected the official discourse within NATO. When the WEU was recognized as NATO's European pillar, in January 1994, and perceived as a possible bridge between NATO and the EU, Denmark became more supportive of both the CFSP and the WEU. This decision was perceived as a confirmation that NATO remained Denmark's main framework for European security, and some political parties even began to argue for full membership in the WEU. The government therefore charged an independent Commission on Disarmament and Security Affairs (SNU) with preparing a report on the changing circumstances of Denmark's security policy. However, while the Commission recommended full membership, the government did not follow this advice, although it did admit that full membership might prove necessary if the Commission's predictions about the WEU's role were realized. This attitude was based on the calculation that it could be difficult to win a referendum on the WEU issue. Underlying the government's policy was the negative feedback from the referendum in June 1992, and the fear of a popular backlash (Petersen 2000c: 105–6).

Beyond territorial defence

At the same time as the ratification process came the first major change in the composition of the national Danish defence forces. In April 1992, one month before Denmark rejected the Maastricht Treaty, an official committee attached to the Ministry of Defence concluded that the traditional threat had disappeared and that economic, social and political instability was now the main concern for Danish defence (Archer 1996). While the gap between the elites and the public in relation to the Maastricht Treaty means that we cannot rule out a certain Europeanization of the Danish political elites in the early 1990s, the impact of the EU is not obvious. After all, the defence dimension of the EU was only vaguely described in the Treaty. It is more likely that these changes were a direct result of the end of the Cold War, the changed security context and the changes within NATO.

In November 1992, the first post-Cold War defence agreement was negotiated between the six main parties in the Folketing. The agreement covered the period 1992–4, and aimed at initiating a restructuring of the Danish defence forces. The agreement was based on the absence of a well-defined military threat and the conclusion that any risk of an invasion of Danish territory was close to zero. The international situation at that time was characterized by actual and potential conflicts of nationalistic, religious, and/or ethnic character, and it was argued that Denmark should be able to make a contribution to alleviating these (Petersen 2000c: 101).

The main feature of the defence agreement was therefore a shift of emphasis, away from territorial defence and toward participation in international security tasks. This was confirmed by the announcement that a Danish International Brigade (DIB) of 4,500 men with a 'dual assignment' had been established. This meant that they could participate in peacekeeping, peace-enforcement, humanitarian and other similar operations under the UN and the CSCE, and simultaneously be a brigade for NATO defence, primarily in the context of the Alliance's Rapid Reaction Forces (ibid.: 110).

Changes in Denmark's security discourse continued, as can be seen in a Foreign Office report – published in the summer of 1993 – containing a comprehensive statement of the world situation. The report referred to the changed security context, but the tone was somewhat more concerned than earlier. While emphasizing that the risk of major war had disappeared from Western Europe, it stressed that this had been replaced by political and economic instability on the periphery. In addition, the report pointed to problems such as the spread of weapons of mass destruction, growing nationalism, terrorism, the drug trade and organized crime, the possibility of mass migrations, growing ecological risks and the widening gap between North and South (ibid.: 102).

In December 1993, the Folketing passed a package of laws and decisions clarifying the legal and organizational basis for the future deployment of the Danish defence forces. A new law on the purposes, tasks, organization, etc. of the defence forces gave them three operational tasks. The first was to contribute with military forces, either directly or through NATO, and on mandates from either the UN or the CSCE, 'to the solution of conflict preventing, peace-keeping, peace-enforcement, humanitarian and other similar tasks'. The second was the defence of Denmark proper, including national conflict prevention and management of conflicts in the vicinity of Denmark. The third and final operational task was 'to participate in conflict management and defence within the whole NATO area, including the demonstration of solidarity by deploying reaction forces' (quoted in Petersen 2000c: 111). With the Defence Act of 1993 the task repertoire of the Danish defence forces was significantly widened, both geographically and functionally, which clearly shows that Denmark's national security identity had moved beyond the Cold War. In this document the government and the Folketing stated that there was no longer any direct military threat to fundamental Danish security interests, such as the nation's existence, its integrity and sovereignty. Thus, in only a few years, Danish defence discourse had changed from a concerned preoccupation with the possibility of negative threats to national security, to a constructive approach to new task opportunities.

As the discussion in this section has shown, Denmark's early adaptation of its national defence forces seems to have been a direct consequence of the end of the Cold War and the changes in NATO. The Danish rejection of the Maastricht Treaty, however, made NATO the sole arena in which Denmark could make itself heard in the realm of European security. It meant that Denmark opted out as a full member of the WEU and later also the ESDP. The rapid internationalization of the Danish defence forces may therefore also be understood as an indirect consequence of Denmark's rejection of the Maastricht Treaty in 1992 (Frantzen 2003: 179).

Impact of the ESDP

A true Europeanization of the Danish security discourse can be identified only after 1995. Increasingly, the EU is referred to as a security actor; and, with the incorporation of the Petersberg tasks into the Treaty, even the defence dimension was becoming more acceptable. All the same, the defence exemption remained in place, so Denmark was still excluded from a security dimension that actually had been developing in accordance with its views. With the further concretization and institutionalization of the ESDP after the St Malo summit in December 1998, the problems related to the Danish exemption became even more apparent. Several initiatives were taken to abolish the exemption. However, as this could only be done through a new referendum, the negative result in Denmark's referendum on the euro (which was one of the four exemptions) in September 2000 slowed down this process. On the other hand, we can see a more active Danish approach – presumably intended to help prevent marginalization – in the parts of CFSP in which Denmark participates fully.

The Danish paradox

By 1995 the EU was presented as the major pillar in Danish security. Helveg Petersen, foreign minister at the time, explained the importance of the EU in the following way:

> Today we need the Union for four main reasons . . . First, we need the Union for reasons of security . . . The theory of 'peace through integration' has stood the test of History. Today war is literally unthinkable among members of the European Union . . . Secondly, we need the Union to produce common solutions to common problems . . . More and more policy problems have international aspects that demand international action . . . Had the Union not already been in place, we would have to invent it . . . Thirdly, we need the Union to promote our values and defend our interests at the global level. No European state can any longer play a leading role on its own.
>
> (Petersen 1995)

This meant that the only remaining contentious issue in Danish security policy was how to handle the defence implications of the EU and Denmark's relationship with the WEU. After 1995 the Danish government explicitly supported not only a soft security role but also a soft *defence* policy role for the EU. This approach was presented in a very low-key manner, but is nevertheless unmistakable. The first clear manifestation of this can be found in the formulations expressing the Danish standpoint at the 1996 IGC negotiations:

> A number of European Countries wish to improve ways of effectively taking on humanitarian tasks, crisis management and peacekeeping efforts in accordance with the provisions of the UN Charter. The Danish Government believes that EU Member States should have the opportunity of participating in the performance of such tasks if they so desire. This would increase the EU's ability to help in resolving foreign and security problems.
>
> (Quoted in Larsen 2000b: 100)

This constituted a change from the position at the 1990/1 IGC, where the Danish political leadership had been sceptical about everything linked to the defence dimension of the EU. However, the change is not so much a change in approach as one of clarification. In the early 1990s there was considerable uncertainty attached to the Union's future defence dimension. Once it became clear that this was not going to include collective defence guarantees, it was easier for the Danish political elites to express their support.

The government interpreted the Danish defence exemption to mean that Denmark should not participate in decisions and actions of the EU which had defence implications with reference to article J.4.2 of the Maastricht Treaty. This meant 'the eventual framing of a common defence policy, which might in time lead to a common defence' – but, more importantly than opting out from a potential EU collective defence arrangement, it also included actions that touched on areas to which Denmark had traditionally attributed great importance, such as peacekeeping, mine clearance and humanitarian aid (Larsen 2000b: 101–2). Denmark therefore found itself in a paradoxical situation – despite being one of the first countries to move beyond territorial defence and to adapt its national defence forces to the new tasks of international crisis management, it had to abstain from future participation in international crisis management operations led by the EU. There was an increased gap between what Denmark officially supported in the EU with regard to the European defence dimension, and what Denmark actually could take part in (Petersen 1996: 195).

Despite these tendencies towards a slight Europeanization of the Danish security discourse after 1995, the Atlantic dimension is still given priority. This is illustrated by the Danish reactions to the Amsterdam Treaty. While this treaty was interpreted by many as the first step towards a more independent European security dimension, a different view was presented in the 1998 annual declaration from the Danish Ministry of Defence. Here the emphasis was on confirming both the intergovernmental character of the CFSP and the fact that the Treaty recognizes the importance of NATO (Forsvarsministeriet 1998: ch. 8).

It has been argued that the Danish political leadership only vaguely supported the development of a European security and defence policy because it feared that the Amsterdam Treaty would be rejected by the Danish public (Nehring 2001: 157). In fact, what it feared was that the public would not understand that the incorporation of the Petersberg tasks into the Treaty actually made a difference. In order to avoid arguments linked to the defence dimension, the government focused instead on arguments concerning employment, consumer policy and the environment in the campaign leading up to the referendum on the Amsterdam Treaty. The aim was to give a picture of a Union in conformity with Danish values. The accession of Sweden and Finland to the EU in 1995 also made such arguments more credible, and the defence dimension was therefore left aside. This strategy succeeded, and the Treaty was ratified on 28 May 1998.

The change in the British attitude towards a European security dimension also made it easier for the Danish government take a more active approach. In October 1998 the Danish Prime Minister stated that Denmark could participate in the debate about the development of the EU as an actor in the field of defence, and that this was compatible with the Danish exemption. This can only be interpreted as a sign that the government's space for manoeuvring had widened after the Amsterdam Treaty had been ratified (Larsen 1997: 102).

However, the exemption persisted and the EU had not yet become an important part of the Danish security discourse. This is evident from the report of the 1997 Defence Commission, presented in November 1998.[5] The references to the EU as a security actor were not frequent in the main volume, and the report from the sub-group on European security policy starts the section on 'EU, WEU and the security policy' by arguing that 'Denmark's entry into European co-operation has been market-oriented' (Forsvarskommissionen 1998: 25, my translation). The security role of the integration process – especially in relation to the enlargement process – was emphasized, while less attention was given to the development towards an independent security and defence dimension in the EU. The report referred to the NATO process, emphasizing that the EU process was a separate but not an independent process. It was also argued that a possible EU action would be likely to occur only in a rather distant future (ibid.: 26). One month after the presentation of the report, the French–British summit in St Malo took place, launching the process towards what today is known as the ESDP. This summit was not mentioned in the declaration published by the Ministry of Defence (Forsvarsministeriet 1998).

Combining 'Atlanticism' with 'Europeanism'

While the St Malo summit was not referred to in the annual declaration from the Ministry of Defence, a more active Danish line could be discerned in discussions about the ESDP at the European Council meetings in Cologne (June 1999) and in Helsinki (December 1999) (Larsen 2000b: 103). This must be seen in relation to the change in British policy. This change was interpreted as a guarantee that the ESDP was not going to weaken NATO, which was still perceived as the most important framework for European security (Petersen 1999a).

The Danish government now started to speak more explicitly about the problems related to the defence exemption. In a speech to the Folketing on 13 October, the Foreign Minister at the time, Niels Helveg Petersen, argued:

The defence exemption is a political reality. It has impact on

Denmark's participation in European crisis management. It put limits to our role in European security. This was not what we had in mind when we negotiated the national compromise.

(Petersen 1999c: 211, my translation)

Plans concerning the ESDP had now become so concrete that the government decided to inform the other EU countries as to the implications of the Danish defence exemption in a report on military crisis management. The report was prepared for the European Council in Helsinki (Forsvarsministeriet 1999: ch. 3).

The report was based on a legal opinion from the Ministry of Foreign Affairs presented in July 1999, which analysed the scope of the Danish defence exemption in light of the entry into force of the Amsterdam Treaty and the new dynamism in discussions about an EU defence dimension since the declaration of the European Council in Cologne. It concluded that Denmark could participate in negotiations and in issuing political declarations, but that the country could not participate in any decisions or actions of the Union which had defence implications (Larsen 2000b: 103). On the other hand, this meant that Denmark could take part in EU civilian crisis management operations (Politiken 2000b).

Despite this clarification, there remained problems related to the defence exemption, and they became even more evident both for Denmark and the other EU countries once the new structures to implement the defence dimension were set up. When Denmark participated in electing the first leader of the Military Committee (and voted for the Finnish candidate General Hägglund), the EU countries that had narrowly lost in this election demanded to know more precisely what Denmark could and could not participate in.[6] For Denmark itself it was not all that clear what 'defence implications' really meant. In addition, the concretization of 'appropriate arrangements' for the participation of third countries at the European Council meeting in Feira in June 2000, implying that non-members like Norway and Turkey could participate in future EU operations, made the possible marginalization of Denmark even more apparent (Politiken 2000a). This was especially difficult to accept since Denmark had already come much further than either Norway or Turkey in making its national defence forces more oriented towards participation in international crisis management.[7] All these factors probably explain why the Danish government now began to argue for having the exemption removed (Petersen 2000b).

The result of Denmark's referendum on the euro on 28 September 2000 did not, however, strengthen the prospects for removing one of the other opt-outs in the near future. But to avoid having the Danish 'no' to the euro interpreted as a vote against European integration as such, the Danish government realized it would have to provide the basis for a national dialogue on Denmark's role in the EU. In October 2000 it therefore decided to produce a White Paper on the issue. It was important to clarify Denmark's role before the country was to take over the Presidency in July 2002.[8]

While the defence exemption prevailed, Denmark's growing interest in the ESDP was confirmed in the annual declaration from the Ministry of Defence in 2000. In the preamble, the newly appointed Defence Minister, Jan Trøjborg, warned explicitly that Denmark might become marginalized if a debate concerning the defence exemption were not launched. For the first time, the annual declaration devoted a whole section to the ESDP and Denmark's complicated position. It also emphasized the importance of NATO, and stressed that the Danish non-participation in the ESDP might possibly complicate its participation in NATO (Forsvarsministeriet 2000: 39–44).

In an article in the Danish newspaper *Politiken*, in January 2001, Mogens Lykketoft, the newly appointed Foreign Minister, also claimed that Denmark supported development towards a European security and defence policy, emphasizing the role of the USA in this process. He argued, 'the USA has been an important driving force' in the establishment of the ESDP, and 'that it was a decision at the NATO summit in 1999 that created the framework for the European project' (Lykketoft 2001b, my translation). In another article in *Jyllandsposten*, in March 2001, he emphasized that it was important for Denmark that NATO should remain the most important defence organization in Europe:

> even though Denmark, because of its defence exemption, cannot participate in EU-led military operations, it is in our interest that the transatlantic ties are strengthened in this process and that NATO keep its position as the main defence organization in Europe.
> (Lykketoft 2001a, my translation)

In the Danish discourse, the European security dimension continues to be perceived as a process within NATO (Lykketoft 2001d). This was seen as the only way of convincing sceptics that the ESDP would not be a threat to NATO. This priority to NATO in the Danish discourse is also evident in the most recent Defence Agreement, in which the main tasks for the defence forces are defined as follows: (1) providing a credible contribution to NATO, (2) contributing to a positive development in European security through a strengthening of the co-operation between the European countries, (3) continuing to be an active member of the UN, OSCE and NATO and participating in humanitarian and peace support operations (Hillingsø 2001: 5).

Early in 2001 two political parties (SF and Enhedslisten) submitted a joint proposal concerning the need for abandoning the defence exemption (Informationen 2001); and with reference to the opt-out, the White Paper presented 12 June 2001 emphasized that 'Denmark could lose influence not only with regard to the ESDP but also the CFSP as such' (Udenrigsministeriet 2001a: 279, my translation). The problems related to the Danish exemption continued to be emphasized in the preparations preceding the Danish Presidency, with Lykketoft claiming that the Danish exemptions represented a real challenge (Lykketoft 2001c). In order to avoid further confusion about this special situation, the government presented a new report on the defence exemption at the General Affairs Council meeting on 8 October 2001 (Udenrigsministeriet 2001b).

Still, there were no prospects of a quick referendum on this issue. This was made clear by the new government coming into office in November 2001.[9] In an interview in the Danish daily *Politiken* on 16 May 2002 the newly appointed Danish Minister for European Affairs, Bertel Haarder, argued that 'Denmark is not going to have a new referendum concerning the exemptions before the next Treaty is to be ratified'.[10]

During the Danish Presidency an important agreement was signed between NATO and the EU, allowing the EU to take over NATO's operation in Macedonia. Because of the Danish exemption, however, it was Greece that was tasked with the Presidency in this particular area. The Danish Minister of Foreign Affairs, Per Stig Møller, welcomed the agreement, but he also pointed to the unfortunate consequences for Denmark as long as the defence exemption had to be followed:

> During the Presidency progress has been made in the NATO–EU relationship. The agreement paves the way for EU's first military crisis management operation. The agreement was made at the European Council and means that the EU may take over the NATO operation in Macedonia and probably also SFOR in Bosnia. The government of course welcome this agreement. But we should all be aware that when the EU takes over some of NATO's operations on the Balkans, we have to send our soldiers home because of the defence exemption.
>
> (Møller 2003, my translation)

While the concretization of EU's security dimension has led to an increased recognition of the EU as a security actor and made it more common to question the value of a continued exemption in this area, there is not much evidence of a Europeanization of the Danish security identity. Rather, the dominant Danish security discourse seems to have been influenced by Danish activism within NATO, with the result that the security identity has been that is both militarized and Americanized[11] (Jakobsen 2000). The fact that the decision to participate in NATO's operation against Serbia at the end of the 1990s was adopted without much resistance is a clear indication of this. As events unfolded in Kosovo, Denmark came to support military intervention based on the idea of 'humanitarian intervention'[12] (Frantzen 2003: 198). Although Denmark has supported peacekeeping since 1957, and has held a high profile in the UN, the use of force had in cases like Korea and the Gulf War traditionally been more controversial. This means that the Kosovo war was Denmark's first real war since 1864 – and it was a war without a UN mandate. The Danish Foreign Minister at the time, Niels Helveg Petersen, stresses that although the starting point should be a mandate, the question should be handled flexibly on the basis of a concrete assessment of each individual incident (Petersen 1999b).

This 'new' policy based on the principle of human intervention represent a break with Denmark's long-standing non-militarist or semi-pacifist policy dating back to 1864, including the 1930s and the Cold War period. As Poul Villaume argues:

> What has happened in the 1990s is that Denmark as a NATO-member has abandoned its status as a more or less low-profile ally with scepticism and reservations towards great powers, including the United States, towards power politics, towards black and white images of the appointed enemy, towards excessive belief in military means as solutions to complicated international ands social conflicts, towards out-of-area operations, towards nuclear strategies, etc. Instead, Denmark has chosen a status as a staunch ally without reservations worth mentioning towards the policies of dominant great powers in NATO, the United States in particular, towards active military participation in unilateral NATO out-of-area operations and engagements.
>
> (Villaume 1999: 56–7)

Denmark's support of and participation in the US-led war against Iraq in March 2003 also confirm this view.

Impact of the EU's comprehensive security approach

While the EU's security approach in the post-Cold War period has become increasingly comprehensive, the Danish approach can be said to have moved in the opposite direction. However, recent developments indicate a trend towards a more comprehensive approach in Danish security discourse in relation to both the 'internal' and the 'external' dimensions of security.

Internal security

The internal security dimension has until recently been dominated by a rather traditional approach. This means that while Denmark was one of the first countries to introduce an internationalized discourse on security, which in turn led to an important modernization and internationalization of the national defence forces, less emphasis has been put on the need to modernize the way one approaches the internal security of the country. In the annual declarations from the Ministry of Defence from 1997 to 2001, this aspect is barely referred to.

According to the Defence Commission international crisis management is characterized as 'indirect security' while 'direct security' refers to Denmark's collective defence engagement in NATO and 'other traditional tasks' for the defence forces, such as defending Danish sovereignty and Denmark's existence and integrity (Forsvarskommissionen 1998: 110–14). While military means are in focus here as well, the traditional total defence concept is presented as an appropriate framework for handling such threats:

> The defence of Denmark is not only a military task. Society has become increasingly vulnerable. In the event of a future crisis or war – or a possible greater catastrophe in peace time – this will require a coordinated approach by all four components of the total defence force in order to keep in place the crucial functions of society and make the most of the resources available. The need to prepare for the co-ordinated use of the defence forces, the police and civilian preparedness within the framework of total defence still exists.
>
> (Forsvarskommissionen 1998: 114, my translation)

But while the need for a comprehensive approach is recognized in principle, less attention has been given to the need to modernize this part of the defence forces. How best to protect vulnerable modern societies is addressed only briefly, and then only in relation to the traditional concept of total defence – no reorganization is proposed.

In March 2001 the editor of a small Danish magazine called *Ingeniøren* ('The Engineer') stressed the need to rethink this dimension of the country's security approach. He emphasized the problems related to the lack of co-ordination between different institutions responsible for national security. He also noted that Denmark had been much slower than either Norway or Sweden in this particular area:

> In Norway and Sweden progress has been made, based on the recommendations from independent commissions, with regard to adapting to current and future threats. In Denmark we have just made small adjustments to the old war preparedness capacity . . . the preparedness is fragmented . . . There is no-one at the ministerial level who feels responsible for overall crisis management preparedness.
>
> (Ingeniøren 2001, my translation)

But while few changes in the Danish discourse at that time can be identified, the Union's competence in the field of internal security is recognized. The White Paper on Denmark and Europe presented in June 2001 states that:

Since the Second World War, it has been clear that Denmark's security must be shaped in relations to other states. Denmark has therefore in the post war period strongly promoted and been active member in international organizations. With the end of the Cold War this tendency has been stronger. . . . Partly because the current security policy challenges includes a number of other questions than military ones – as for instance international crime and pollution. . . . EU is of course not the only framework for handling these challenges. But in most cases it is the most important one.

(Udenrigsministeriet 2001a: 261–3)

However, in relation to some of these questions Denmark also has a self-imposed exception, which means that it cannot participate in any EU activities related to justice and home affairs that have a supranational character. With the acceleration of the integration process in this area at the European Council meetings in Amsterdam (1997) and in Tampere (1999) in addition to post-11 September developments, problems related to this exemption also became increasingly obvious. With the decision to incorporate Schengen into the EU and to transfer some parts of co-operation on this issue from the third to the first pillar, Denmark has been forced to opt out from areas in which it could have taken part as long as these were intergovernmental. The implementation of the Schengen Area and the increased focus on the threat from terrorism, for instance, have led to several initiatives aimed at strengthening integration in this field. The Danish government explicitly supports this development, while admitting the possibility of Denmark being marginalized (ibid.: 289). Thus, it is interesting to note that, besides the enlargement process, the priorities of the Danish Presidency in 2002 were areas linked to the Union's internal security approach – such as 'an area for freedom, security and justice', 'sustainable development', 'food safety' and 'global responsibility' (Udenrigsministeriet 2003).

After the terrorist events of 11 September, however, the Danish authorities recognized the need for rethinking internal security. The prime minister at that time, Poul Nyrup Rasmussen, argued that:

We . . . now face a situation that demands a number of important decisions. In order to enable the Government and the Danish Parliament, Folketinget, to choose and prioritize in the years ahead, we must make a thorough analysis of Denmark's situation after 11 September, as concerns foreign policy and security policy. It is time to reflect, and it is time to co-operate.

(Rasmussen 2001)

This resulted in an agreement between the major political parties in the Folketing concerning civilian preparedness capacity after 2002. The agreement, signed on 21 June 2002, instructed a Commission (composed of representatives from several ministries and relevant institutions) to prepare a report on the issue. The report was presented in January 2004 and gives an evaluation of the appropriateness of the current civilian preparedness capacity and proposes possible changes to reduce the vulnerability of Danish society. It also proposes ways of increasing cooperation between the military and civilian instruments (Udvalget for National Sårbarhedsudredning 2004). While the Commission's secretariat was the Department for Civilian Preparedness and the Ministry for Internal Affairs, the need for increased coordination in the area of civilian preparedness is also emphasized in the 2004 defence agreement and other recent documents from the Ministry of Defence (Forsvarsministeriet 2004: 17).

While the attention still is limited and cannot be said to have become a dominant part of the overall Danish discourse on security, it indicates the beginning of a more important change. It is interesting to note that there has been an increased interest in the concept of 'homeland security'. In a recent speech on this issue, the Danish defence minister, Søren Gade, argued that:

> As minister with responsibility for not just the military defence but also the rescue preparedness – and to top it off a coordinating role with regard to general preparedness in the civil sector in Denmark, I can assure you that Homeland Security and society's general resilience are items high on my agenda. . . . One of the other central recommendations in the vulnerability assessment from January 2004 is that the cross-sector coordination needs to be better. This we've tried to accomplish by creating various forums. Firstly, we've set up a national coordinating forum, where all the central authorities will meet and coordinate the operative response to a given crisis or catastrophe. Secondly, we've created a number of sector forums, where associated authorities and actors meet to be informed and inform each other on matters regarding preparedness and resilience. Thirdly, I will mention that we've gathered both the civil emergency management and the military defence under one ministry – the ministry of Defence. This is meant to create more coordination and synergy. The transfer happened about a year ago, and the preliminary results are good. With regard to both operative and strategic cooperation we've seen a positive development.
>
> (Gade 2005)

He also emphasizes the importance of the current development in the EU in this area:

> With regard to homeland security issues, I want to mention that the EU Commission is for example working on creating a programme

for the protection of cross border critical infrastructure. Cross border critical infrastructure is for instance transportation routes, electricity supply and the like. We have not yet seen the actual proposal, but it serves as an example of how international cooperation may be instrumental in elevating national safety.

(Ibid.)

This means that there is a move towards an increased emphasis on comprehensive internal security also in the Danish discourse and that these changes, to some extent, are related to the processes at the EU level.

External security

Even though Denmark was one of the first countries to adapt its security discourse to the post-Cold War context, and thus moved beyond a discourse dominated by national territorial defence, it has not been among the first to make civilian aspects an important part of the dominant discourse on external security. The Defence Commission's report from 1998, for instance, focuses on the military aspects of international crisis management and pays scant attention to the need for improved co-ordination between civilian and military security policy tools (Forsvarskommissionen 1998). The new defence agreement from 1999 and the annual declarations from the Ministry of Defence also put relatively little emphasis on these aspects.

The Ministry of Foreign Affairs, however, has put more stress on comprehensive external security – for instance, through active support of both EU and NATO enlargement processes combined with an extensive engagement in the Baltic region. Denmark has also, like the other Nordic countries, contributed to conflict prevention and civilian crisis management within the framework of the UN and OSCE for a long time. While these initiatives are important, they have been implemented independently of military crisis management. While the Ministry of Foreign Affairs has shown little interest in hard security, the Ministry of Defence has been focusing precisely on that.

As Peter Viggo Jakobsen argues, the Ministry of Foreign Affairs has now begun to stress the importance also of CIMIC (Jakobsen, forthcoming). But as long as the Ministry of Defence is only moderately interested in this dimension, a real comprehensive external security cannot be viewed as an integral part of the dominant Danish security discourse. This reluctance on the part of the Ministry of Defence may be due to the Danish position in the EU. The opt-outs have limited Denmark's traditional international activism to NATO alone, and thus led to an Americanized and militarized security discourse.

At the same time, the opt-out from the Union's defence policy has been compensated by an increasingly active Danish foreign policy line in relation to conflict prevention and civilian crisis management also within the EU.

144

While the Danish government has been reluctant towards the future tasks the EU might take on in relation to conflict resolution that potentially involves military tasks, the government has been far more supportive of the Union's soft security initiatives. For instance, Denmark has been the most prominent promoter of a broad enlargement and has strongly supporte the Europe Agreements and the pre-accession strategy. Since the middle of the 1990s Denmark has also been amongst the states voting most in line with the EU position at the UN general Assembly (Larsen 2000a: 50–2). More specifically, in relation to the ESDP process, the Danish governments have been increasingly active in emphasizing the need for a civilian crisis management capacity. Together with the Netherlands, Denmark, as early as in 1999, presented a proposal regarding the development of a permanent EU mechanism that should make EU police forces able to intervene at an early stage when needed (Politiken 1999).

As the Permanent Secretary in the Ministry of Foreign Affairs, Friis Arne Petersen characterizes the EU as a comprehensive security actor in an article that describes Danish foreign policy in 1999:

> The European Union is well prepared for dealing with tomorrow's complex problems. Because of its broad range of instruments – diplomatic, political, economic, social and cultural – soon to be supplemented by military means, it is in a position to assume greater responsibility for stable and secure development in Europe. Thus, the European Union has the potential to become a global political actor – also in crisis management.
>
> (Petersen 2000: 29)

The Minister of Foreign Affairs at the time, Mogens Lykketoft, indicated his support for the Union's comprehensive security approach in a speech held at the General Affairs Council on 22 January 2001. He refers to the Solana/Patten report on how to improve EU's coherence and effectiveness in the field of conflict prevention, which was presented at the Nice summit in December, and expresses his full support for the conclusions in this report (Lykketoft 2001e). Within the framework of the Political and Security Committee (PSC), Denmark has also promoted its views on all broad issues linked to conflict prevention and civilian crisis management (Larsen 2002a: 138); and in order to show its commitment it also doubled the level of its announced contribution to the civilian commitment conference in May 2001 (Politiken 2001).

In the report on the Danish defence exemption presented in October 2001 the Danish government emphasized that Denmark will opt out of joint actions which involve military units or have derived effects on military units, but that it allows participation in the civilian parts of certain operations, as long as they can be separated from the military part. The report makes it clear that the government will attempt to distinguish on a case-by-case basis between military and civilian elements (Udenrigsministeriet 2001b). The Danish interest in the civilian parts of the ESDP have been noticed in the EU, and on 11 March 2002 the General Affairs Council decided to appoint the Danish police officer, Sven Fredriksen, to head EU's first civilian crisis management operation in Bosnia.[13]

While this activism can be viewed as a continuation of the softer sides of Denmark's security approach, traditionally pursued through UN and/or CSCE/OSCE, it may also be interpreted as an attempt to avoid marginalization in ESDP due to the defence exemption. It is interesting to note that Danish officials explicitly support a closer co-ordination of military and non-military elements in EU crisis management. In fact, such an approach, if implemented, will actually undermine the opportunity for Denmark to take part in the civilian operations (Nielsen 2001: 321).

But while Danish officials explicitly support a comprehensive security approach in the EU, it is only recently that such a comprehensive security approach has been incorporated into the dominant discourse on security and defence (Frantzen 2003: 211). While the defence agreement from 1999 continued to focus on the internationalization of the defence forces, rather than on the need for developing a more comprehensive external approach, the former Defence Minister, Hans Hækkerup, expressed in November 2000 the importance of such a development, emphasizing the EU as an example:

> It is completely artificial to try to distinguish between civilian and military crisis management. The strength of what is happening in the EU now is exactly that one combines the military with the civilian. It is very difficult to pursue civilian crisis management without having military capacities at the same time. One must have the whole toolbox at one's disposal.
>
> (Politiken 2000c, my translation)

In addition, there seem to be some changes towards a more comprehensive external security policy in the new defence agreement that was adopted by the main political parties in the Folketing in June 2004. The agreement covers the period from 2005 to 2009 and focuses explicitly on the need to strengthen coordination between civilian and military capabilities in international operations. In a recent speech the Danish Defence Minister even emphasizes the importance of the EU in that regard, recognizing that the self-imposed exception may create problems for Danish participation in the civilian parts of EU operations (Gade 2004). The government also plans to set up a unit responsible for civil–military coordination in the Ministry of Foreign Affairs (Forsvarsministeriet 2004).

Europeanization and socialization

Main findings

Compared to the other Nordic states, the Europeanization of Denmark's security discourse is somewhat more difficult to grasp. As argued above, the Danish security identity after the end of the Cold War can be characterized as *Atlantic-oriented universalism*. Although this is a change from traditional Danish resistance to NATO during the Cold War, it seems to be more of a general adaptation to the contextual changes and less a function of the European integration process. Denmark was one of the first countries to move beyond territorial defence, with internationalization not only of the national security discourse, but also of the organization of the defence forces. As early as in 1993, the main task of the defence forces was defined as 'international crisis management'. This change may be understood as a consequence of both the Danish security context having changed more fundamentally than was the case in the other Nordic states, and of Denmark's intention to play an important role in the new NATO. The EU, however, was not totally neglected in the Danish discourse in the early 1990s. While priority went to the new NATO, the Danish political leadership also supported the process towards the establishment of a political union, as a complementary security actor on the soft security side. However, the country's rejection of the Union Treaty and the subsequent national compromise put Denmark on the sidelines in important areas of the integration process.

While the content of the Maastricht Treaty in itself did not seem to have had any direct influence on changes in the Danish security approach, the opt-out from this dimension in the EU actually made it increasingly important for Denmark to be a 'good pupil' in NATO, the sole remaining arena for Danish participation in European security. Thus, while the rejection of the Treaty seems to have contributed indirectly to the internationalization of the Danish defence forces, it also led to an increased militarization and Americanization of the Danish approach. References to the EU as a security actor were in fact toned down after 1992.

A more direct European influence can be identified after 1995, especially in relation to the gradual concretization of the Union's security and defence dimension. Once it had become clear that the security dimension would focus on international crisis management, and not on collective defence, Denmark found its opt-outs increasingly difficult to maintain. They actually excluded Denmark from participating in the very kinds of security tasks that it had adapted itself to within the framework of NATO over the preceding five years. In an attempt to avoid further marginalization, Denmark argued strongly that the European dimension should be developed in close relationship with NATO. When the ESDP instead established its own institutions in 1999, Denmark's political leadership realized that it was time to begin to discuss and re-evaluate the value of the exemption. However, the 'no' vote in the referendum on the euro (in September 2000) showed that this was not yet the time for a second referendum. So while the political leadership supported the development in principle, in practice Denmark was unable to change its policy due to the opt-outs.

While the Danish security approach in the 1990s was both Americanized and militarized, a tendency which was further reinforced after the Kosovo war, 11 September and the Iraq war, the recent development towards a European comprehensive security approach has also had some impact on parts of the Danish discourse. In relation to the external dimension, the Ministry of Foreign Affairs in particular has shown a certain activism with regard to the enlargement process, conflict prevention, civilian crisis management, and increased focus on civilian military relations. While the Ministry of Defence has been slower in adopting such a discourse, comprehensive security and the importance of the EU in this regard are now increasingly referred to. This is especially interesting since the implementation of a such a comprehensive external security approach, as for instance in Bosnia, will make it increasingly difficult for Denmark to participate even in civilian operations.

While less attention has been given to the internal dimension of comprehensive security, this is also starting to change, with the Ministry of Foreign Affairs starting to show some interest in these questions. In a White Book on Denmark and Europe, presented in June 2001, it emphasized the importance of the EU in relation to internal security. But while the Union's competence in this area is recognized, Denmark's participation is limited due to yet another opt-out. After 11 September 2001, however, it is possible to identify a slight move in the dominant national security discourse towards greater emphasis on internal security. For instance, a decision was then taken to create a commission tasked with evaluating the vulnerability of Danish society. In addition, there is an increased interest in the concept of 'homeland security' and the role of the EU in that regard.

In general, the relationship between the European integration process and the changes in the national security approach has been less than straightforward in Denmark. The rejection of the Maastricht Treaty, followed by opt-outs, could be interpreted as demonstrating that no Europeanization existed. However, closer study of the Danish discourse reveals that the political elites have become somewhat Europeanized, but that the clearly defined opt-outs and the continued gap between the Danish people and the elites have placed important limitations on possibilities for incorporating these ideas into the dominant discourse on security.

Instrumental adaptation or identity change?

As we have seen, a traditional security discourse dominated by territorial defence characterized the Swedish security discourse until the late 1990s and is still a central part of the Finnish one. In Denmark, however, the primacy of territorial defence was abandoned in the early 1990s, followed by a broad process towards internationalization of the national defence forces. Cold War scepticism towards NATO was also replaced by strong support for the 'new' alliance. In addition, the political leadership at that time expressed its support for the establishment of a European political union, now referred to as the 'anchor for European security'.

While these early changes in Denmark's security discourse seemed radical, they can also be seen as a continuation of the active foreign policy tradition from the Cold War period. In fact, the new NATO was more in line with the security priorities that Denmark had widely emphasized during the Cold War. It is therefore possible to argue that these changes only reaffirmed the status quo, and thus do not indicate a move beyond the first phase in the socialization model. The most important change, however, was that instead of being an important part of a general Danish foreign policy and linked to the UN and CSCE, this internationalism was now also seen in relation to the Atlantic dimension. In other words, instead of representing a development towards an increase in comprehensive security thinking, it rather led to greater focus on *military* international crisis management and less emphasis on other security policy tools. As mentioned, this has led some to argue that the Danish security approach has been both 'militarized and Americanized', a tendency that seemed further reinforced after the rejection of the Maastricht Treaty.

During the Cold War, Denmark's relationship to the EU was basically of an economic nature. While there was some acceptance of the political dimensions of the integration process in the early 1990s, after the rejection of the Maastricht Treaty the Danish security discourse focused primarily on NATO. This does not mean that the European elements of the security discourse disappeared, but they became less visible and more linked to the EU as a soft security actor. Instead of being characterized by the introduction of a clearly and easily identifiable new discourse, this phase is marked by gradual acceptance of the idea of *two* centres for European security: the EU for issues related to soft security, and NATO for issues related to hard security. While the Ministry of Foreign Affairs was preoccupied with the former, the Ministry of Defence has been more concerned by the latter. This also contributed to a prevailing separation of the two discourses. Influenced by the EU, however, the Ministry of Foreign Affairs began focusing more on comprehensive security, and this indicates a move into the second phase of the socialization process.

A process of instrumental adaptation, which is characteristic for the next phase, can be identified from 1995 onwards, especially after the St Malo summit in 1998 (phase 3). At first, the Danish political leadership seemed rather resistant towards the development of a European security dimension, but when the ideas launched at the French–British summit were made concrete in the late 1990s, the Danish government changed its views and began actively to search for ways to participate and to avoid becoming marginalized. First, attempts were made to remove the defence exemption, so that Denmark might participate fully in this dimension. Second, Danish political leaders supported a process taking place within the framework of an European Security and Defence Identity (ESDI) and anchored in NATO. Third, Denmark started to actively support and participate in the civilian part of ESDP to compensate for non-participation in the military part. All these efforts must be understood as adaptation for instrumental reasons.

It has become increasingly evident that what many Danes feared with regard to the future of political union in 1992 has not been realized. The EU has, for instance, not developed into a fully fledged federation, nor into a traditional military superpower. This is now increasingly emphasized by the political elites, and support for the ESDP and the problems related to the defence exemption are now expressed more openly. The ESDP is also mentioned in more positive terms. The Union's role as a comprehensive external security actor is increasingly accepted by parts of the political elites, even though such a development, as long as the opt-out is upheld, will actually make Danish participation more difficult. However, this approach must also be understood as a way of compensating for the opt-out and making the Danish population understand the real meaning of the EU's security dimension.

But while we may note a heightened interest in the European Union as a security actor and in comprehensive security in general on the part of the Ministry of Foreign Affairs and recently also by the Ministry of Defence, it cannot yet be said to have become the dominant part of the Danish security discourse or policy. There are, as we have seen, changes that indicate instrumental adaptation to some of the processes in the EU, but few indications of a real identity change.

7

NORWAY

Adaptive non-member

The previous case studies have been analyses of three EU members. Norway is not yet a member of the EU, but it enjoys close relations with the Union through a wide range of special agreements, informal contacts and *ad hoc* constellations. Thus, it seems reasonable to assume that the European integration process influences the Norwegian security approach, and that this takes place through a Europeanization process similar to the one that affects member states.

As noted, the Norwegian political and administrative system has made substantial changes in order to cope with the challenges and opportunities raised by European integration. Thus, formal EU membership is not necessary condition for Europeanization.[1] This chapter will inquire whether the development of a distinct EU security approach also has influenced Norway's security approach and identity.

Also this chapter begins by presenting the development of the Norwegian security identity at the end of the Cold War. Then it goes on to investigate the impact that three dimensions characteristic of the EU as a security actor – the establishment of the European Union, the development towards an ESDP and the comprehensive European security approach – have had on this identity. The chapter ends with a discussion of the degree and character of Europeanization in the case of Norway.

Towards an Atlantic identity

Norway's security identity may be characterized as an Atlantic identity. We can identify three periods in the development of this Atlantic identity: first, the period from independence in 1905 until NATO membership in 1949; second, the Cold War period and Norway's special position in the Alliance; third, the end of the Cold War and a continued emphasis on Atlanticism and territorial defence.

From neutrality to NATO membership (1905–1949)

The decision to join NATO represented a dramatic change for a country with little experience in foreign policy. Olav Riste has discerned three formative periods in the development of Norway's foreign policy prior to Norwegian membership in NATO (Riste 2002: 206). The first period (1905–14) clarified the basis of Norway's *neutralism*; the second (1918–40) was characterized by continued neutrality and active engagement in the League of Nations; and the third (1940–9) started with the Nazi occupation and ended with NATO membership.

In 1905 Norway gained its independence after nearly 500 years under Denmark (1380–1814) and Sweden (1814–1905). The first Norwegian Foreign Minister, Jørgen Løvland (1905–8), emphasized two aims of Norway's new and independent foreign and security policy: to defend Norwegian economic interests, and to keep the country out of war between the European powers. An active trade policy was assumed to protect Norway's economic interests while non-alignment in peace and neutrality in war was the main strategy for protecting the nation against international conflicts. Foreign and security policy was not a major concern for Norway at that time. There was general agreement that conflicts and wars were the result of a hidden great-power game, and that small states were better off isolating themselves from this game. Løvland's negative conception of other European states is evident in the following well-known statement:

> the aim is to keep us outside participation in those combinations of alliances and alliances that might drag us into wars together with some of the European warrior states.
> (Quoted in Neumann and Ulriksen 1997: 110, my translation)

The second formative period was the inter-war period. Norwegian neutralism prevailed but now in combination with efforts to defend international norms and respect for international law. This was especially evident in the country's active engagement in the League of Nations. The main ingredient in this policy was to promote a moralistic advocacy of international law as the civilized way of settling international disputes. This policy was also seen as the only way to guarantee the interests of a small state such as Norway.

The third period was characterized by the Nazi German occupation during the Second World War, followed by a new concern with the USSR's expansionist policies. These experiences gradually eliminated neutrality as a viable security policy orientation for Norway. When attempts to create a Nordic defence co-operation failed in 1948/9, membership in the new Atlantic Alliance gradually emerged as the best policy option.

An alliance within the alliance (1949–1989)

Throughout the Cold War period, Norway's main concern was to avoid pro-voking the Soviet Union. A set of self-imposed restraints including a 'no foreign bases' policy,[2] a 'no nuclear weapons' policy,[3] and a 'no-go area' for NATO forces in peacetime, east of 24° longitude (250 km from Soviet borders), were introduced in the 1950s. Initially Norway was therefore (like Denmark) perceived as a NATO member state with reservations. While Norway's struggle to raise allied concerns about the northern area remained generally fruitless throughout the 1950s,[4] Riste argues that Norway neverthe-less remained an important ally of the USA through its co-operation in the field of intelligence (Riste 2002: 217–25). This combined policy of integra-tion and shielding characterized Norway's NATO policy throughout the Cold War period.

While the Atlantic orientation was well established in the dominant national security discourse as early as the 1960s, a national debate concern-ing the character and the content of this co-operation continued. This debate resulted in the break-out of a faction of the Labour Party and the establish-ment a socialist anti-NATO party in 1961 (Sosialistisk Folkeparti). In the early 1970s, the NATO question was overshadowed by the first national dispute concerning EC membership, but after the Norwegian 'no' vote in 1972, new disagreement emerged concerning the national security approach (Tamnes 1997: 93).

Despite this disagreement, Norway's security approach was dominated by its special relationship to the USA. The approach was largely defined by the *new Atlanticists*, who were inspired by the new trend in American security studies, with civilian analysts functioning as important players in interpret-ing the power game in the nuclear age. Fear of a nuclear disaster led them to seek new methods to limit or control the use of this power, and concepts such as *deterrence* and *arms control* gained widespread currency. This new strategic thinking began to interest Norwegian security analysts and politi-cians. Johan Jørgen Holst was the most important representative of this approach, both as an analyst and as a politician.

The influence of this new Atlanticism made the Norwegian Ministry of Defence a more important actor in defining the country's security policy, not only its defence policy. In addition, in Norway security policy had tradition-ally been the main responsibility of the Ministry of Foreign Affairs. But when this ministry began to devote more resources to other fields, such as development, this gave the Ministry of Defence room for involvement in security policy as well. In addition, the defence forces were now given expanded responsibilities, through Norway's participation in UN operations and various political issues in the North (ibid.: 65).

Throughout this period, NATO – and the USA in particular – also showed increased interest in Norway and in the Northern areas. The reason for this was that Norway's geopolitical position was of particular interest to the USA during this period, when the Soviet Union was building up its military capabilities on the Kola Peninsula. By the 1970s, Norway was attracting attention and diplomatic interest quite out of proportion to its size (military, economic or in terms of population). According to Rolf Tamnes, Norway was the NATO country that received most support from the USA in proportion to its population. He therefore describes Norway's relationship with the USA as so close as to represent 'an alliance within the alliance' (ibid.: 61).

The influence of both the new Atlanticism and this greater US interest in Norway have helped to strengthen the Atlantic dimension in the Norwegian security discourse. Thus, although Norway's decision to join NATO had been somewhat reluctant in the immediate post-war period, more than forty years within NATO seem to have transformed the Norwegian security identity into a true 'Atlanticism'. It is interesting to note that popular support for NATO was, in fact, at its peak when the threat from the East diminished: at the end of the Cold War, NATO was seen as a guarantee in a new and uncertain period (ibid.: 63).

Atlanticism and territorial defence (1990–1991)

Norway's special position within NATO was seriously challenged with the end of the Cold War. This explains why Norway has been ambivalent with respect to this historically important transition. On the one hand, the end of the Cold War was something Norway had long worked for through the UN and the CSCE. On the other hand, Norwegian politicians feared that this change would lead to lessened international interest in the Nordic region.[5]

While the breakdown of the Soviet Union, which reduced military concerns and automatically increased the influence of the European integration process, was seen as a positive development by most other European states, in Norway the political leadership was sceptical. It feared that a more independent EU security policy would lessen US interest in Europe, leaving Norway more vulnerable to possible pressure from Russia. The concept of territorial defence against a potential invasion from the East therefore continued to be highly emphasized.

While the 1990 report of the Norwegian Defence Commission underlined the idea that NATO remained the cornerstone of Norwegian security (NOU 1992: 94), it also stressed the importance of developments in Europe, even noting that Norwegian membership in both the EU and the WEU would augment Norway's security (ibid.: 100). However, not all members of the Commission agreed with this statement, so some special remarks were added. For instance, it was argued that:

> Norway under no circumstances wishes to send signals that might contribute to a reduction of NATO's role or weaken the basis for US

engagement in the Alliance. To support membership in the EU on this basis is therefore unacceptable.

(Ibid.: 100, my translation)

On the basis of the Commission's report and recommendations from the Chief of Defence, in January 1993 the government presented a White Book on long-term plans for Norwegian defence. In this document Russia was still seen as the main threat to Norwegian security, and territorial defence strengthened by NATO's security guarantees was perceived as crucial to Norwegian security (Forsvarsdepartement 1992–3: 26–41). The establishment of a political union with a common foreign and security policy was not ignored, but it was viewed as important only in the area of soft security (ibid.: 40), which was considered as less important at the time. Although the political leadership expressed interest in bringing Norway closer to the EU, NATO was still perceived as the most important security actor. Norway's need for a close relationship to the EU must rather be characterized as seeking assurance in case the status quo should change (Sjursen 1999: 51).

The traditional security approach is also evident in Norway's reactions towards the changes in NATO. In negotiations on the reduction of conventional forces in Europe, Norway was perceived as a country that had not managed to move beyond the Cold War. That Norway continued to argue for maintaining its flank defence, and that it was one of the last countries to adapt to NATO's new strategic concept of 1991 (ibid.: 54), indicates that the Norwegian political leadership had difficulties in moving beyond the Cold War, and that this change in the security context did not lead to major changes in the national defence approach.

Still, some changes may be identified in the early 1990s. On the basis of the recommendations from the Defence Commission, various cuts were made in the defence budgets. However, this was not followed up by qualitative changes in the dominant national security discourse or in security policy. These changes were merely adaptations to reduced budgets or to a situation without US weapons assistance (Ulriksen 2002: 230). While reference was made to the changed security context, the specific proposals that were made represented a continuation of the fifteen-year plan for the defence forces from 1978 – a plan that came to term in 1993 (Archer and Sogner 1998: 119–20).

Combining 'Atlanticism' with 'Europeanism'

The changes in the first part of the 1990s were first characterized by instrumental adaptation to the end of the Cold War and to the establishment of a political union in the EU. While the former led to some minor qualitative adaptations of the defence forces, the latter led to a greater emphasis on soft security and the establishment of closer relations with the EU.

Adapting to the end of the Cold War

In the period from 1992 to 1994, however, some decisions were taken that also aimed at improving the the country's capacity to participate in international operations. It was claimed that fulfilling international expectations and obligations was a main objective of Norwegian defence. In 1993, for instance, a decision was taken to increase the total number of personnel for such operations from 1,300 (unchanged since 1963) to 2,000 (Ulriksen 2002: 236). In this respect Norway was in line with the same trends as the rest of Western Europe. But while Norway had long experience with participation in international operations within the framework of the UN – for instance in UNIFIL in Lebanon since 1978 – forces were recruited on an *ad hoc* basis; groups of volunteers from different defence branches were briefly trained, and then disbanded on their return. This indicates that the Chief of Defence saw this only as a secondary task for the national defence forces.

Participation in international operations increased throughout the 1990s (in Lebanon, Macedonia, Somalia, the Gulf War, Bosnia and Kosovo), but the Chief of Defence, supported by some politicians, continued for some time to express his concern that this trend could weaken Norway's defence capabilities (ibid.: 237). While the Norwegian Parliament (the Storting) decided to establish the 'Telemark Battalion' in 1992, a battalion earmarked for international operations, there were still disagreements in relation to its main purpose. Whereas Johan Jørgen Holst, Minister of Defence at the time, saw this force as a contribution both to NATO's collective defence function and to international peacekeeping operations undertaken by the OSCE, the UN or NATO, Arne Solli, the Chief of Defence, argued as late as in 1995 that 'I cannot see that the Telemark Battalion, which now is established at Heistadmoen, will have any role in the PfP [Partnership for Peace] co-operation' (quoted in Ulriksen 2002: 238, my translation). If it was not intended for PfP, this should indicate that it was not intended to have a role in the UN or the OSCE either. The creation of the Telemark Battalion must be understood as a political signal to the other allies, making them continue to pay interest to the Northern area. Norway's intention of participating in international operations therefore did not indicate any qualitative change in the Norwegian security discourse.

Thus, the changes made in the early 1990s had few implications for the country's actual security policy. Throughout the 1990s, Norway remained one of the most conservative members of NATO. While countries like Denmark and the Netherlands complied with the changes undertaken in NATO, Norway continued to defend the maintenance of NATO's old functions (Ulriksen 2002: 238). This may be explained by a combination of a 'never again 9 April syndrome'[6] and successful societal resistance at the local and regional level (Jakobsen, forthcoming: ch. 5).

As to Norway's interest in and policy towards the European integration process, it had been rather limited since the 'no' vote in 1972. While a slight change may be identified after 1986 in reaction to the Single European Act and the project of creating an internal European market, it was not until the Maastricht Treaty and the establishment of a political union that Norwegian politicians began to emphasize the security aspects of the European integration process. Even though the Atlantic security identity prevailed after 1992, the Maastricht Treaty introduced a European dimension into the discourse. As we shall see in the next section, this dimension grew stronger after Norway began to move closer to the EU despite (or to compensate for) its second 'no' vote.

The European dimension

Although Norway considered NATO as the main framework for its European security, the Maastricht Treaty and the establishment of a political union, were, as mentioned, also seen as a development that enhanced security on the continent. While the Ministry of Defence paid little attention to this development, in the early 1990s the Ministry of Foreign Affairs – with its tradition of internationalism and humanitarian work and long-term conflict prevention through the UN and OSCE – became increasingly engaged in various non-military security initiatives which were to introduce the EU as an important soft security actor (Archer and Sogner 1998: 126). The first initiative came in March 1992, when the Danish and German foreign ministers invited their colleagues in Estonia, Finland, Latvia, Lithuania, Norway, Poland, Russia, Sweden, and a representative of the European Commission, to meet in Copenhagen. The aim was to strengthen co-operation among the Baltic Sea states and to decide on the establishment of a Council of the Baltic Sea States (CBSS). The foreign ministers found that the recent dramatic changes in Europe heralded a new era of European relations, in which the confrontation and division of the past were to be replaced by partnership and co-operation. An enhanced and strengthened Baltic Sea co-operation was seen as a natural and logical consequence. It was agreed that the Council of the Baltic Sea States should serve as an overall regional forum focusing on intensified co-operation and co-ordination among the Baltic Sea States. The aim of such co-operation should be to achieve a genuinely democratic development in the Baltic Sea region, as well as greater unity between the member countries, and also to ensure favourable economic development.

While participation in this framework was seen as important for Norway, developing a similar framework for co-operation in the Barents region was even more important. The Norwegian Foreign Minister, Thorvald Stoltenberg, therefore presented the Barents Region Initiative, calling for co-operation between north-western Russia and the Nordic states north of the Arctic Circle. The initiative presupposed a lasting community of interest between East and West and emphasized civilian issues more than military problems.[7] The Kirkenes Declaration, which established the Barents Council in January 1993, followed the same logic as the Council of the Baltic Sea States, with representatives from all the Nordic countries, Russia and the European Commission.[8]

While Norway's national security approach continued to be dominated by NATO and territorial defence, the country's power elite had now found a compromise in the Barents co-operation initiative that leaned to the 'European' side. NATO was still perceived as the most important security actor, but Norwegian policymakers began to recognize the potential of the EU in the field of soft security. Johan Jørgen Holst, foreign minister at the time, described the Barents Region as a Euro-Arctic Nordic-Russian 'meeting place' which required attention from the EU, aimed at 'normalizing and stabilizing' the relationships between East and West. He saw this initiative as a contribution to 'a new European security structure' (Tunander 1996: 55; Archer and Sogner 1998: 126). Prime Minister Gro Harlem Brundtland stressed the importance of the European dimension in this co-operation initiative by arguing that 'we need a stronger European basis when developing the cooperation eastwards' (quoted in Tamnes 1997: 240). A further indication of such a compromise was the explicit support for Norwegian EU membership given by such avowed 'Atlanticists' as General Fredrik Bull Hansen and Professor Olav Riste, who emphasized the important security role of the Union (Tunander 1996: 55). Reference was also made to the European dimension in the 1993/4 defence budget proposal from the Ministry of Defence. This discursive account, given by the Minister of Defence at the time, Jørgen Kosmo, contained three elements that represented Norway's considered response to the changes in the international context: a confirmation of Norway's Atlantic identity; that security had to be widely defined; and that the EU was seen as the core institution of Europe, membership of which would prevent Norway from being marginalized (Archer and Sogner 1998: 130). This Europeanization must be understood as a reaction to the recently signed Maastricht Treaty, which transformed the European Community to a European Union with a Common Foreign and Security Policy CFSP. However, despite increased recognition of the importance of the EU's role in European security, there remained a mis-match between how the security context was described and what were seen as the most appropriate security policy tools. The latter continued to be based on a traditional understanding of security, characterized by territorial defence against a potential military invasion.

The new European dimension in Norwegian foreign policy, however, marked the beginning of a process which was to result in a closer relationship between Norway and the EU. Important elements in this process were the signing of the European Economic Agreement (EEA),[9] Norway's application for EU membership,[10] associated membership in the WEU and explicit support for the integration aims set out in the Maastricht Treaty (Godal 1993).

This did not mean any radical change in Norway's security identity, but the EU was now perceived as a complement to NATO in European security:

> Security and stability are not only a military challenge. Political and economic means are increasingly important. It is the EU that possesses the broadest range of such means. . . . NATO membership and the co-operation between North America and Europe are still essential for the security of Norway.
>   (Utenriksdepartementet 1993–4: 14, my translation)

These changes may also be seen in relation to the changes that were taking place within NATO at that time. At its 1994 summit in Brussels, NATO made decisions concerning its organizational structure, so as to adapt to the new security context. Thus, NATO established the Combined Joint Task Forces (CJTF) and the Partnership for Peace (PfP), but it also recognized EU's security policy ambitions as set out in the Maastricht Treaty and it started to develop a European Security and Defence Identity (ESDI) within NATO.

While official Norwegian policy still gave priority to the 'old' NATO and collective defence, some voices – especially within parts of the research establishment and among the political elites – started to emphasize the need for both a modernization of the national defence forces and a closer relationship to the CFSP (Neumann and Ulriksen 1995, 1996; Kosmo 1995). These voices becoming stronger, with more and more members of the military leadership as well as the younger generation of officers with direct experience from the Balkans arguing for internationalization of the defence forces (Jakobsen, forthcoming: ch. 5).

The interval between the signing of Norway's Treaty of Accession to the EU in June 1994 and the membership referendum held on 28 November 1994 led to a major change of attitude among members of the Norwegian foreign policy elite. This period was crucial, since it made the Norwegian political elite understand how foreign policy co-operation was conducted within the EU. Throughout this short period, Norway participated fully in the various working groups established under the CFSP, and was also connected to the Correspondance européenne (COREU) network, a restricted data forum for exchange of information on foreign and security policy issues. Even though the negative result of the 1994 Norwegian referendum brought an abrupt end to this learning process, it led to an greater understanding of the EU as a political project which played an increasingly important role in the field of security policy (Sjursen 1999: 52). The result of the referendum did not lead to Norwegian membership in the EU, but the compromise achieved between 'Atlanticism' and 'Europeanism' in the Norwegian discourse opened the way for a closer relationship with the EU.

Moving closer to the EU

The period after the Norwegian referendum in 1994 is characterized by several moves aimed at strengthening relations between Norway and the EU. Since the EEA Agreement already regulated Norway's relationship with the EU's first pillar, efforts were undertaken especially in relation to the second and third pillars.

First, a *political dialogue* concerning the EU's CFSP was established. Although co-operation in the sphere of foreign policy in the EU had been initiated in the 1970s with the establishment of European Political Co-operation (EPC) Norway had evinced little interest in this co-operation. At that time Norway conducted its foreign and security policies through NATO, and any other (competing) multilateral fora which did not include the United States were regarded with suspicion (Knutsen 2000). Since 1980, however, Norway had had informal contacts with the EPC, under the terms of a bilateral agreement of 1988. Soon after Norway submitted its application for membership, this contact was broadened (Archer and Sogner 1998: 129). The new dialogue of the 1990s gave Norway a chance to embrace the EU's foreign and security policy statements and common positions, and the number of such joint statements increased throughout the period. This was partly because Norway was invited more often by the EU to do so, but also due to an unofficial Norwegian policy of underwriting EU statements as far as possible. In addition, Norway was invited to participate in several working groups under the CFSP, covering areas such as security, the peace process in the Middle East, Western Balkans, Russia/CIS, the OSCE, disarmament, weapons export and non-proliferation. The Norwegian government also managed to obtain access to meetings twice a year at the political level. However, the importance of these meetings has proven to be rather limited, and the EU countries are seldom represented by members of their governments.

Second, the Norwegian government also worked at establishing a closer link to the EU's third pillar, concerned with justice and home affairs. These efforts started with an agreement between the Schengen countries and Norway and Iceland in 1996. The agreement aimed at regulating the two countries' participation in the Schengen co-operation's common border control, which entered into force in 1995. Such an agreement was necessary in order to maintain the existing Nordic passport union. At that time the Schengen co-operative scheme was not yet integrated into the EU's structure, but when the agreement was to enter into force in June 2000, the situation was different. As we shall see, in view of the changes introduced with the Amsterdam Treaty, and with Schengen becoming an integrated part of the EU, it became necessary to renegotiate the agreement.

As a result of the EEA Agreement, the political dialogue and the Schengen Agreement, by 1996 Norway had managed to establish a close link to several major areas of the integration process. This special relationship has been characterized as a 'Class B' membership in the European Union – extended participation, but without the possibility of influencing decisions taken at the EU level (Claes and Tranøy 1999). Concerning the dominant national security discourse, this closer relationship with the EU led, as we have seen, to a greater focus on the European dimension (see for instance Kosmo 1995).

The Amsterdam Treaty, decided upon in June and signed in October 1997, introduced several changes that had consequences for Norway's relationship to the EU. Concerning the second pillar, the decisions taken in Amsterdam allowed for a future integration of the WEU into the EU 'should the European Council so decide' (Amsterdam Treaty). Such a development represented a challenge to Norway, as this could lead to a loss of the associated member status it had obtained in the WEU. This arrangement had become an important channel for influence, guaranteeing Norwegian participation at all levels – the sole limitation being that Norway did not have the right to vote. The Norwegian government therefore expressed its ambitions of obtaining a similar status in future EU arrangements. However, as we shall see below, it was somewhat later and after the French–British summit in St Malo in December 1998, that the Norwegian political leaders came to realize that this would represent a real challenge for Norway.

The Amsterdam Treaty also introduced some important changes with regard to the third pillar. The EU countries decided to integrate the inter-governmental Schengen co-operative scheme into the EU structure, divided between the first and the third pillars. Since this area now would be handled within EU institutions, the agreement with Norway and Iceland from 1996 had to be renegotiated. A new agreement, signed in May 1999, resulted in the establishment of a Mixed Committee for consultation in questions related to Schengen, and as part of this arrangement Norway in March 2001 joined the Schengen Area – the European passport-free zone – together with the other Nordic states. Norway obtained associated membership within Schengen, which meant that it would participate in the common border control and to some degree in police co-operation,[11] but without any connection to the EU process towards the establishment of an area of freedom, security and justice. Concerning third-pillar issues, Norway's participation is limited to the Schengen Area, the Dublin Convention[12] and the MLA convention,[13] and an agreement with EUROPOL, signed in June 2001.

Thus we see that Norway, in seeking to compensate for its non-membership, has managed to reach a high level of co-operation with the EU. With the EU having become an increasingly important security actor, we may assume that this close relationship will lead to some degree of Europeanization of the Norwegian security approach. In the following two sections I will take a closer look at a possible influence from the ESDP process and the development of a comprehensive European security approach.

Impact of the ESDP

Even though NATO was still viewed as the principal security actor, we may discern a certain Europeanization of Norway's security approach towards the late 1990s. This led to greater interest in the ESDP process, and accelerated the process of internationalizing the national defence forces. The fact that the Norwegian government at that time consisted of a coalition of parties who were all opposed to EU membership makes the influence of the EU process on Norwegian security discourse and policy even more notable (Knutsen 2000: 26).

Recognizing the ESDP

As late as 1998, the Norwegian government was paying only scant attention to the ongoing processes within the EU's security dimension. Emphasis was on the importance of NATO and the OSCE (see for example Bondevik 1998). In relation to the EU there was suspicion relating to the possibilities of an EU–WEU merger. Here the argument was that this could lead to a future collective defence role for the EU, and that this could harm relations with Russia. In fact, the EU had by then moved away from its initial collective defence ambition with the incorporation of the Petersberg tasks into the treaty, but this fact was ignored:

> the development of the EU into a 'defence alliance' could harm the forthcoming EU enlargement since an EU role in the sphere of security and defence could alienate Russia and hence cause strains in the EU–Russian relationship.
> (Forsvarsdepartement 1997–8, my translation)

While the government found it difficult to envisage the EU as an important security actor without a territorial defence dimension, it also feared such a development, as this could mean a potential marginalization of Norway in the European security system. However, the British reluctance towards security co-operation in the EU was taken as a guarantee for the continued dominance of the transatlantic security arrangement. Therefore, the French–British St Malo summit must have come as quite a surprise to the Norwegian government. Indications of change in the Norwegian leadership's discourse when referring to the EU's security dimension can be noticed only a month after St Malo. In January 1999, the Norwegian Minister of Foreign Affairs addressed the Storting, arguing as follows:

> experience gained from the peace process in the Middle East, the implementation and the follow-up of the Dayton Agreement in Bosnia and the efforts to reach cease-fire and a peaceful solution in

Kosovo have strengthened the position of those who feel that the EU should not only make an economic contribution but also play a more prominent role . . . if the EU should become the framework of political decisions on European security and crisis management to a greater extent than at present, the natural result would be for Norway and the EU to deepen their existing cooperation within the framework of the current arrangement for political dialogue.

(Vollebæk 1999)

After the Vienna and the Cologne summits in December 1998 and June 1999, it became clear that the EU wanted to follow up on the French–British declaration. A decision to integrate the WEU gradually into the EU was taken, and work towards establishing a new decision-making structure within the Council was initiated, with the aim of completing it by December 2000.

As a reaction to these decisions the Norwegian government issued a PM (a memo) in October 1999 in connection with the EU's preparation for the European Council meeting to be held in Helsinki in December the same year. The PM expressed Norwegian support for the development of an ESDP, but included a proposal for how the six non-EU allies[14] could be involved in the new decision-making structures. This specific proposal involved obtaining day-to-day consultations in the proposed Political and Security Committee, the Military Committee, and the subsidiary working groups.

Such an arrangement would give the non-EU allies the right to speak and to put forward motions, as well as have access to all relevant documents and information.[15] In short, Norway's initial ambition aimed at persuading the EU members to transfer its special WEU member status to the new EU structure (Missiroli 2001a). However, the EU soon made it clear that this was a highly unrealistic ambition. The EU fully intended to retain its autonomous decision-making capacity.

A comparison of Norway's ambitions with the actual outcome of the Helsinki European Council in December 1999 clearly shows that Norway's diplomatic efforts failed. The European Council instead suggested the establishment of 'appropriate arrangements' for the participation of non-EU allies, making it clear that third-country participation should not affect the decision-making autonomy of the EU. Later (at the European Council in Feira and Nice) this rather vague suggestion was made more concrete, and opened up the possibility of meetings between the EU and all candidate countries together with Iceland and Norway (the '15+15'), as well as special meetings between the EU and the non-EU allies (the '15+6').[16] While the long-term importance of these meetings is difficult to foresee, the ones that already have taken place have been rather disappointing from the Norwegian point of view. Instead of being invited to participate constructively in the debate on how to conduct European security policy, the six have been allocated the rather passive role of being mostly informed of the status of the EU's work in this area.[17]

When Vollebæk emphasized that it was important for Norway to participate in the ESDP in order to avoid losing influence in NATO, this shows that Norway's prime concern was to avoid becoming marginalized within the European security system. Participation in the ESDP was important for maintaining a status similar to the one Norway had achieved as an associated member of the WEU:

> The continuation of full Norwegian participation in European security policy cooperation is also important, especially for our position in NATO. . . . Norway's rights as an ally, and as an associated member of WEU, should be maintained in any future solutions that may change the cooperation between the EU, the WEU and NATO.
>
> (Vollebæk 1999)

In other words, the significant change in Norway's attitude towards the security and defence dimension in the EU must be understood as an attempt to avoid becoming marginalized, rather than as a sign of strong support for EU's ambitions in the area of security.

The change of government in March 2000 led to some changes in the new Norwegian approach. Instead of continuing to ask the EU for special arrangements, the new government now focused on making Norway attractive to the EU, realizing that Norway would have to make a contribution in order to get something in return. The most obvious result was a concrete contribution to the headline goal at the commitment conference in November 2000. While this was an interesting change of approach, it does not represent any major change in the Norwegian security discourse. Avoiding marginalization was still the main objective. Nina Græger has characterized this as the Norwegian 'troops for influence' strategy (Græger 2002: 68).

Adapting the national defence forces

In June 1999, the Norwegian government submitted a White Book to the Storting that (finally) stressed the need to reform Norway's defence forces in order to improve national capabilities for participating in peace support operations led by primarily by NATO, but potentially also by the WEU (Forsvarsdepartementet 1998–9). This report should be seen as the first *qualitative* change proposed to the defence forces after the end of the Cold War. While the previous White Book concerning long-term plans for national defence, presented in February 1998, had stated that that active international involvement, substantive contributions to NATO's mutual defence arrangements and participation in peace operations outside NATO's borders together should form an important part of Norway's security and defence policy (Forsvarsdepartement 1997–8), it had not proposed any specific changes. By contrast, the June 1999 White Book recommended the establishment of an Armed Forces Task Force for international operations, to consist of units from all branches of the armed forces, altogether more than 3,500 personnel. It aimed at fulfilling NATO Article 5 as well as non-Article 5 missions and tasks, but also at being answerable to the WEU (Forsvarsdepartementet 1998–9).

The need for a more radical adaptation of Norway's security approach was soon recognized, and by July 1999 the government had decided to establish a Defence Commission (Forsvarspolitisk Utvalg) to 'review Norwegian defence policy, its scope and objectives' (quoted in Knutsen 2000: 30). The conclusions of the Defence Commission, presented in late June 2000, indicated that the Norwegian armed forces were in a deep crisis:

> The idea of nationally balanced forces exists only in rhetoric. The adjustments made during the 1990s have to a considerable extent failed, despite good intentions and high ambitions. The infrastructure and organization of the forces are too large. . . . A continued turn away from the singular focus on traditional invasion defence towards a broader and more balanced structuring of the forces is needed. The future forces must be flexible, i.e. able to meet the challenges that may arise in the short and medium term, and able to adapt to a fundamentally different situation in the longer term.
>
> (Quoted in Knutsen 2000: 47)

On the basis of these conclusions as well as a report from the Chief of Defence (Forsvarssjefen 2000), the government submitted a report to the Storting in February 2001 (Forsvarsdepartementet 2001), proposing the first radical changes in the country's approach to its defence forces after the end of the Cold War. The most important change was the introduction of a 'niche defence' based on a more focused organization of troops trained for international crisis management. Instead of the Armed Forces Task Force for international operations set up in 1998, there would now be established a more sophisticated system for training and recruitment. International crisis management became the main task of the defence forces. While in the early 1990s there had been a poor link between the description of the new security context and Norway's security policy, the government had now managed to take these changes into account (ibid.).

These changes must be seen, first and foremost, as an adaptation to the changes that had taken place in NATO throughout the 1990s, and particularly the Defence Capability Initiative (DCI). This initative, launched at the Alliance's fiftieth anniversary Washington summit in April 1999, is, in the words of Secretary General Lord Robertson, designed 'to ensure that all Allies not only remain interoperable, but that they also improve and update their capabilities to face the new security challenges'.[18] DCI covers almost all areas of military capability – the mobility of forces; their logistical support; their ability to protect themselves and engage an enemy; and the command and control and information systems they use in order to ensure that, if necessary, they can deploy rapidly and efficiently to the locations where they may be needed to manage crises, if necessary for extended periods.

However, this does not rule out a process of Europeanization. While the changes in NATO initiated the changes, there is reason to believe that the ESDP process has accelerated and intensified these changes. In fact, these changes enabled Norway to contribute to the new European Rapid Reaction Force: at the capability conference in November 2000, Norway decided to make the totality of the newly established task force of 3,500 personnel available for the EU's headline goal.

While official reports show a gradual change in the dominant security discourse of the political leadership, the reactions to these changes reflect a continued traditional understanding of security in public opinion. When the Defence Minister, Bjørn Tore Godal, declared in an interview with Norway's main newspaper, *Aftenposten*, that Russia no longer represented a threat to Norway, he was widely criticized (Aftenposten 2001b). Reactions to the speech held by NATO's Secretary General, Lord Robertson, in Oslo in February 2001 also reveal the disparities between Norwegian public opinion and the dominant line within NATO (Aftenposten 2001a). While the Norwegian establishment may recognize the changed European security context, the EU's security dimension and the need for greater Europeanism and international crisis management, the Norwegian public has tended to view territorial defence and NATO as the main ingredients of the national security identity. The conclusions of the Parliamentary Standing Committee on Defence concerning the governmental proposal showed that the members of the Storting were not yet ready for fundamental changes. The conservative parties, in particular, have insisted on the traditional understanding of 'security' (Forsvarskomiteen 2001). Despite this continued traditionalism, we may note a development towards greater acceptance of the EU as an important security actor, and towards a stronger focus on international crisis management among the political elites, which has made some changes possible in actual security policy as well. This tendency has also been further strengthened in the later reports from the Ministry of Defence (Forsvarsdepartementet 2002, 2004, 2005) as well as the Norwegian government's pronounced interest in participating in one of the EU's battle groups, which is planned within the framework of the renewed Headline Goal for the period 2004–10 and is to be led by Sweden (Devold 2004).

The discussion in this section has indicated a change in the Norwegian security discourse towards a stronger focus on international crisis management and an increased interest in EU's security dimension. The next section will look at the non-military aspects of both external and internal security, in order to find out whether there has also been a change in the national security discourse towards a comprehensive security approach similar to the one identified in the EU.

Impact of the EU's comprehensive security approach

Since the end of the Cold War, there has in Norway been a considerable lack of clarity in how the security context is described. In 1998, Foreign Minister Knut Vollebæk gave a comprehensive definition of the current security context:

> Security policy has become a more complex matter. This means that the Foreign Minister's overall responsibility for security policy is getting more challenging. The distinction between domestic and foreign policy is totally different today . . . and this is affecting how one defines security. For instance, parts of our environmental policy are now defined as a security aspect.
>
> (Vollebæk 1998)

But he still concluded by arguing that NATO and collective defence constitute the main basis of Norway's security:

> Even though Europe has changed, it is the cooperation in NATO that remains the main basis for our and Europe's security . . . The capability and will to collective defence remain the most important elements of the NATO cooperation.
>
> (Ibid.)

This indicates a continued traditionalism, but let us see whether the development of a European comprehensive security approach has had any impact on the Norwegian security discourse.

Internal security

Towards the end of the 1990s the Norwegian political leadership had already recognized the EU's competence in relation to *internal* security. In a speech to the Storting in January 1999, Knut Vollebæk began by recognizing organized crime as a security threat:

> Security and stability also involve taking steps to protect individuals from crime and violence. All over Europe, the crime scene is becoming increasingly dominated by international organized crime. This is something that affects all countries, and the prevention of cross-border crime requires international collaboration.
>
> (Ibid.)

167

He then went on to refer to the importance of the EU's work in this field, emphasizing the government's intention of following this development closely:

> the EU countries have over the last few years expressed their desire to strengthen their cooperation in justice and home affairs. . . . In future [this cooperation] will cover a broad range of areas, including judicial cooperation in criminal and military matters, police cooperation on controls at the EU's external frontiers, and combating racism. The aim is to lay the basis for what the EU refers to as an area of greater freedom, safety and security for all. The purpose is to ensure the free movement of persons while at the same time taking action to strengthen controls at the external frontiers. . . . The government will keep abreast of the development in EU cooperation within the field of Justice and Home Affairs.
>
> (Ibid.)

Towards the end of that year, the first concrete follow-up can be identified, with the presentation of a government bill on Norwegian participation in international police co-operation by the Ministry of Justice. The strengthening of the justice and home affairs dimension in the EU since 1997, in particular the strengthening of EUROPOL, were among the reasons behind this proposal. A negotiated agreement concerning Norway's association to EUROPOL was annexed to it. The agreement, implemented as of 1 August 2002, means that Norway now has one liaison police officer working in this institution.

In parallel with the work on this report there was recognition of the need to examine the overall security discourse on the civilian and the military sides. In September 1999 the government decided to establish an independent commission to evaluate the current Norwegian security environment with a focus on internationalization. This 'Vulnerability Commission' delivered its report on 14 August 2000 (NOU 2000b), at the same time as the Defence Commission (NOU 2000a) and the Chief of Defence (Forsvarsjefen 2000) presented their reports on the transformation of the Norwegian defence forces. The Vulnerability Commission's report identifies a long list of current challenges to national security (terrorism, cyber warfare, pollution, diseases, etc.), and includes a proposal that indicates the need for the establishment of a ministry specifically responsible for co-ordinating the various instruments of national security policy.

Initially, it had been intended that the three reports should together provide a comprehensive basis for the government's work on the forthcoming bill on the transformation of the Norwegian security policy in general and the defence forces in particular. In a speech held by Øystein Singsås (Former Deputy Minister in the Ministry of Defence) (Singsås 2000), on a 'new defence in a new time', four groups of risks were identified:

1 The traditional territorial threat (which in Singsås' view could not be totally excluded);
2 Regional instability in NATO' s near abroad;
3 The proliferation of weapons of mass destruction;
4 Terrorism and international crime.

Even though Singsås emphasized the need for increased and improved co-operation with the police forces, especially in relation to the last group of risks, there was no reference to this in the government bill presented by the Ministry of Defence in April 2001. The reports from the Defence Commission and the Chief of Defence were both mentioned, but the report from the Vulnerability Commission was not referred to (Forsvarsdepartementet 2001). That these aspects were not included must indicate the difficulties of achieving radical changes in the security approach that would lead to integration of non-military security tools into the overall national security approach. While there is general agreement on the need to focus on a broader range of threats, it seems far more difficult to follow this up by adopting radical changes in the security policy approach to meet these new challenges.

However, the bill presented did contain one important proposal which had an impact on the security approach. This was a proposal concerning the establishment of a national body for the co-ordination of national security. On the other hand, this particular proposal did not attract much attention compared to the proposals concerning the transformation of the defence forces.

After 11 September 2001, these security challenges have received increased attention in Norway. The 'Sem declaration', creating the basis for the coalition government established in October 2001, emphasizes that it is the Ministry of Justice that will have the major responsibility for societal security, and it is this ministry that is given the overall co-ordination role in this area. The April 2002 White Book on societal security indicates a strong political will to put greater emphasis on a national comprehensive security approach.

While these questions are still handled by the Ministry of Justice, the Ministry of Defence has also begun to focus more on such matters, especially after 11 September. In the implementation bill for the reorganization of the defence forces, an entire chapter was devoted to the fight against terrorism and the role of the Ministry of Defence (Forsvarsdepartementet 2002: ch. 3). Reference is also made to the work done by the Ministry of Justice, and it is argued that there exists a need for a comprehensive approach to security that can combine different political, lawmaking, police, economic, diplomatic, international, humanitarian and military tools. The role of the military in this area is defined as providing assistance to the civilian authorities nationally, and participating in anti-terrorist operations internationally (ibid.: ch. 3.2).

Considerable emphasis has been placed on the need for better co-ordination between the various institutions responsible for national security. While a civilian–military co-operation group was established on a central level as early as in 1994,[19] this is now to have a permanent secretariat. The White Book referred to the committee as an important instrument for improving inter-ministerial co-ordination, especially in the fight against terrorism and international crime (Justisdepartementet 2002: chs 7 and 9).

Additionally, a new directorate for national security (NSM) was established as of 1 January 2003. This directorate, which was proposed in the report from the Ministry of Defence in 2000, has been placed under the authority of the Ministry of Defence and reports to it in military matters. However, in civilian matters it reports to the Ministry of Justice. This is done in order to assure a comprehensive approach to security[20] (ibid.: 85).

The parliamentary debate on the White Book on societal security revealed great interest in a continued focus on these questions. However, 11 September has been important here as well, and has led to a proposal from the government to increase the budgets for civilian defence and police by 106.5 million NOK in order to improve work on anti-terrorism.

In 1999, Norway signed a new Schengen Agreement and joined the EU's action plan for civilian protection. This may well have led to recognition of many potential 'new' threats and the need to handle these within a European context. These were first identified in the government bill of 1999 (Justis-departementet 1999–2000), and then followed up by the Vulnerability Commission. As we have seen above, the Ministry of Defence has seemed less interested in the challenges from Norwegian participation in the Schengen Area.[21] For instance, there is no reference to recent developments within the EU in this area. When the EU is mentioned in official documents produced by the Ministry of Defence, this is still in relation to the ESDP.

As indicated, the Ministry of Foreign Affairs has shown greater interest in these questions. The government's political platform for Europe, presented in February 2002, emphasizes the need for Norway to strengthen its co-operation with the EU in the areas of justice and home affairs. With reference to developments in the EU, it argues that the government should:

> consider the possibilities for co-operation when questions in the area of justice become a part of EU's foreign policy (relations with third countries) or security policy (ESDP), and seek a comprehensive approach with regards to the relationship between foreign affairs and the policy of justice and home affairs in Norway as well.
>
> (Utenriksdepartementet 2002: 15, my translation)

But while the Ministry of Defence has showed less interest in the EU's competences in this area, it is possible to notice an increased emphasis on societal security. A recent report, presenting a strategic concept for the Norwegian

Defence forces, explicitly emphasizes that there has been a move from 'state security' to 'societal security' (Forsvarsdepartementet 2005: 16). A more comprehensive approach to security and a modernized concept of total defence is also given increased attention (ibid.: 51–2).

External security

As Jakobsen argues, 'the Norwegian case presents a stark contrast of civilian activism and military foot-dragging' (Jakobsen, forthcoming: ch. 5). While Norway was among the first countries to develop a civilian standby capacity for international peace operations in the early 1990s,[22] the first qualitative changes in Norway's defence forces were, as we have noted, not initiated until the late 1990s. In addition, it was not until 2001 that civilian military co-operation (CIMIC) in international crisis management received any attention in an official publication from the Ministry of Defence. The need for better inter-ministrial co-ordination and improved co-operation with NGOs in order to enhance a comprehensive crisis management capacity was emphasized in a report in 2001 (Forsvarsdepartementet 2001: 36).

While Norway has had broad experience with civilian crisis management, this dimension has been organized independently of the military dimension. In other words, this has been a point long ignored by the Ministry of Defence. Since 1989 Norway has participated in more than twenty international police operations through the UN, the WEU and the OSCE,[23] and Norwegian competence in this area has been internationally recognized[24] (Justisdepartementet 1999–2000: ch. 6; Jakobsen, forthcoming: ch. 5). The Norwegian government has also made eighty police officers available for the EU's civilian headline goal, and these now participate in the first EU-led civilian crisis management operation in Bosnia.

But despite this competence and willingness, participation in civilian international peacekeeping operations has traditionally been administrated independently of the military aspects and by the Ministry of Justice and by the police itself. The need for more focus on civilian-military co-operation has been emphasized by these institutions for some time, but until recently the Ministry of Defence has paid little attention to this aspect. The 2002 White Book on societal security, presented by the Ministry of Justice, discussed these matters to some extent (Justisdepartementet 2002: ch. 10). The fact that these aspects received far less attention in both the Ministry of Foreign Affairs and in the Ministry of Defence indicates that the non-military aspects have not become an integral part of the dominant Norwegian security discourse.

As described in Chapter 2, the EU has paid considerable attention to comprehensive conflict prevention and to the need for better co-ordination between civil and military tools for crisis management. While the Norwegian government has emphasized the importance of such an approach, no reference is made to the processes within the EU. As Foreign Minister Torbjørn Jagland argued:

> Complex conflicts are difficult to solve. There has to be an overall approach and extended cooperation between different actors. The contribution may vary between military units, assistance in order to build up national police forces and functioning legal systems to humanitarian aid or more traditional and long-term economic aid.
>
> (Jagland 2001, my translation)

In this speech there is no reference to the EU, even though developing a comprehensive conflict prevention approach was the main focus of the Swedish EU Presidency at that time. In addition, the programme on conflict prevention was not referred to in the Norwegian government's platform European policy, adopted the year after the Gothenburg summit and only a few months before the EU programme was to be evaluated at the European summit in Seville in June 2002. As a result of increased participation in crisis management operations, however, there is reason to believe that gradually there is greater recognition of the need to focus on such aspects (Jensen 2003; Jakobsen, forthcoming: ch. 5). Still there is a tendency for the CIMIC concept, when it is used, to be more closely linked to the NATO definition, which gives priority to military operations (see note 17 of Chapter 1).

In the latest publications from the Ministry of Defence (Forsvarsdepartmentet 2004, 2005), which present an important modernization of the Norwegian defence force, there is still surprisingly little emphasis on comprehensive external security. The need to strengthen the co-ordination between civilian and military personnel in international operations is barely mentioned. There is also little indication that the Norwegian government sees the recent development in the EU, such as the adoption of a European Security Strategy, the new Headline Goal and the Constitutional Treaty, as the institutionalization of a comprehensive European security approach. Instead it is seen as a step towards an independent military capacity and thus as a potential competitor of NATO (Forsvarsdepartementet 2005: 35).

Europeanization and socialization

Main findings

In contrast to Sweden and Finland, Norway did not choose to join the EU in 1995. Still, the country's political and administrative political leadership gradually developed a close relationship to the EU in the years after the referendum. This close relationship has led to a certain Europeanization of Norway's security approach as well. This is not to say that the Norwegian security approach is exclusively driven by the European integration process

(Archer and Sogner 1998: 172), but rather that we can identify a certain degree of Europeanization. As we have seen, the EU has had some impact in relation to the three dimensions of the EU's security approach (the establishment of a political union, the ESDP process and the development of a comprehensive security approach) in focus here. However, some aspects have received more attention than others.

First, the Maastricht Treaty and the establishment of a political union led to some changes in the Norwegian discourse, towards greater recognition of the EU's soft security dimension. This did not replace the Norwegian Atlantic identity, but has been seen to complement it. Some have referred to this change 'as a compromise between Atlanticism and Europeanism', indicating that NATO and territorial defence continued to have priority, but that the EU had a great potential in the field of soft security. The Union's role in the Barents co-operation was emphasized. The establishment of a political union with a CFSP also led to a debate concerning possible membership for Norway. While the general interest in EU questions was toned down after the 'no' vote in 1994, the country's administrative and political elites worked hard to establish a range of co-operation arrangements with the Union in most policy areas.

Second, the St Malo summit and the subsequent development towards an ESDP made it clear that the EU had ambitions beyond soft security. Despite the close relationship to the EU, this development seemed to come as a surprise to Norway's political leaders. Although the process was launched at the Amsterdam summit in June 1997, it was largely ignored by the Norwegian political leadership until a change in the British approach made the Union's ambitions more real and relevant for Norway. Various diplomatic efforts were then initiated by the Norwegian political elites in order to obtain some influence in the structures under development. The fact that the government then in office in Norway was a coalition of no-to-EU parties makes this adaptation even more striking. In addition to this Europeanization, a modernization of the Norwegian national defence forces was also initiated. While the recent changes in NATO were probably the main explanation for these changes, the ESDP may also have been important here. The creation of an Armed Force Task Force for international operations in 1999 made it possible for Norway to contribute to the EU's headline goal, and thus reduce the possibilities of becoming marginalized in the European security system. The subsequent modernization of the national defence forces and the government's wish to participate also in the Union's new Headline Goal (the so-called battle groups) must be understood in the same way.

Third, while the Union's recent focus on comprehensive security may have had little influence on the dominant Norwegian discourse on security, it still seems to have been met with interest by some parts of the political leadership. The Ministry of Foreign Affairs, however, has showed surprisingly little interest in the EU's external comprehensive approach, given Norway's interest in long-term security-building within other multilateral frameworks such as the UN and OSCE. But the need for a comprehensive approach was emphasized in the Vulnerability Reports. In the Ministry of Defence external comprehensiveness was initially evident only in relation to CIMIC in international operations, and has only recently been introduced in the dominant security discourse. In relation to the internal dimension, Norwegian participation in the Schengen arrangement seems to have highlighted the need for improving instruments to handle threats from international crime and terrorism. While this has been emphasized by both the Ministry of Justice and the Ministry of Foreign Affairs for some time, the Ministry of Defence has shown only limited interest in these questions. The need for a comprehensive national approach to security was stressed in the report of the Vulnerability Commission and the subsequent White Book. While these questions have not yet become an important part of the dominant national discourse, there has been greater interest after the events of 11 September 2001 and this led to an increased emphasis on societal security in the more recent reports from the Ministry of Defence.

The analysis in this chapter shows that, while Norway did uphold a rather traditional security approach until the end of the 1990s, there have recently been some changes towards internationalization and comprehensiveness. Some of these changes seem to have been a result of some kind of Europeanization process, while others appear to involve a largely independent but parallel process. Norway's Atlantic identity seems to have been supplemented by a European dimension, and some elements of a comprehensive security approach have been introduced, although they have not yet become a major part of the dominant national discourse of security.

In relation to the internal dimension, we note an increasing number of references to the EU process. However, also here comprehensive security is referred to only by some sections of the political elite, not as a part of the dominant security discourse. While Norway's participation in the Schengen arrangement has led the Ministry of Foreign Affairs and Ministry of Justice to emphasize the need to fight international crime, the Ministry of Defence has made few references to Schengen except to note that it has some consequences for the work and the responsibilities of the Coast Guard. The most important work on the part of political elites in relation to comprehensive security was the White Book on Vulnerability, which was based on the report from the Vulnerability Commission. In it the government argued for a more co-ordinated approach to security, but without this becoming an important part of the dominant discourse; also this view was promoted only by the Ministry of Justice. It was not until after 11 September 2001 that the Ministry of Defence presented a report (in April 2002) with an entire chapter devoted to these questions, and with explicit references to the work done by the Ministry of Justice on these issues. The strategic concept for the national defence forces, presented in January 2005, also shows that a comprehensive internal approach now is seen as an integrated part of the Norwegian security discourse.

While this change in the dominant discourse represents a move towards greater comprehensiveness, it is difficult to identify a direct influence from the processes in the EU. At best, the EU has had an indirect effect on the security discourse in the Ministry of Defence through the Ministry of Justice or the Ministry of Foreign Affairs. In fact, a study of documents and speeches from the Ministry of Defence shows that the EU is seen as a security actor only in relation to the ESDP, especially to the military parts of the ESDP and its relations to NATO. In the Ministry of Foreign Affairs and in the Ministry of Justice, however, security developments within the EU have received increased attention and interest, and here the need for a comprehensive security approach also seems to be viewed as 'the right thing', not merely a necessary adaptation to external processes.

Instrumental adaptation or identity change?

The socialization model presented in Chapter 3 takes as its starting point a situation where the traditional discourse continues to dominate policy-making. As argued above, a traditional security discourse with emphasis on an Atlantic-oriented territorial defence was characteristic of Norway until the late 1990s. This discourse involved a continued emphasis on territorial and collective defence against a potential military invasion from the East. The main security policy instrument was NATO membership. There was general scepticism towards any security ambition presented by the EU that might undermine transatlantic relations, and thus lead to reduced interest in the Northern area among Norway's NATO allies (phase 1).

Gradually, however, some voices started to argue for change. The establishment of the EU with a Common Foreign and Security Policy led to the growth of the EU's potential in terms of soft security. Norwegian participation in the Baltic Sea and Barents co-operation initiatives, and its application for EU membership, indicate a slight Europeanization of the Norwegian security discourse. The strong Atlanticism of the Cold War period still prevailed, now complemented by a European dimension. Although the Norwegian public rejected EU membership in November 1994, the country's political elite continued to strengthen Norway's relationship to the EU throughout the 1990s. This close relationship would increase the possibilities of further Europeanization (phase 2).

Norway's political leaders began to realize that some changes were necessary on the domestic level in order to retain influence and to defend the same unchanged national interests in a changed international context. Such an instrumental adaptation is especially evident in response to the establishment of the ESDP. Initially, the attitude of the Norwegian political leadership towards the Union's security dimension was rather reluctant, as they remained attached to Atlanticism and territorial defence. After the French–British summit in 1998, however, the Norwegian government began to fear that their country could become marginalized within the European security context, and there ensued diplomatic efforts to assure an association to the ESDP. While this process did not lead to the modernization of the national defence forces, it did make the need for such a change even more apparent. This strategy has been referred to as the 'troops for influence strategy', and is a good example of instrumental adaptation (phase 3).

According to the socialization model presented in Chapter 3, governments slowly but surely become entrapped by their own rhetoric and policy statements, and thereby move into the next phase in which instrumental adaptation is replaced by an emerging identity change. This occurs when they become convinced and/or persuaded that norm compliance is not only necessary but also appropriate, i.e. the 'right thing'. The fact that Norway's traditional Atlantic identity has now been supplemented by a European dimension could indicate a slight change in this direction, as could the circumstance that the need for such a change in the Norwegian defence forces is no longer disputed. On the other hand, the fact that NATO continues to be seen as the main security organization, and that the wish to participate in the ESDP seems motivated by fear of becoming marginalized in European security, would indicate that this is an instance of instrumental adaptation rather than learning.

While military aspects still dominate the security approach, we have also noted an emerging interest in comprehensive security. Concerning comprehensive external security, however, only some segments of the political elite have begun to argue for such an approach, which means that the process has barely moved beyond the second phase in the socialization model. It is interesting to note, however, that there has been an increased interest in comprehensive internal security and that this also has been integrated into the dominant security discourse. Still, the degree of Europeanization is somewhat limited and uncertain, and the references to the EU as a comprehensive security actor are fragmented, found only in certain parts of the political elite.

The fact that, in the Norwegian case, Europeanization is both more limited and more fragmented than was the case in Sweden and Finland is mainly due to the low level of participation in the integration process. There is reason to believe that Europeanization beyond the three first phases requires a certain level of participation. Norwegian officials and policymakers cannot participate directly in the discussions and debates on EU security issues, and hence Norway's Atlantic security identity does not get truly challenged. As we have seen in the previous chapter, a similar argument can be made in relation to Denmark as well.

8

COMPARISONS, CONCLUSIONS AND IMPLICATIONS

The aim of this study has been to find out how and to what extent the development of a distinct EU security identity has influenced the security approaches and identities of the four largest Nordic states. The following two assumptions were presented in the introduction:

* The emergence of a distinct European security identity influences the security approaches and the identities of the Nordic countries.
* The character and the strength of the Europeanization process vary according to national security policy traditions and the character of the relationship to the EU.

This concluding chapter is divided into three main parts. The first part provides a summary of the main findings in each chapter and compares them with respect to the three dimensions (Maastricht Treaty, ESDP and comprehensive security) in the development of a distinct EU security actor. On the basis of these findings, the second part suggests which phase in the socialization process each of the four states has reached, indicating some possible reasons for the differences observed among the four. Finally, the last part presents some possible implications for further research in the area of security studies, EU studies and studies of Europeanization.

Comparisons

While Norden is often perceived as a unity, the region consists of states that have both differing relationships to the EU and differing security policy traditions. The starting point of this study was the Cold War security identities of the four largest Nordic states. Together these have been commonly known as the Nordic Balance – a term referring to a combination of different approaches aimed at keeping the two superpowers out of Norden as much as possible, during the Cold War era. With the end of the Cold War, this special arrangement came under pressure. While it took time before the Nordic states actually changed their security approaches, it is argued here that the development of the EU as a security actor has accelerated or facilitated such changes.

Despite differences in approaches, all four countries, except Denmark, have upheld security identities dominated by territorial defence until recently. Denmark made its military forces capable of participating in international operations at a rather early stage, but, at the same time, it upheld a security identity that was dominated by a focus on the military. However, as this analysis has shown, the EU's security identity, which has developed gradually since the early 1990s, has indeed influenced the security approaches and identities of the four Nordic states. The special character of the Union – something between an international organization and a federal state – was in Chapter 2 referred to as a 'tightly coupled security community'. It was suggested that the high level of integration of such a community influences the national security approaches and identities of both its members and states closely linked to it. The case studies presented here also indicate that the security identities of the Nordic states have, to a various degree, been challenged by the European integration process – gradually, through a process of adaptation and learning.

An additional aim of this analysis, beyond seeking to show that there has been a Europeanization process, has been to determine how and to what extent the EU has affected the security identities of these nation-states. The analysis has been based on an interpretative process-tracing approach, coupled with a 'soft' discourse analysis as the main analytical tool. Systematic comparisons have been made possible by investigating the impact of the three major changes in the development of the EU as a distinct security actor: the Maastricht Treaty and the establishment of a political union, the development towards a European Security and Defence Policy, and the emergence of a comprehensive European security identity.

Impact of the Maastricht Treaty

The resistance towards the European integration process that existed in Norway and Sweden in the early 1990s was partly due to security policy considerations. In Norway it was feared that a European political union with a common foreign and security policy would weaken NATO, and hence Norway's position in the European system. In Sweden, the Union's security policy ambitions were seen as incompatible with the doctrine of Swedish neutrality. Despite this general scepticism, parts of the political elite in both countries recognized the importance of the integration process and began to work for closer relations with the Union. Once Sweden had submitted its application for membership, an intense debate concerning neutrality took place, and some revision was perceived as necessary in order to achieve membership. While a first change in this doctrine was made in 1992, the debate concerning the need for more radical change continued after Sweden

178

had joined the EU. In addition, there was also an increased focus on the need to reorganize the national defence forces.

In contrast, Norway's security policy approach was compatible with EU membership, but at this time NATO membership and transatlanticism dominated the Norwegian security policy. After the Maastricht Treaty, however, the Norwegian political elites wished to strengthen their country's relationship with the EU. The dominant security discourse also changed towards a more balanced view of the EU and NATO, emphasizing the Union's role as a soft security actor. While the majority of the Norwegian political leadership largely favoured membership, the negative result of the referendum kept Norway formally outside the integration process. However, during the years following the referendum, the Norwegian political elites managed to achieve a close relationship with the EU, resulting in several agreements and co-operation arrangements and also exposing Norway to even further Europeanization.

The Finnish political leadership was in general far more favourably inclined to the integration process than its Norwegian and Swedish counterparts. With the end of Cold War constraints, EU membership was seen as a way for Finland to confirm its long-repressed Western identity, and not as a threat to national sovereignty or freedom of action. The establishment of a political union made EU membership interesting with reference to security political considerations, and it was actually seen as a possible substitute for the country's traditional policy of neutrality. While Finnish neutrality was abandoned and the EU was recognized as a security policy actor, there was no national debate concerning the role of the defence forces at that time. Finland's EU membership continued to be based on traditional security policy arguments, and was seen as a complement to a national independent and credible defence.

While tendencies towards increased interest in the EU can be identified in all the Nordic non-members of this period – although for different reasons – the opposite seemed to hold for EU-member Denmark. In the early 1990s the Danish political leadership actually supported the Maastricht Treaty and the establishment of a political union. The rejection of the Treaty, however, led to a (self-imposed) exemption of Denmark from important parts of the integration process, including the security dimension. This resulted in few references to the EU in the Danish security discourse, and the EU continued to be perceived as primarily an economic project. Despite this weak interest in the EU's security dimension, the Danish security discourse and policy underwent important changes in the early 1990s. In fact, the reorganization of the national defence forces was initiated earlier in Denmark than in most of the other European states. Rather than a result of the Maastricht Treaty, it should be seen as an early response to the end of the Cold War. Indirectly, however, the rejection of the Maastricht Treaty may have contributed to this change. The opt-out made it even more important for Denmark to be a 'good pupil' in the new NATO (in which international crisis management now was becoming the major task), as this was the sole arena within which Denmark could participate in terms of European security.

Thus we can see that the Maastricht Treaty and the establishment of a political union have had an impact on the changes in the Nordic countries security discourses in the period between 1992 and 1995. The degree and the character of Europeanization have varied, however, and historical and geopolitical differences have arguably contributed to these differences. During this period there was in all four countries a recognition of EU's security dimension, but this was interpreted differently in each country. As argued above, the impact was most evident in Sweden and Finland, where it led to changes in the national security policy doctrines.

Impact of the ESDP

The process towards the establishment of a European security and defence policy started with the Maastricht Treaty, but the framework for this policy had been set out in the Amsterdam Treaty of 1997. For Sweden the future security and defence dimension of the EU was particularly problematic. Thus, once inside the Union, Sweden considered it important to influence this process, to prevent it from developing into a collective defence arrangement. With support from Finland, Sweden managed to have the 'Petersberg tasks'[1] included in the Amsterdam Treaty. While this was perceived as a successful policy action in both countries, the fact that these tasks go beyond traditional peacekeeping with regard to the use of military force also indicates an important change in the security identity of the two countries. This change was most important for Sweden, which was more attached to a policy of neutrality than Finland.

The inclusion of the Petersberg tasks also made it easier for Denmark to accept and support the EU's security dimension. This is evident in the Danish security discourse, but there was still no clear indication of a willingness to give up the defence exemption. The Defence Commission's report of 1998 emphasized that Denmark's relationship to the EU was still based on arguments linked to economic co-operation and free market structures.

As argued above, Finland, Sweden and Norway have been slow to transform their national defence forces by increasing their focus on international crisis management. While the changes in the Danish defence forces were a (rather immediate) reaction to the end of the Cold War, this was not the case in the other three countries. There was still the danger of a negative development in the East, and this was used to legitimize the continued emphasis on having a significant territorial defence capacity. Not until the late 1990s, and thus after the ESDP was launched, were concrete proposals for transforming the national defence forces presented in Norway, Sweden and Finland. Although the ESDP process is not the only explanation, it seems to have accelerated the transformation processes in all three countries. While the important changes that have been introduced into the defence structures of Norway and Sweden, in recent years have been combined with a change in the dominant security discourse, the Finns have retained a more traditional security discourse, legitimizing any alterations by reference to their importance for bolstering the Finnish national defence capacity. While Denmark has undertaken such a transformation of the defence forces at an earlier stage, the launch of the ESDP also had an impact on the Danish discourse. In fact, this process led to a discussion about the value of the Danish defence exemption, focusing especially on the risk that Denmark could become marginalized within the European security system.

This shows that the St Malo process and the development towards an ESDP have influenced the national security discourse in all the Nordic countries, but that the relationship to the EU and security policy traditions in each case can explain the differences. In Norway and Sweden it accelerated the process towards a modernization of the defence forces, also involving some changes in the conception of security. In Finland it led to greater emphasis on the international dimension, but combined with a continued traditional view of security. In Denmark, which already had undergone such changes, it led to a debate concerning the value of the defence opt-out.

Impact of the EU's comprehensive security approach

The impact of the Union's comprehensive security approach is to some extent evident in all countries, but also here there are important differences – both among the four countries and with relation to the internal and external dimensions.

Internal security

For a long time, national defence was exclusively concerned with defending national territories against military threats. The first change came with an increased focus on the external dimension (international crisis management) while national defence, although toned down, still was characterized by territorial defence. Today, the need for a more comprehensive approach in this internal (or domestic) area has also become increasingly evident. The EU has been focusing on what we have called 'internal comprehensive security' for some time, but the '9/11' terrorist attacks on the USA brought home the importance of such a development also to other actors. While these attacks put the need for a more co-ordinated security approach to internal security on the agenda, the EU also had a certain impact on these developments in the national security discourses – a development that started prior to 9/11.

Norway was the first to put these questions on the agenda with its decision to establish a commission tasked with writing a report on questions related to the vulnerability of Norwegian society. Some references to the processes in the EU can be identified before this decision was taken. At the time, however, this was treated separately, not as a part of the dominant national discourse on security but by the Ministry of Justice. However, there were some references to the EU and especially to Norwegian participation in the Schengen arrangements. Later, references to the EU were replaced by terrorism and 9/11, but these aspects gradually become an integral part of the dominant discourse. Recently, there has been some emphasis on the need to improve inter-ministerial co-ordination, and a high-level civilian military co-operation group and a new directorate have been established for that purpose. The traditional concept of total defence has been somewhat redefined, with more emphasis on societal defence civilian preparedness. While there is a close co-operation with the EU in these areas, the EU is not explicitly recognized as a comprehensive security actor in the dominant security discourse.

In Sweden and Finland a similar process started somewhat later than in Norway. In contrast, it has from the very outset been viewed as an integral part of the dominant discourse on security. This has been facilitated by a greater importance of the concept of total defence in these countries, having both civilian and military defence under the authority of the ministries of defence. In both countries it was also the respective ministries of defence that initiated the debate. Interest in these questions has been especially strong in Sweden; and while we find few specific references to the European integration process in this connection, there may be an indirect influence here. Similar to its influence as to the external dimension, the problem of having two different discourses is also relevant here. In fact, when a country is part of a tightly coupled security community like the EU, talking about comprehensive security in the EU and having a continued focus on territorial defence and military defence on the national level seems more difficult. In Finland, where the changes are more recent, they are also better integrated into the dominant discourse and more explicitly linked to the EU processes.

In Denmark, the political leadership showed little or no interest in these comprehensive internal security issues prior to 11 September. Only after these tragic events did such questions begin to appear in the Danish security discourse. As in Norway, this was initially a separate process, not part of the discourse within the Ministry of Defence, and few references are made to the EU in relation to these questions in the Danish discourse. Recently there has been a move towards increased focus on 'homeland security' and the importance of the EU in this regard is increasingly recognized.

External security

All the four Nordic countries have had long experience with civilian crisis management and conflict prevention, especially through the UN. Still, these have been viewed largely as tasks separated from those that define national security policy. This explains why these aspects have received scant attention in the documents and speeches presenting the national security approach in each country. As international crisis management has become an increasingly important function of the defence forces in all four states, we can also note that all four have begun to show greater interest in civil-military cooperation, and in integrating non-military capabilities into this dimension of the national security approach. However, here too there are important differences with respect to how well these aspects are integrated into the dominant national discourse on security.

Among the Nordic states, Sweden has been most committed to a comprehensive security approach. Even though parts of the Swedish political elites, especially as represented by the Ministry of Foreign Affairs, have promoted this approach for some time, it is only recently that this has become an important part of the dominant Swedish discourse on security expressed in the Ministry of Defence. This is why it is possible to talk about the Europeanization of the Swedish approach even though Sweden has actually been the most important promoter of these aspects within the EU. In fact, we can identify a 'feedback' from the Swedish Ministry of Foreign Affairs' own discourse in the EU into the Swedish Ministry of Defence. This has resulted in a heightened focus on comprehensive security also here, with greater interest in CIMIC, but also more generally with a clear ambition to base policy on a broader security concept. The establishment of an academy for training of both civilian and military personnel for international crisis management operations is important. While this institution is put under the authority of the Ministry of Foreign Affairs and will mainly focus on civilian crisis management, the objective is enhanced cooperation with SWEDINT (Swedish Armed Forces International Centre).

Also in Finland the need for greater comprehensiveness in relation to external security has recently been introduced into the discourse. Explicit references to the processes within the EU indicate that this is a direct result of the process of Europeanization. While comprehensive external security also builds on Finland's traditional activism in the UN, this comprehensive dimension has not led to a change in the dominant security discourse – a discourse still very much focused on traditional defence. Every alteration is, in fact, viewed in relation to whether or not it strengthens Finland's traditional defence capability or national security in the changed security context. The fact that these aspects are so well integrated into the discourse is a result of Europeanization, but is also facilitated by the strong Finnish tradition of interministerial co-ordination – the security discourse in the Ministry of Foreign Affairs and the Ministry of Defence being more co-ordinated than in most other countries.

In Norway and Denmark, less emphasis has been put on such a comprehensive external security approach in the dominant discourse even though some recent changes have been identified. As a result, civilian and military aspects of international crisis management have remained separated. Some emphasis on the need for greater comprehensiveness can be identified in parts of the discourse (especially in the ministries of foreign affairs and, in Norway, also in the Ministry of Justice). However, this has not yet become an important part of the dominant discourse, despite the greater attention to CIMIC in the ministries of defence in both countries. This is interesting, since Norway and Denmark have been front-runners on the civilian and the military side, respectively. However, co-ordination has been more limited, and the dominant discourse in both countries remains very much military-dominated. Still, in Denmark we can note a special eagerness to participate in the EU's civilian crisis management forces, and even to support the comprehensive security approach at the EU level. While this must be understood as a way in which Denmark can compensate for its non-participation in the EU's military co-operation, it is interesting to note that the implementation of such an approach at the EU level will in fact limit Denmark's participation also in the civilian dimension. In Norway, the comprehensive dimension and the EU's role in this regard has also been increasingly emphasized by the Ministry of Foreign Affairs and the Ministry of Justice. This should indicate a certain level of Europeanization of also the Danish and the Norwegian approaches.

Comparison

Both in relation to internal and external comprehensive security, the EU seems to have had some impact on the national discourse, even though the link is not always made that explicit. The degree of influence also varies among the four countries and is facilitated or slowed down by different institutional and historical factors.

The integration of civilian and military aspects, with regards to both internal and external security, is most extensive in Sweden and Finland. While comprehensive security is presented as an end in itself in the Swedish discourse, the changes in the Finnish approach are consistently legitimized by reference to traditional security arguments. At the same time, the changes in the Finnish approach seem to be more directly linked to the processes in the EU. While, the importance of the EU in this area is explicitly emphasized in the Finnish discourse, the effect of the EU on Sweden seems to happen indirectly through the Ministry of Foreign Affairs. In Denmark and Norway comprehensive security has only recently become an integrated part of the dominant national security discourse and the EU's role in this area is also increasingly recognized. It is also in relation to internal security that the changes are the most obvious. While this may have been initiated as a result of Europeanization, it was intensified after the terrorist incidents of 11 September 2001 in the US and of 11 March 2004 in Spain.

In fact, since 9/11, there has been an increased emphasis on comprehensive internal security (referred to either as societal security, societal defence or homeland security) in the EU as well as in the four Nordic countries. The fact that comprehensive internal security has been more integrated into the national discourse on security in Sweden and Finland than in Denmark and Norway, however, may also be explained by different institutional factors. In fact, a stronger and perhaps more coordinated total defence concept (civilian and military defence being the responsibility of the Ministry of Defence) in Sweden and Finland and the special tradition of interministerial co-ordination in Finland may have facilitated the move towards a more holistic approach to internal security, and perhaps also the Europeanization process.

Conclusions

We can identify important changes in the security approaches in all four cases – Denmark, Finland, Norway and Sweden – in the period from 1990 to 2004. As already indicated, all changes we observe are not a result of Euro-peanization, but in some cases this seems to be the case. However, even when we identify such a influence from the EU level, it is important to note that there are different degrees of Europeanization and all four countries have not experienced a profound change in the dominant security discourse. Such a change would have resulted in a change in security identity and would have led to a more stable and enduring change in security policy orientation. On the basis of the main findings presented above, this section will attempt to determine which phase in the socialization process (model presented in Chapter 3) each of the Nordic nation-states has reached, and then indicate some possible explanations for any variations.

Europeanization and socialization

Developments in the national post-Cold War security discourses seem to have followed a pattern similar to the five-phase socialization model pre-sented in Chapter 3. According to this model, such a process begins when an actor starts to adjust its actions to a community norm. Such adjustments are first characterized by instrumental adaptation to external changes, with the actor trying to find 'new' ways of preserving its traditional interests. The original identity is challenged, and the actor searches for new ways of defending it. The more the identity is challenged, however, the more con-vincing arguments are needed. It is assumed that the actor gradually becomes convinced by the 'challenger's' arguments, and that the chances for socialization or learning then increase. This means that the actor becomes convinced by the community's norms and discourse. The final phase in this socialization process comes when the new discourse has become insti-tutionalized. Adapted to the empirical focus of this book, the five phases presented were expressed in the form of the following steps:

1   Maintenance of a traditional national security discourse;
2   Parts of the national political leadership become convinced by the community norm and start to question their own traditional national security discourse;
3   Instrumental adaptation of the dominant national security discourse to the community norm;
4   The new security approach has become part of the dominant national security discourse and is viewed as 'the right thing' (identity change/learning);
5   The new ideas in this security discourse get institutionalized, becoming part of the national security policy (socialization).

Developments in the security approaches of the Nordic states indicate that all four have reached the phase where changes must be understood as instrumental adaptation (phase 3). But – have some of them moved beyond this point and into the two final phases, characterized respectively by identity change and institutionalization? This would indicate a more stable and enduring change in security policy.

As we have seen, European integration and a comprehensive security policy have become important parts of the Swedish security identity. Neutrality and territorial defence have been toned down, and comprehensive security is now defined as one of the main tasks for Sweden's security and defence policy. References to neutrality are reduced to a minimum, and co-operation within the EU is now seen as an important part of the Swedish security approach. Sweden's Cold War identity, which was characterized by a credible territorial defence and neutrality, would certainly seem to have been replaced by a comprehensive security identity within an EU framework. Thus, we may argue that Sweden has reached the final phase in the socialization process – institutionalization of these new ideas (phase 5). This seems to be a result of Europeanization, even though the influence is not always obvious, or explicitly referred to. To some extent, the ideas promoted in the EU by the Swedish Ministry of Foreign Affairs seem to have led to a feed-back on the dominant Swedish discourse on security.

While Sweden is the only one among the four studied here to have institutionalized a comprehensive security approach, a process of Europeanization is even more evident in Finland. Here all of the three phases in the development of an EU-specific security identity seem to have had a direct impact on the country's security approach. All the same, this has not yet led to a change in the Finnish security identity. Even though neutrality has been abandoned, the Finnish discourse continues to be based on a highly traditional understanding of security. Neutrality was painlessly replaced by EU membership as the main security policy orientation, but the changes in the Finnish approach must be understood as a pragmatic and instrumental adaptation to a new security context rather than as a change in identity.

Finland's security approach is very much Europeanized, but this Europeanization does not seem to have moved beyond the third phase of instrumental adaptation. However, Finland's decision to finally sign the Ottawa Convention in 2012 (and destroy its land mines by the end of 2016) may indicate the beginning of an identity change.

The Danish security approach has also been Europeanized, but the impact of the EU seems more fragmented than in Sweden and Finland. The Danish approach changed rather early after the end of the Cold War. At that time, the Danish political leadership also supported the Maastricht Treaty and the EU as a security actor, which indicates that the Danish security discourse had already reached the second phase in the socialization process at that time. International crisis management became the most important task for the Danish defence forces in the early 1990s, but it is difficult to argue that this change was a *direct* consequence of the Maastricht Treaty. It seems more likely that it was an immediate response to the altered security context. However, it has been claimed that this change *indirectly* was a result of instrumental adaptation to the EU process. The fact that the Danish people rejected the Maastricht Treaty left NATO as the only framework through which Denmark could participate in European security. It therefore became crucial to be perceived as a relevant player in the post-Cold War NATO, for which international crisis management had become the main task. While this change was important, it did not really represent a rupture with the Danish Cold War discourse. In fact, that Cold War security discourse had been dominated by strong support for co-operative security arrangements, and NATO's new profile was nicely in accordance with this discourse.

More recently, and after the ESDP process was initiated, we may note a more *direct* impact of the EU. Denmark's need to compensate for its opt-out led to more explicit recognition of the European security dimension as well as a debate concerning the defence exemption. Despite the recent interest in the EU's civilian crisis management dimension, CIMIC and vulnerability questions in recent documents, however, a comprehensive security approach has not become a central part of the dominant Danish security discourse, and the focus on military tools continue to be dominant. So, while the changes in Denmark's security approach referred to here are important, they do not challenge profoundly the country's traditional identity of Atlantic Universalism, and must therefore be seen as instrumental adaptation.

Atlanticism and a militaristic conception of security also continue to dominate the Norwegian discourse. Also in Norway, the changes we have identified must first of all be understood as a way of limiting the potential marginalization of the country within the European security system (transformation of the defence forces, contribution to and participation in the ESDP). In addition there are some important changes that indicate that the traditional security identity is increasingly being challenged. There has been increased interest in the security dimension of the EU beyond ESDP, as well as a development towards a comprehensive security approach by parts of the political leadership. Recently the dominant security discourse has also concentration on these aspects; there has been more focus on CIMIC and comprehensive external security; and a new institution has been established (NSM) for co-ordination between the civilian and the military at the national level. While the latter have been fairly well integrated into the dominant discourse, comprehensive external security has not yet become a priority in the security discourse.

National differences

From the discussion above, we may conclude that only in Sweden has there been a true change in identity, while the other three have remained in the phase of instrumental adaptation. However, there are also differences between these three. While Finland has adapted instrumentally to all major changes in the EU's security dimension, Denmark and Norway have been far more reluctant. In addition, Norway seems slightly more influenced by the EU process than Denmark. The reasons for these differences seem related to two main differences between these countries – relationships to the EU, and security policy traditions.

Our analysis has shown that type of relationship to the EU is important. However, this does not mean that *formal EU membership* necessarily leads to the highest levels of Europeanization. The Swedish and the Finnish security approaches have been most Europeanized; but when we turn to developments in Denmark and in Norway, formal EU membership seems even less important. Both countries are less Europeanized than Sweden and Finland, but the Norwegian approach seems slightly more affected by the EU than is the case in Denmark – and yet Denmark has been an EC/EU member since 1973. While this is an interesting finding, it can be explained as a consequence of Norway's closeness to the EU and Denmark's habit of opting out. This would mean that it is the *level* of participation in the EU structures that is of importance, not the form of the relationship itself. A first conclusion is therefore that the more integrated into the EU system a nation-state is (formally or informally), the more exposed it is to Europeanization in one way or the other.

Security policy traditions such as neutrality and non-alignment, combined with a strong concept of total defence, may also explain why Sweden and Finland have been better at developing an integrated comprehensive approach. While our analysis has indicated that Finland and Sweden have been the most affected by the EU, it has also shown that these two countries have been better at incorporating the civilian dimension into the dominant national discourse, and in relation to both internal and external security. Denmark and Norway have no restrictions on participation in international military operations, and the total defence concept has a less dominant position. Here such a comprehensive discourse in relation to external secur-ity is less present in the ministries of defence, and is merely referred to by other parts of the political leadership (in particular by the ministries of foreign affairs). A more comprehensive discourse in relation to internal security, however, has recently become part of the security discourse also in Denmark and Norway. But this seems to be a result of 9/11 and the increased focus on the threat from international terrorism rather than a result of Europeanization.

However, the level of integration and security policy traditions like neu-trality are not sufficient for understanding the variations, since they do not account for the differences between Sweden and Finland. In order to account for these differences, one has to include yet another aspect – historical experiences and geopolitical positions. While both Sweden and Finland have traditions of neutrality (although with some different interpretations) and a strong concept of total defence, Finland must be considered as being more integrated into the EU structures than Sweden and thus more directly affected by the EU. At the same time, Sweden seems to have undergone the most profound changes with regard to the dominant discourse. In Sweden, neutrality has been largely abandoned. There seems to have been an insti-tutionalization of a comprehensive security identity, internally with the trad-itional total defence concept having been replaced by something that, using Bengt Sundelius' term, may be referred to as *societal defence* (Sundelius 2001) and externally, with the increased focus on comprehensive crisis man-agement, conflict prevention and CIMIC. In Finland, however, the high degree of Europeanization is evident in relation to both the internal and the external dimension, but the character of the changes is very different from the case in Sweden. In Finland many important changes have been made, but these are systematically legitimized in terms of traditional security policy arguments. This indicates that historical experiences and geopolitical posi-tions are also of importance. While the absence of 'recent' war experiences in Sweden may have accelerated the socialization process and favoured identity change, Finland's Winter War experience and its continued vulnerable geopolitical position have until now prevented profound changes.

Implications

This book has aimed at contributing to a better understanding of the pro-cesses of Europeanization of the security approaches and identities of the Nordic states. We have sought to identify the dominant security discourse and to determine whether this has been challenged by the European integra-tion process. While the aim has not been to provide generalizable conclu-sions, we may indicate some observations of general value. This study has combined theoretical approaches that are normally employed separately, and, on the basis of the empirical findings presented above, we may highlight some insights of value for security studies, EU studies and also studies of Europeanization.

Security, integration and identity change

Our analysis has shown that security is a flexible concept, and that the current security context requires an approach based on comprehensiveness and co-ordination among the various tools of security policy, rather than a security approach focused exclusively on military security. While a traditional approach operates with a clear soft/hard and external/internal distinction (Walt 1991), a more relevant distinction in the current security context would seem to be between various efforts at crisis *prevention*, and crisis *management*. Moreover, the conventional view in security studies fails to distinguish between a nation-state's security policy and its security identity. The analysis in this book, however, has indicated that in order for there to be a long-term, stable change in policy, there must first be an identity change. Such identity changes are slow, which explains why nation-state security policies also tend to be out of touch with the current security context.

Instrumental adaptations to changes in the security context do occur, but as long as the political leadership has not adopted a new understanding of the security context (new 'codes'), these changes are likely to be less stable and enduring. In order to identify changes in the national security identity, however, one needs a framework that is more open. The framework must also be able to distinguish between adaptations and identity change, to permit us to determine the significance of the changes that occur. An actor's security identity can be captured only by studying that actor's dominant discourse on security over a certain period of time. Employing such an approach enables us to distinguish 'latent' from 'manifest' change. While the former is only an adaptation to external challenges without challenging the 'identity codes' that are defining for policy options, the latter is a result of a learning process whereby the ideas inherent in the discourse (identity codes) are challenged.

Institutions that have no security legacy will have a greater potential for developing a security approach more in accordance with the current security context – and this is precisely what has happened in the EU since the early 1990s. This book has emphasized that a new framework for understanding the EU as security actor is needed, since the existing literature does not take into account the importance of the special character of the EU. More frequently, the EU has been viewed either as an international organization or as a fully fledged federation.

Seeking to capture the special character of the Union as being something between the two, we have presented the EU as a tightly coupled security community. For many years the dominant view was that the EC/EU could not be considered as a serious actor in the international system as long as it did not have an efficient military capability. This argument was first put forward as a criticism of François Duchêne's 'civilian power' argument (Bull 1982). With the end of the Cold War came a renewed interest in the possibilities for such a civilian power Europe (Lodge 1993), but the militarization of the EU through the ESDP process was not perceived as compatible with the civilian power argument (Whitmann 1998; Zielonka 1998; Smith 2000). Since then most of the literature on the EU's security dimension has focused on the CFSP and/or ESDP (Lodge and Flynn 1998; Peterson and Sjursen 1998; Duke 2000; Heisbourg 2000; Howorth 2000; Kupchan 2000; Larsen 2002b; Youngs 2002). This means that research on this topic, although characterized by a wide range of approaches, has been dominated by an interest in the external dimension: few studies have attempted to see this dimension as a part of a whole. The approach in this book has attempted to fill this gap and to provide a framework for understanding how the EU functions as a security actor. This means that instead of investigating what kind of security actor one thinks the EU *should be* (whether a military or civilian power) the aim here has been to uncover what it *is* and what it *does*. This has been done by applying a 'soft' discourse analysis approach. As argued in Chapter 2, the fact that the EU/EC did not have a clearly defined security identity developed during the Cold War period has facilitated the development of a comprehensive security discourse and policy better adapted to the current security context.

This tightly coupled European security community with a comprehensive security approach seems to produce a special framework which in turn also challenges the security approaches and identities of both member states and states closely linked to the community. For that reason, this analysis also may contribute to an improved understanding of how processes of Europeanization take place. The literature on Europeanization has generally focused on adaptation and changes in nation-state policies and administrative institutions, and some work has been published on the Europeanization of national foreign and security polities and policies (Manners and Withman 2000; Tonra 2001; Featherstone 2002). However, there has been far less interest in the Europeanization of national identities (some exceptions are Boekle *et al.* 2001; Risse 2001). The analysis in this book provides some observations that might be of added value for this field of study as well.

First, we have seen that it is necessary to follow the security discourses and policies of states *over time* in order to capture a possible Europeanization of a nation-state's security identity. While long-term and stable change in security policy tends to be preceded by a change in national security identities, identities generally change slowly and through a process that often starts with deliberations and instrumental adaptations. Identifying these changes requires studying dominant discourses over several years.

Second, the EU influences both its members and countries that are closely linked to the Union. While this fits in with existing research on the Europeanization of national policies and administrative systems (see for instance Sverdrup 2000), this study indicates that the level of Europeanization varies according to the degree of participation in the EU, whereas that the type of relationship to the EU is less important. In addition, different security policy traditions and historical experiences may reduce or strengthen the impact of the EU.

Third, the analysis has shown that we may distinguish between direct and indirect Europeanization. Direct Europeanization can most easily be identified in the discourse, since the importance of the processes at the EU level is explicitly referred to in it. With the second type, there are no explicit references, but the timing of the changes at the national level indicates a process of Europeanization. This could be the case when changes at the EU level are followed up by similar changes at the national level, whether by a change in discourse or in a specific decision. Examples of indirect influence could include the impact of the Maastricht Treaty on Denmark's reorganization of its defence forces in the early 1990s, the influence of the ESDP process on the same development in Norway in the late 1990s and the impact of the EU's comprehensive security approach on the Swedish and the Norwegian discourse.

Concluding remarks

This analysis has shown that community norms influence nation-state identities and interests, but that such changes take time and are often preceded by a phase of instrumental adaptation. To argue that the development of the EU's security dimension has influenced the security approaches of the Nordic states, however, is not to say that the integration process constitutes the sole reason for change. Other factors, both external and internal, are also important for understanding changes in the various national security approaches throughout the 1990s. The aim of this study has not been to provide a comprehensive explanation, but to contribute to greater understanding of the EU's impact on the security approaches and security identities of these four countries.

The empirical findings have shown that the special Nordic security community – characterized by being different from Europe and commonly known as the 'Nordic balance' – is gradually being replaced by an ongoing process of Europeanization. While only Sweden that has gone through an identity change, the others seem to be moving in the same direction. This indicates that, despite differences, changes in national security identities seem to follow a similar pattern. This does not mean that Europeanization is a rigid process, but rather that any change in identity seems to take place gradually. The dominant discourse or the main 'codes' that define a nation-state's security policy orientation may change – but slowly, and most often as a reaction to changes in the external environment. Security identities of nation-states within a tightly coupled security community – like the EU – gradually seem to converge with the identity of the community itself.

NOTES

1 INTRODUCTION

1 The Nordic countries or 'Norden' – the Nordic term for this area – consist of the Scandinavian countries (Denmark, Norway, Sweden), together with Finland and Iceland.
2 Other comparative studies have been done earlier, but this is the first in the period after the establishment of the EU in 1992.
3 For an introduction to this debate see Rosamond (2000).
4 The problems related to the EU as an actor is discussed in greater detail in Chapter 2.
5 With the end of the Cold War 'comprehensive' conceptions of security have become a growth industry. While the concept is generally referred to in relation to studies of environmental security (Westing 1989; Dokken 1997), it will here be used to refer to a holistic security approach that includes both internal and external security mechanisms.
6 In a recent book, Cooper distinguishes between three different phases in European history. He describes the period before the establishment of the system of nation-states in 1648 as the pre-modern phase, the period after 1648 as the modern phase and finally the post-Cold War era as the post-modern period, which is characterized by the final abandon of a power of balance system and the acceleration of a period of political integration (Cooper 2003).
7 The fact that the EU has developed institutional features beyond the original design and certainly beyond the purpose of managing economic interdependence also indicates that it is more than simply a successful intergovernmental regime (Christiansen et al. 2001: 13).
8 Iceland is not included in this study. The reason for this is that Iceland is very different from the other four – a small country with no military forces, making systematic comparison difficult.
9 The Copenhagen School distinguishes between 'referent objects', 'securitizing actors', and 'functional actors'. While referent objects refer to things/people that/who are seen to be existentially threatened and have a legitimate claim to survival, securitizing actor refers to actors who securitize issues by declaring something/someone – a referent object – existentially threatened. Functional actors are actors who affect the dynamics of a sector by significantly influencing decisions in the field of security (Buzan et al. 1998: 36).
10 The issue-driven widening of the security concept in the 1980s triggered its own reaction, creating a plea that security studies be confined to issues centred on threat or the use of force. A key argument was that progressive widening

194

endangered the intellectual coherence of the notion of security, making it so broad that it becomes essentially meaningless (Walt 1991). The securitization approach was an attempt to provide an answer to this critique.

11 Henrik Larsen defines 'dominant discourse' as 'a discourse which predominantly determines the use of language and hence promotes certain meanings in the . . . documents that are analysed' (Larsen 2002b: 288). In this book 'dominant security discourse' is understood as 'the overall understanding of security' presented by the political leadership, and especially through the official statements from the Ministries of Defence.

12 In contrast to studies interested in uncovering the historical roots of a certain security identity – identity formation (Neumann 1999, 2001b) – the aim of this study is to identify well-established security identities, how they change and what kind of impact they have on policy orientations.

13 The period under study is 1990–2004. The starting point is the end of the Cold War; that the study ends in December 2004 is due solely to practical reasons connected with the submission of this manuscript. The Europeanization process, however, is seen as a continuous process.

14 This discussion aims at clarifying how the relationship between national security identity and the national security discourse is understood here. A more detailed discussion of this methodological choice is undertaken towards the end of this chapter under the heading 'soft discourse analysis'.

15 This identity is explained in more detail in Chapter 2.

16 For an overview of the research on Europeanization see for instance Radaelli (2000).

17 The NATO definition is as follows: 'The co-ordination and co-operation, in support of the mission, between the NATO Commander and civil actors, including national population and local authorities, as well as international, national and non-governmental organizations and agencies' (quoted in Jensen 2003: 9).

18 The UN defines civil–military co-ordination as 'the system of interaction, involving exchange of information, negotiation, de-confliction, mutual support, and planning at all levels between military elements and humanitarian organizations, development organizations, or the local civilian population, to achieve respective objectives' (quoted in Jensen 2003: 10).

19 This socialisation process is discussed further in Chapter 3.

2 THE EU: A COMPREHENSIVE SECURITY ACTOR

1 For an introduction to this debate see Rosamond (2000).

2 The multi-level governance literature seeks to avoid two traps: state-centrism and the treatment of the EU as operating solely at the European level. It argues that the EU has become a polity where authority is dispersed between levels of governance and amongst actors, and where there are significant sectoral variations in governance patterns (ibid.: 109–13).

3 In the following 'community' is used when referring to EU as a tightly coupled security community. 'Community', however, will refer to the European Community (pillar I).

4 For an overview of the literature on the EU as a security actor see Ginsberg (1999) or Bretherton and Vogler (1999).

5 Such as direct threats to the sovereignty of Norway, Greece, Turkey and other Western European countries, the June 1948 coup in Czechoslovakia, and the illegal blockade of Berlin which began in April of the same year.

6 In 1952, Greece and Turkey acceded to the Treaty. The Federal Republic of

Germany joined the Alliance in 1955. Spain became a member of NATO in 1982.

7 This section is largely based on Martin Sæter's doctoral book from 1971 (Sæter 1971), which provides a comprehensive and detailed analysis of the first decades of the European integration process.

8 The events in Korea in the early 1950s led to the establishment of the North Atlantic Treaty Organization (NATO) with an integrated military structure.

9 While it is often held that the French gaullists were strongly opposed to both the Schuman Plan and the Pleven Plan because of their supranational character, this view does not take into consideration the changes that took place during the first years after the war and which radically changed the gaullists' opinion about French independence. The development in East–West relations just after the Second World War made earlier ideas about French independence illusory, and thus led de Gaulle and his political allies to be supportive of the initial European integration initiatives. These initiatives were not seen in contrast to *la grandeur de la France* but rather as a necessary condition for it. When French finally rejected the Pleven Plan in 1954, it was because this project had abandoned much of its original ideas. Instead of being an independent European defence community it became a European defence community subordinated to NATO and American dominance (Sæter 1971: 239–41; Rieker 1998b).

10 This organization was revitalized in 1984. Portugal and Spain joined the WEU in 1988.

11 The Merger Treaty of 1965, which entered into force 1 July 1967, established a single Council of Ministers and a single Commission integrating the executives of the ECSC, the EEC and Euratom. From 1 July 1970, the term 'EC' was used officially to denote the three communities.

12 It was the implementation of the already adopted Common Agriculture Policy that was the direct cause of this crisis. However, there are good reasons to believe that France favoured this common policy, but that it wanted the EC to come to a conclusion before they started membership negotiations with Great Britain. This would have forced Great Britain to accept the highly supranational result and would thus have been a guarantee for France that there would be no special British–Atlantic role within the Community (Sæter 1992: 52).

13 Since the five other member states were in favour of the idea, set down in the Treaty of Rome, of making qualified majority voting the rule, de Gaulle feared that France, through its integration in the EC, could at a later stage also lose its sovereignty in NATO. As the Luxembourg Compromise did not give any guarantee that qualified majority voting would not be used at a later stage, de Gaulle's decision to withdraw France from the integrated military structures in NATO must be seen as a way to safeguard itself on this point (Rieker 1998b, 1998a).

14 Gunnar Sjöstedt introduced this distinction in international relations theory in the 1970s (Sjöstedt 1977). He maintained that an actor was synonymous with the ability for active and goal-oriented behaviour towards other actors in the international arena. More recently, several scholars have addressed this question in different forms (Allen and Smith 1990; Ginsberg 1999).

15 http://ue.eu.int/cms3_fo/showPage.ASP?id=406andlang=EN.

16 EU Action Plan on Combating Terrorism – Update (14 December 2004).

17 http://europa.eu.int/pol/justice/overview_en.htm.

18 Referring to a WEU Ministerial Council meeting in June 1992, held at Petersberg Hotel near Bonn, where the member states of this organization had decided that the WEU should aim at carrying out 'humanitarian and rescue tasks,

peace-keeping tasks and tasks of combat forces in crisis management, including peace-making' (the Petersberg tasks).
19 The headline goals consisted of a military Rapid Reaction Force of 60,000 troops to be deployable within sixty days for a period of up to one year, and specific civilian capabilities in policing, civilian administration, rule of law and civil protection.

3 EUROPEANIZATION AS SOCIALIZATION

1 Defined as those expectations of appropriate behaviour that are shared by most of the states in an international community.
2 Defined as those expectations of appropriate behaviour that are shared by the majority of the citizens in a state.
3 These arguments have been emphasized by Jeffrey Checkel (1997, 1998, 1999) and Frank Schimmelfenning (1999b).
4 Argumentative rationality is different from 'rhetorical action' (Schimmelfenning 1999b). Actors engaging in rhetoric are not prepared to change their own beliefs or to be persuaded themselves by the 'better argument'. As Risse points out: 'If everybody in a communicative situation engages in rhetoric – the speaker, the target, and the audience – they can argue strategically until they are blue in the face and still not change anyone's mind' (Risse 2000: 8).

4 SWEDEN: TEACHER AND PUPIL

1 During the Crimean War the Anglo-French fleet was allowed to use Swedish ports as bases for attacks against Russian fortifications on the Åland islands and against Russian ports and shipping. Another challenge to the policy of neutrality was the Scandinavianist movement. In the 1860s plans were discussed for a defensive alliance with Denmark in order to protect Schleswig. The final argument, however, was that the military resources were too limited and the political and military risks too great. The Danes had to fight Prussia alone, and Sweden returned to a more peripheral position.
2 Since the end of the Cold War there have been many analyses that show the limits of this policy of neutrality, and that Sweden maintained close contacts with NATO throughout the Cold War period. Ola Tunander has thus claimed that Sweden was 'plugged into NATO' (Tunander 1999: 183). While the end of the Cold War provoked a debate concerning the future of Swedish security policy, it also led to an increased demand for the past to be examined. This is why in 1992 a commission was established to examine Sweden's military co-operation with the West from 1949 to 1969. The commission's report showed that links, both formal and informal, had been far more extensive than previously admitted and beyond those that might be expected of a non-aligned state (Archer 1996: 24).
3 This led the Nordic countries to initiate discussions on a Nordic economic community (NORDEK). However, it soon became apparent that Denmark and Norway considered NORDEK as merely a complement to EEC membership; the final blow to this project came when Finland, after negative reactions from the Soviet Union, decided that it was not able to sign the agreement.
4 The PfP programme, launched at the NATO summit in Brussels in January 1994, enabled Sweden to participate in NATO's peacekeeping operations.
5 This was not the case for other neutral countries such as Austria and Switzerland.
6 The EEA agreement, signed in 1992, included the EFTA countries in the internal market and gave Sweden, as well as all the other EFTA countries that had

accepted the agreement, most of the benefits of membership except political influence. The agreement entered into force in January 1994, one year before Sweden joined the Union.

7 The Swedes voted for membership by a majority of 52.27 per cent (46.83 per cent against) (Miles 1997: 248).
8 See Chapter 2, note 18.
9 http://forsvar.regeringen.se/inenglish/issues/internationellt.htm
10 These included a command resource, a mechanized battalion, an engineering company with ammunition and minesweeping capabilities, a military police company, a naval minesweeping unit, a corvette unit, one submarine, reconnaissance and fighter aircrafts units (8 JAS), and a transport aircraft unit.
11 http://www.sweden.gov.se/sb/d/2060/a/21983.
12 http://www.sweden.gov.se/sb/d/2237/a/21793.
13 http://www.folkebernadotteacademy.se/fba.htlm.
14 http://www.regeringen.se/sb/d/658/a/34054 (my translation).
15 http://www.sweden.gov.se/sb/d/2060/a/21983.

5 FINLAND: PRAGMATIC ADAPTER

1 According to Penttilä, discussions on the question of neutrality were initiated in Finland as early as in 1863 in a newspaper article in *Helsingfors Dagblad* (Penttilä 1994: 9).
2 The government and Supreme Court of Justice in the Grand Duchy of Finland from 1816 to 1917. The Senate was divided into judicial and financial departments. The judicial department was replaced by the Supreme Court in 1918, and the Senate became the Council of State.
3 The Diet was based on simultaneous meetings of the four Estates – nobility, clergy, burgesses and peasants. The meetings of the nobility were open to the heads of noble families. The other Estates elected their representatives to the Diet. The Estates were the social classes of the time, internally united by privileges and rules. A significant proportion of the population did not belong to any of the Estates.
4 The first edition of the *Kalevala* appeared in 1835, compiled and edited by Elias Lönnrot on the basis of the epic folk poems he had collected in the Finnish heartland. This poetic song tradition, sung in an unusual, archaic trochaic tetrameter, had been part of the oral tradition among speakers of Balto-Finnic languages for two thousand years. When the *Kalevala* appeared in print for the first time, Finland had been an Autonomous Grand Duchy for a quarter of a century. Prior to this, until 1809, Finland had been a part of the Swedish empire. The publication of the *Kalevala* marked an important turning point for Finnish-language culture and caused a stir abroad as well. It brought a small, unknown people to the attention of other Europeans, and bolstered the Finns' self-confidence and faith in the possibilities of their own language and culture.
5 Finland thus became the first European country to grant women the vote; and nineteen women were elected to the 200-person Parliament in 1906 (http://www.iwdc.org/timeline.htm).
6 This tragedy left deep wounds. The Whites and Reds continued their battle on the political arena, and as one country after another fell under totalitarian or authoritarian rule, Finland too experienced a wave of Fascism. This trend was influenced by the fear of the Soviet Union, and the fact that the Social Democrats and Liberals were perceived to be too soft on Communism. However, Finland was one of the few countries to resist these antidemocratic forces (Jakobson 1998: 22).

7 http://memory.loc.gov/frd/cs/finland/fi_appnb.html.

8 This policy was shaped, with broad political support, by two successive Finnish presidents in particular – Paasikivi and Kekkonen – who enjoyed supreme constitutional responsibility for foreign policy. Finland's old constitution from 1919 stipulated that 'the relations of Finland with foreign powers shall be determined by the president' (quoted in Forsberg 2001b: 4). Although the paragraph dealing with the president's power in the field of foreign policy gave a general mandate, foreign policy decision-making did not develop as president-centric before the Second World War. Of the post-Cold War presidents, Urho Kekkonen in particular concentrated all power in foreign policy in himself, so that the government including the foreign minister (unless he was Kekkonen's trusted man), let alone the Parliament, were not able to influence foreign policy decision-making. Criticized by some, this practice was not changed until after the end of the Cold War. Kekkonen dominated Finnish political life from 1962 until his retirement for reasons of health in September 1982.

9 For an overview of Finland's economic relationship to the EC/EC see Ojanen (1997: ch. 5).

10 He admits that he refrained from saying so publicly before Finland had actually been accepted as a member, so that the country might not be perceived as less secure, in the event that Finland's entry bid was unsuccessful (Jakobson 1998: 111).

11 The Finns voted for EU membership by a majority of 57 per cent to 43 per cent on 16 October 1994 (Tiilikainen 1996: 129).

12 The differences are greater between him and the current President, Tarjo Halonen, who has been far more sceptical about the development of a European defence policy. However, recently her attitude seems to have changed towards being more in line with that of the former Finnish prime minister (Lipponen) and the former president (Ahtisaari) (Forsberg 2001a).

13 Finland is the only Nordic country to rule out participation in peace enforcement operations by law (Jakobsen, forthcoming: ch. 4).

14 The debate continued, however. The reservation on 'peace enforcement' led to embarrassing problems of interpretation in specific operations, as it was not clear what the Finnish troops could do and what the legislation impeded them from doing. A committee was established in 1999 to examine the need for further amendments to the legislation. It did not suggest any changes in the main principles – that a participation required a mandate from the UN or OSCE, or that Finland would not take part in operations where the parties of the conflict were forced by coercive means to give up their weapons – but the committee did recommend removing the conditions, so that once a political decision was made to send Finnish troops to a mission, there would be no limits as to what the mission could involve itself in (Ojanen et al. 2000: 134–5).

15 Despite this continued traditionalism the Finnish defence budgets have remained relatively modest. Less than 2 per cent of GNP is used on defence. Due to a strong public will to participate in the Finnish defence forces it has been possible to keep soldiers' salaries low. This, in turn, has made it possible to use a certain percentage on procurement. But as the investments have primarily been used to buy F-18s and upgrade the three rapid reactions brigades, it has left the rest of the defence Finnish defence forces unchanged (Holmen and Ulriksen 2000: 49).

16 The other crises are regional crises that may have repercussions on Finland; political, economic and military pressure, associated with a threat of or a limited use of military force; a surprise attack ('strategic strike') with standing forces, aimed at paralysing or seizing key areas and objectives in Finland, as well as subjugating the Finnish national leadership.

17 In the 1997 report the wartime strength of the Finnish defence forces was to be cut from 540,000 to 430,000 by the year 2008 and the number of army brigades was to be reduced from 27 to 22 (Council of State 2001: 22).

18 The same trend continues: according to the review, the total number is brought down to 350,000 by the year 2008 (Council of State 2001: 10). Assuming that the situation in Northern Europe remains stable, the number of mobilizable troops might even decrease further.

19 The 1997 report was to be reviewed at intervals; the first review was presented in 2001, and a comprehensive report on long-term plans for Finland's defence system was made in 2004.

6 DENMARK: RELUCTANT ADAPTER

1 The Danish historian, Carsten Holbraad, argues that neutrality is what has defined Denmark's security policy since 1720, including the Cold War period. He distinguishes between *aligned neutrality* (1720–1807), *isolated neutrality* (1814–1920), *defenceless neutrality* (1920–45), *non-aligned neutrality* (1945–9) and *latent neutrality* (1949–89) (Holbraad 1991). In using this concept in relation to the two latter periods he cites the Danish scepticism in relation to international commitments after the Second World War, the reluctance of the Danish government in 1948–9 to join the new Atlantic Pact, and the country's subsequent hesitant, low-profile policy as a NATO member. While the validity of this argument may seem to have been confirmed by Denmark's reluctance to take part in the European integration process, as expressed not least in the four exemptions from the Maastricht Treaty obtained in 1992, it has also been strongly criticized. Hans Branner, for instance, argues that neutrality is both an inadequate and a misleading term to describe the Danish foreign policy tradition after 1949, which, he maintains, is a tradition based on an active international engagement (Branner 2000: 213). Referring to the current policy, Uffe Østergaard agrees with Branner, arguing that Holbraad's approach does not allow for the present Danish policy of 'active internationalism'. He also argues that Holbraad misconceives the very meaning of 'Denmark' and 'Danish' in seeing 'Denmark' of the different periods as one and the same entity (Østergaard 2000: 141). Branner also points out that Danish politicians have never considered a return to the policy of neutrality. He argues 'in 1949, the alliance is chosen, although half-heartedly, over the alternative of continued neutrality, and at no point since then has there been any question of altering this fundamental choice' (Branner 2000: 190).

2 Since these wars were 'local' conflicts, and Denmark was not an ally of a great power in a major war, its participation may be understood as being compatible with neutrality (Holbraad 1991: 20–3).

3 The 'footnote' policy referred to a situation where the Conservative-Liberal minority government had to run a foreign policy to which it was itself opposed. When their parliamentary 'partner' – the Social Liberals – voted with the opposition, the government, rather than taking the parliamentary consequence of having a majority against it in an important issue such as defence, stayed in power but inserted footnotes in a number of NATO communiqués. The starting point was the new, 'second Cold War' US security priorities, which were seen as confrontational, based on marked nuclear rearmament, abandonment of arms control and heightened demands on the USSR on the arms control negotiation front. In this situation, the government chose to pursue a policy in NATO which expressed Danish reservations towards NATO's general policy on nuclear arms in East–West negotiations (Heurlin 2001: 10).

4 Towards the end of the year Denmark became an observer in the WEU. Shortly after this, the opposition parties started to argue for full membership.

5 As part of the Defence Agreement of 8 December 1995 concerning the organization of the defence forces for the period 1995–99, it was decided to appoint a Defence Commission to review the organization of the defence forces in light of developments in the security political context. On 15 January 1997 the Defence Commission started its work. The overall conclusion, presented in November 1998, was that international efforts should be strengthened and that territorial defence should be toned down in priority (Forsvarskommissionen 1998).

6 A clarification was made at the General Affairs Council, 8 October 2001. In a report on the Danish defence exception the government made it clear that Denmark should not to participate in any decision taken in the Military Committee (Udenrigsministeriet 2001b).

7 On 25 May 1999, six political parties, representing 80 per cent of the seats in the Danish Parliament, signed the Defence Agreement for the period 2000–4. Thus, three times in the last decade, Danish representatives agreed to put more emphasis on international as opposed to national defence (Hillingsø 2001: 5).

8 On Wednesday 20 December, the long-time Danish Foreign Minister Niels Helveg Petersen (1993–2000) suddenly resigned. At a local press conference he admitted that he had resigned 'because he was not able to act as a Foreign Minister as long as Denmark had exceptions concerning the EU Treaty'. In fact, he found the exceptions to be in conflict with Danish interests. During the same period, the Minister of Defence, Hans Hækkerup, was appointed head of the UN mission in Bosnia, thus necessitating the appointment of a new Minister of Defence. Prime Minister Nyrup Rasmussen rearranged the cabinet on December 21. The former Minister of Finance, Mogens Lykketoft, became the new Foreign Minister, while the former Minister of Foreign Aid, Jan Trøjborg, was appointed Minister of Defence (http://www.folkestyre.dk/Nyhed/update_danmark.htm).

9 As a result of the Danish elections of 20 November, a new Liberal-Conservative government was brought into power. The government consisted of, among others, Anders Fogh Rasmussen as Prime Minister, Per Stig Møller as Minister of Foreign Affairs and Svend Aage Jensby as Minister of Defence.

10 As I am writing this book, Denmark has not yet had its referendum on the Constitutional Treaty, and there is a disagreement among the political leadership whether Denmark should have a second referendum on its opt-outs if the Treaty is accepted.

11 The fact that Denmark did not react to the US National Missile Defence is a clear expression of this (Larsen 2002a: 139).

12 A humanitarian intervention is an armed intervention in another state, without the agreement of that state, to address (the threat of) a humanitarian disaster, in particular caused by grave and large-scale violations of fundamental human rights (DUPI 1999: 11).

13 Fredriksen has a broad experience in international civilian crisis management through the UN and was recently in charge of the UN police operation in Kosovo.

7 NORWAY: ADAPTIVE NON-MEMBER

1 See for instance Sverdrup (1998).

2 While no permanent NATO bases existed in Norway, it would be possible for NATO to stock various types of materiel for use in the case of a crisis.

3 While the Norwegian political leadership was against nuclear weapons being stocked or used in Norway, the anti-nuclear weapons position was somewhat

modified later, when the government tried to reassure the alliance by making it clear that the ban on nuclear weapons might at any time be reconsidered if so warranted by changed circumstances. Then Norway might consider allowing allied forces coming to Norway's assistance in a crisis to be equipped with nuclear weapons.

4 This was not due to these 'self-imposed restraints', but rather a consequence of the slow build-up of NATO's conventional military strength in Europe, and the concentration of attention on the problems of the Central Front (Riste 2002: 217–25).

5 During the Cold War, Norway distinguished between two international external policy arenas. In the arena of narrow security policy and military defence, Norway kept as low a profile as possible in NATO (integration and shielding) in order not to provoke the Soviet Union. In the arena of foreign policy, development assistance and conflict resolution, however, Norway sought a high profile in the UN and the CSCE (Thune and Ulriksen 2002: 113–14).

6 It was on 9 April 1940 that Norway was invaded and thereafter occupied by Nazi forces.

7 The Barents Initiative includes the following fields of co-operation: economy, trade, science and technology, tourism, the environment, infrastructure, educational and cultural exchange as well as the improvement of the situation of the indigenous peoples in the North. At the second meeting of the Barents Council in 1994, health issues were included as the eighth area of co-operation. Finally, the Council also decided at its sixth meeting in 1999 to include youth policy as one of its development areas.

8 Apart from its seven members (Denmark, European Commission, Finland, Iceland, Norway, Russian Federation and Sweden) there are nine observers: Canada, France, Germany, Italy, Japan, the Netherlands, Poland, the United Kingdom and the USA.

9 The signing of the EEA Agreement in 1992 was the result of a process that started in 1986. When the EC signed the Single European Act (SEA), it became important for Norway to examine its relationship to the integration process. The EEA Agreement, which was an agreement between the EFTA countries and the EC, gave Norway access to the internal market. The agreement included common rules and common conditions for competition. But the EFTA countries did not gain any influence over decisions taken in the EC, and had to incorporate the Community's directives and regulations in this area into their national legislation. Even though some common institutions were established (the EEA Council and EEA Committee), these were used only for consultations. The EEA Agreement – the most important international agreement that Norway ever had signed – was adopted in October 1992.

10 Norway's application was submitted in November 1992 after a heavy debate within the ruling Labour Party under the leadership of Prime Minister Gro Harlem Brundtland.

11 This co-operation has been limited to the exchange of information and assistance in police investigations. An electronic network for information, SIS, has been established with a central base in Strasbourg and local bases in each country.

12 The Dublin Convention, which entered into force in September 1997, sets up a detailed system to allocate responsibility for the examination of asylum applications.

13 Mutual Legal Assistance in Criminal Matters, adopted in May 2000.

14 The Czech Republic, Hungary, Iceland, Norway, Poland and Turkey.

15 http://www.atlanterhavskomiteen.no/publikasjoner/andre/dokumenter/ memo.htm.

16 In the event of an operational phase where the contributing non-members are invited to participate in an *ad hoc* committee of contributors. In such a phase, the 'appropriate arrangements' will imply day-to-day consultations and discussions concerning how to conduct the operation.
17 Information based on interviews with the representatives at the Norwegian delegation to the EU, June 2001.
18 Quoted in NATO fact sheet on DCI (http://www.nato.int/docu/facts/2000/nato-dci.htm).
19 A co-operation committee was established in 1994 with the participation of the Ministry of Foreign Affairs, Ministry of Defence, Ministry of Justice, the military intelligence units (FO and FOE) and the police intelligence unit (POT).
20 Former Prime Minister Kåre Willoch, who led the Vulnerability Commission 2000, has criticized the White Book. In his view, only an independent ministry can ensure independence from the political leaders who have responsibility for the economy that they will control.
21 Except for an increase in the tasks and responsibilities of the Coast Guard and the forces supervising Norway's borders with Russia (Forsvarsdepartementet 2001: 33).
22 The number of civilian personnel has increased significantly due to the establishment of three rapid reaction forces: NORSTAFF, NORDEM and the NST. NORSTAFF is a civilian standby force set up after the humanitarian crisis in Northern Iraq in 1991 to enhance the UN's capacity to help and protect refugees and internally displaced persons in humanitarian emergencies. Today NORSTAFF has emergency response agreements with eight UN organizations but has also made personnel available for the OSCE. NORDEM, established in 1993, is made up of a Resource Bank and a Standby Force. It has expertise in the areas of election assistance, democratic organizations, news mass media, minority protection, constitutional reform, rule of law, good governance, and human rights education. The NST is part of the Norwegian civilian defence and was established in 1997. Its standby teams can provide assistance in connection with international disasters at short notice.
23 Norway participated in twenty-four international police operations between 1989 and 2000; 600 Norwegian police officers were engaged in such operations. It has also been decided that 1 per cent of the national police force shall be earmarked for international operations (http://www.politi.no/tema/civpol.shtml)
24 As a result, Norwegian police are represented as advisers both in the UN headquarters in New York and at the Norwegian EU delegation in Brussels (http://www.politi.no/tema/civpol.shtml).

8 COMPARISONS, CONCLUSIONS AND IMPLICATIONS

1 Humanitarian and rescue tasks, peacekeeping tasks and tasks of combat forces in crisis management, including peace-making (see also Chapter 2, note 18)

REFERENCES

Adler, E. (1997a) 'Imagined (Security) Communities: Cognitive Regions in International Relations', *Millennium: Journal of International Studies* 26 (2): 249–77.

Adler, E. (1997b) 'Seizing the Middle Ground. Constructivism in World Politics', *European Journal of International Relations* 3 (3): 319–63.

Adler, E. (2002) 'Constructivism and International Relations', in W. Carlsnaes, T. Risse and B. A. Simmons (eds), *Handbook of International Relations*, London: Sage, pp. 95–118.

Adler, E. and M. Barnett (eds) (1998) *Security Communities*, Cambridge: Cambridge University Press.

Aftenposten (2001a) 'NATOs leder går for langt', 3 February.

Aftenposten (2001b) 'Trusselen om invasjon er forsvunnet', 11 February.

Aftonbladet (2000) 'Var är debatten om svensk neutralitet?', 28 December.

Aggestam, L. (2005) 'Role Theory and European Foreign Policy Analysis', Paper presented at ECPR Joint Session, Granada, 14–19 April.

Agrell, W. (2000) *'Fred och fruktan. Sveriges säkerhetspolitiska historia 1918–2000'*, Falun: Historiska Media.

Allen, D. and M. Smith (1990) 'Western Europe's Presence in the Contemporary International Arena', *Review of International Affairs* 16 (1): 19–37.

Andersen, J. H. (2000) 'Fra atlantisk sikkerhet til europeisk usikkerhet? En studie av utenriksdepartementets og forsvarsdepartementets responser på endrede sikkerhetspolitiske rammebetingelser', *Arena Report* 2, Oslo: Arena.

Andersen, S. S. and K. A. Eliassen (eds) (1993) *Making Policy in Europe. The Europeification of National Policy-making*, London: Sage.

Anderson, B. (1991) *Imagined Communities: Reflections on the Origin and Spread of Nationalism*, New York: Verso.

Andolf, G. (1995) 'Amerikanska flygare i Sverige 1944–45', in B. Huldt and K. R. Böhme (eds), *Horisonten klarnar. 1945 – krigslut*, Stockholm: Norstedts Tryckeri AB, pp. 13–39.

Andrén, N. and Y. Möller (1990) *Från Undén til Palme. Svensk utrikespolitik efter andra världskriget*, Lund: Norstedts.

Antola, E. (1999) 'From the European Rim to the Core: The European Policy of Finland in the 1990's', in *Northern Dimensions*, Helsinki: Finnish Institute of International Affairs, pp. 5–10.

Archer, C. (1996) 'Nordic Perspectives on European Security', in A. Orrenius and

L. Truedson (eds), *Visions of European Security – Focal Point Sweden and Northern Europe*, Stockholm: The Olof Palme International Center, pp. 19–31.

Archer, C. and I. Sogner (1998) *Norway, European Integration and Atlantic Security*, London: Sage.

Argyris, C. and D. A. Schön (1978) *Organizational Learning: A Theory of Action Perspective*, Reading, MA: Addison-Wesley.

Arter, D. (1995) 'The EU Referendum in Finland on 16 October 1994: A Vote for the West, Not for Maastricht', *Journal of Common Market Studies* 33 (3): 677–97.

Baldwin, D. (1995) 'Security Studies and the End of the Cold War', *World Politics*, 48 (October): 117–41.

Bengtsson, R. and M. Ericson (2001) 'La réorganization dans l'internationalisation', in P. Buffotot (ed.), *La défense en Europe*, Paris: La documentation Française (Notes et études documentaires), pp. 189–99.

Bertelsmann Foundation (ed.) (2000) *Enhancing the European Union as an International Security Actor: A Strategy for Action*, Gütersloh: Bertelsmann Foundation.

Bigo, D. (1996) *Policies en réseaux. L'expérience européenne*, Paris: Presses de Science Po.

Björkdahl, A. (2002) 'From Idea to Norm. Promoting Conflict Prevention', PhD thesis, Lund: Department of Political Science, Lund University.

Björklund, L. (2003) 'Sveriges och Europas sikkerhet', Speech given at Folk och Försvars rikskonferens in Sälen, 22 January.

Björklund, L. (2004) 'Swedish Defence Policy in Times of Change', Speech given in Bern, 22 October.

Boekle, H., J. Nadoll and Bernard Stahl (2001) 'European Foreign Policy and National Identity: Detecting the Link', Paper presented at the fourth pan-European International Relations Conference, Canterbury, 6–10 September.

Boekle, H., V. Rittberger and W. Wagner (1999) ' "Norms and Foreign Policy": Constructivist Foreign Policy Theory', *Working Papers* 34a, Tübingen: Center for International Relations, University of Tübingen.

den Boer, M. and J. Monar (2002) '11 September and the Challenge of Global Terrorism to the EU as a Security Actor', *Journal of Common Market Studies* 40 (1, Supplement: The European Union, 2001/2002 Annual review of the EU): 11–28.

Bondevik, K. M. (1998) 'Regjeringens Europapolitikk', *Arena Working Papers* 6, Oslo: Arena.

Branner, H. (2000) 'The Danish Foreign Policy Tradition and the European Context', in H. Branner and M. Kelstrup (eds), *Denmark's Policy Towards Europe After 1945*, Odense: Odense University Press, pp. 185–220.

Bretherton, C. and J. Vogler (1999) *The European Union as a Global Actor*, London and New York: Routledge.

Browning, C. (1999) 'Coming Home or Moving Home? "Westernizing" Narratives in Finnish Foreign Policy and the Re-interpretation of Past Identities', *Working Papers* 16, Helsinki: UPI.

Brundtland, A. O. (1966) 'Nordisk balanse før og nå', *Internasjonal Politikk* 5: 491–541.

Brundtland, A. O. (1981) 'The Nordic Balance and its Possible Relevance for Europe', *Working Papers* 229, Oslo: NUPI.

Brundtland, A. O. (1994) 'Nordic Security at the End of the Cold War: Old Legacies and New Challenges', in Arne Olav Brundtland and Don M. Snider (eds),

Nordic–Baltic Security. An International Perspective, Washington, DC: CSIS/ NUPI, pp. 1–30.

Bull, H. (1977) *The Anarchical Society: A Study of Order in World Politics*, London: Macmillan.

Bull, H. (1982) 'Civilian Power Europe: A Contradiction in Terms?', *Journal of Common Market Studies* 21 (2): 149–64.

Buzan, B. (1991) *People, States and Fear: A Security Agenda for the Post-Cold War Era*, Brighton: Wheatsheaf.

Buzan, B., O. Wæver and J. de Wilde (1998) *Security. A New Framework for Analysis*, Boulder, CO: Lynne Rienner.

Börzel, T. A. (1999) 'Towards Convergence in Europe? Institutional Adaptation to Europeanization in Germany and Spain', *Journal of Common Market Studies* 39 (4): 604–28.

Börzel, T. A. (2002) 'Member State Responses to Europeanization', *Journal of Common Market Studies* 40 (2): 193–214.

Börzel, T. A. and T. Risse (2000) 'When Europe Hits Home. Europeanization and Domestic Change', *Working Papers* 56, Florence: European University Institute.

Carlsnaes, W. (1992) 'The Agency-Structure Problem in Foreign Policy Analysis', *International Studies Quarterly* 36: 245–70.

Carlsnaes, W. (1993a) 'On Analysing the Dynamics of Foreign Policy Change. A Critique and Reconceptualization', *Cooperation and Conflict* 28 (1): 5–30.

Carlsnaes, W. (1993b) 'Sweden Facing the New Europe: Whither Neutrality?' *European Security* 2 (1): 71–89.

Checkel, J. (1997) 'International Norms and Domestic Politics. Bridging the Rationalist-Constructivist Divide', *European Journal of International Relations* 3 (4): 473–95.

Checkel, J. (1998) 'The Constructivist Turn in International Relations', *World Politics* 50 (January): 324–48.

Checkel, J. (1999) 'Why Comply? Constructivism, Social Norms and the Study of International Institutions', *Working Papers* 24, Oslo: Arena.

Checkel, J. (2001) 'Social Learning and European Identity Change', *International Organization* 55 (3): 553–88.

Christiansen, T. (1997) 'The Social Construction of European Integration', in Knud Erik Jørgensen (ed.), *Constructivism, International Relations and European Studies*, Aarhus University: Department of Political Science, pp. 25–36.

Christiansen, T., K. E. Jørgensen and A. Wiener (eds) (2001) *The Social Construction of Europe*, London: Sage.

Claes, D. H. and B. S. Tranøy (eds) (1999) *Utenfor, Annerledes og Suveren*, Bergen: Fagbokforlaget.

Cooper, R. (2003) *The Breaking of Nations. Order and Chaos in the Twenty-First Century*, London: Atlantic Books.

Council of State (1995) 'Security in a Changing World: Guidelines for Finland's Security Policy', *Report by the Council of State to the Parliament*, Helsinki: The Council of State (on-line version: http://virtual.finland.fi/finfo/english/ tpseng.html).

Council of State (1997) 'The European Security Development and Finnish Defence', *Report by the Council of State to Parliament*, Helsinki: The Council of State.

Council of State (2001) 'The Finnish Security and Defence Policy', *Report by the Council of State to the Parliament*, Helsinki: The Council of State.

Cowles, M., J. Caporaso and T. Risse (eds) (2001) *Transforming Europe. Europeanization and Domestic Change*, London: Cornell University Press.

Cramér, P. (1998) *Neutralitet och Europeisk Integration*, Stockholm: Norstedts juridik AB.

Croft, S. (2000) 'The EU, NATO and Europeanization: The Return of Architectural Debate', *European Security* 9 (3): 1–20.

Cronenberg, A. (1986) 'Säkerhetspolitik och krigsplanering. Hovudlinjer i arméns operativa planering 1906–1945', in Bo Hugemark (ed.), *Neutralitet och försvar*, Stockholm: Militärhistoriska Förlaget, pp. 44–165.

Cronin, B. (1999) *Community Under Anarchy*, New York: Columbia University Press.

Dagens Nyheter (2000) 'President Chirac i neutrala Sverige', 12 April.

Dagens Nyheter (2001) 'Neutralitetens tid är utmatt', 18 November.

Dagens Nyheter og *Helsingin Sanomat* (1996) 'Article by Ministers for Foreign Affairs L. Hjelm-Wallén and T. Halonen on a Swedish-Finnish Initiative Designed to Strengthen the EU's Conflict Management Capability', 12 April. http://europa.eu.int/en/agenda/igc-home/ms-doc/state-fi/210496.html

Dagsavisen (2001) 'Vi må lytte til svenskene', 21 January.

Dahl, A. (2002) 'Activist Sweden: The Last Defender of Non-Alignment', in A. Dahl and N. Hillmer (eds), *Activism and (Non) Alignment*, Stockholm: Utenrikspolitiska Institutet (Conference Papers 31), pp. 139–50.

Delors, J. (1991) *European Integration and Security*, Speech at IISS in London, 7 March, Europe Documents 1699.

Deutsch, K. W. (1957) *Political Community and the North Atlantic Area. International Organization in the Light of Historical Experience*, Princeton, NJ: Princeton University Press.

Devold, K. K. (2004) 'Norge og EUs innsatsstyrker', *Dagbladet*, 9 December.

Dokken, K. (1997) 'Environment, Security and Regional Integration in West Africa', Dr philos. dissertation, Oslo: Department of Political Science, University of Oslo.

Duchêne, F. (1972) 'Europe's Role in World Peace', in Richard Mayne (ed.), *Europe Tomorrow*, London: Fontana, pp. 32–47.

Duchêne, F. (1973) 'The European Community and the Uncertainties of Interdependence', in M. Kohnstamm and W. Hager (eds), *A Nation Writ Large? Foreign Policy Problems before the European Communities*, London: Macmillan, pp. 1–21.

Duchêne, F. (2002–2003) 'Mars, Vénus et l'Olympe', *Commentaire* 100 (winter): 773–9.

Duff, A. (1994) 'The Main Reforms', in Andrew Duff, John Pinder and Roy Pryce (eds), *Maastricht and Beyond*, London and New York: Routledge, pp. 19–35.

Duke, S. (2000) *The Elusive Quest for European Security*, Basingstoke: Macmillan (speech given at St Anthony's College, Oxford).

DUPI (1999) *Humanitær intervention, Retlige og politiske aspekter*, Copenhagen: DUPI.

Duval, M. (1996) 'La Crise de la CED (1950–1954)', in Maurice Vaïsse, Pierre Mélandri and Frédéric Bozo (eds), *La France et L'OTAN 1949–1996*, Paris: Edition Complexe, pp. 189–216.

Economist, The (2001) 'Sweden's neutrality. The past is past', 13 October.

Eekelen, V. (1998) *Debating European Security, 1948–1998*, Brussels, The Hague: CEPS/Sdu Publishers.

Ehrhart, H. G. (2001) 'What Model for CFSP?', *Chaillot Papers* 55, Paris: EU ISS.

Ekengren, M. and B. Sundelius (1998) 'Sweden: The State Joins the European Union', in K. Hanf and B. Soetendorp (eds), *Adapting to European Integration. Small States and the European Union*, London: Longman, pp. 131–48.

Eksborg, A. L. (2002) 'An Emergency Management Agency – Why?', Speech given at the Solbacka Course, 20 August (http://www.krisberedskapsmyndigheten.se/english/).

Eriksson, J., U. Bjereld, F., Bynander, E. Noreen and A. Robertson (2001) 'Försvaret skapar egna hotbilder', *Dagens Nyheter*, 7 February.

European Commission (1973) Bulletin of the European Communities, No. 12/1973.

European Commission (2000) 'Shaping the New Europe, Strategic Objectives 2000–2005', COM(2000)154, Brussels.

European Commission (2001) 'Communication on Conflict Prevention', COM(2001)211 final, Brussels.

European Constitution (2004) 'Treaty Establishing a Constitution for Europe', CIG 87/1/04 REV 1.

European Council (1992) 'Treaty on the European Union', Maastricht: European Council.

European Council (1997) 'Treaty on the European Union', Amsterdam: European Council.

European Council (1999) 'Presidency Conclusions', Cologne, 3–4 June.

European Council (2001a) 'Conclusions and Plan of Action', Brussels, 21 September.

European Council (2001b) 'EU Programme for the Prevention of Violent Conflicts', *Presidency Conclusions*: Annexe III, Gothenburg, 15–16 June.

European Council (2001c) 'Presidency Conclusions', Gothenburg, 15–16 June.

European Council (2002a) 'Implementation of the EU Programme of Violent Conflicts', Presidency Conclusions: Annexe VIII, Seville, 18 June.

European Council (2002b) 'Presidency Conclusions', Seville, 21–22 June.

European Council (2003) 'A Secure Europe in a Better World, European Security Strategy', Brussels, 12 December.

Featherstone, K. (2002) 'Europeanization in Theory and Practice', in E. Davidson, A. Eriksson and J. Hallenberg (eds), *Europeanization of Security and Defence Policy*, Stockholm: The Swedish National Defence College, pp. 13–20.

Featherstone, K. and G. Kazamias (eds) (2001) *Europeanization and the Southern Periphery*, London: Frank Cass.

Finnemore, M. (1996) *National Interests in International Society*, Ithaca, NY: Cornell University Press.

Finnemore, M. and K. Sikkink (1998) 'International Norm Dynamics and Political Change', *International Organization* 52 (4): 887–917.

Forsberg, T. (2001a), 'Soft Means to Hard Security, Finland and the Northern Dimension of the European Union', in P. Joenniemi and J. Viktorova (eds), *Regional Dimensions of Security in Border Areas of Northern and Eastern Europe*, Tartu: Peipsi Center for Transboundary Cooperation.

Forsberg, T. (2001b) 'One Foreign Policy or Two?' in *Northern Dimensions*, Helsinki: Finnish Institute of Foreign Affairs, pp. 3–11,

Forsvarsdepartementet (1992–1993) 'Hovedretningslinjer for Forsvarets virksomhet i tiden 1994–98' *Stortingsmelding* 16, Oslo.

Forsvarsdepartementet (1997–1998) 'Hovedretningslinjer for Forsvarets virksomhet og utvikling i tiden 1999–2002', *Stortingsmelding* 22, Oslo.

208

REFERENCES

Forsvarsdepartementet (1998–1999) 'Tilpasning av forsvaret til deltakelse i internasjonale operasjoner', *Stortingsmelding* 38, Oslo.

Forsvarsdepartementet (2001) 'Omleggingen av forsvaret i perioden 2002–2005', *Stortingsproposisjon* 45, Oslo.

Forsvarsdepartementet (2002) 'Gjennomføringsproposisjonen – utfyllende rammer for omleggingen av Forsvaret i perioden 2002–2005', *Stortingsproposisjon* 55, Oslo.

Forsvarsdepartementet (2004) 'Den videre moderninseringen av forsvaret i perioden 2005–2008', *Stortingsproposisjon* 42, Oslo.

Forsvarsdepartementet (2005) *Styrke og relevans – Strategisk konsept for forsvaret*, Oslo

Forsvarsjefen (2000) 'Forsvarsstudie 2000', *Sluttrapport*, Oslo: Forsvaret.

Forsvarskomiteen (2001) 'Instilling fra forsvarskomiteen om omleggingen av forsvaret i perioden 2002–2005', *Innst. S*, 342, Oslo.

Forsvarskommissionen (1998) 'Fremtidens Forsvar', Hovedbind, Copenhagen.

Forsvarsministeriet (1998) 'Årlig redegørelse', Copenhagen, http://www.forsvarsministeriet.dk/index.asp?cat_id=277.

Forsvarsministeriet (1999) 'Årlig redegjørelse', Copenhagen, http://www.forsvarsministeriet.dk/index.asp?cat_id=277.

Forsvarsministeriet (2000) 'Årlig redegørelse', Copenhagen, http://www.forsvarsministeriet.dk/index.asp?cat_id=277.

Forsvarsministeriet (2001) 'Årlig redegørelse', Copenhagen, http://www.forsvarsministeriet.dk/index.asp?cat_id=277.

Forsvarsministeriet (2002) 'Årlig redegørelse', Copenhagen, http://www.forsvarsministeriet.dk/index.asp?cat_id=277.

Forsvarsministeriet (2004) 'En verden i forandring – et forsvar i forandring', Regeringens forsvarsoplæg 2005–2009, Presented in March 2004.

Frantzen, H. A. (2003) 'NATO and Peace Support Operations 1991–1999: Policies and Doctrines. A Study of NATO and Britain, Canada, and Denmark', unpublished thesis, King's College, University of London.

Försvarsberedningen (1999) 'Förandrad omvärld – omdanat försvar', *DS* 12, Stockholm: Försvarsdepartementet.

Försvarsberedningen (2001) 'Gränseöverskridande sårbarhet – gemensam säkerhet', *DS* 14, Stockholm: Försvarsdepartementet.

Försvarsdepartementet (1995) 'Sverige i Europa och världen, Säkerhetspolitisk rapport från Försvarsberedningen', *DS* 28, Stockholm: Försvarsdepartementet.

Försvarsdepartementet (1999–2000) 'Det nya försvaret', *Proposition*, 30, Stockholm: Försvardepartementet.

Försvarsdepartementet (2001–2002) 'Fortsatt förnyelse av totalforsvaret', *Proposition* 10, Stockholm.

Försvarsdepartementet (2001/02) 'Samhällets säkerhet och beredskap', *Proposition* 158, Stockholm: Försvarsdepartementet.

Gade, S. (2004) 'Dansk forsvar som sikkerhetspolitisk instrument', Speech given to the Foreign Policy Society, Copenhagen, 4 October.

Gade, S. (2005) Speech given at the conference 'Homeland Security – The Nordic Challenges', Copenhagen, 18 April.

George, A. L. (1979) 'Case Studies and Theory Development: The Method of Structured, Focused Comparison', in P. G. Lauren (ed.), *Diplomacy: New Approaches in History, Theory, and Policy*, New York: Free Press, pp. 43–68.

Ginsberg, R. H. (1999) 'Conceptualizing the European Union as an International Actor: Narrowing the Theoretical Capability–Expectation Gap', *Journal of Common Market Studies* 37 (3): 429–54.

Ginsberg, R. H. (2001) *The European Union in International Politics: Baptism by Fire*, Lanham: Rowman and Littlefield.

Godal, B. T. (1993) 'Innlegg holdt ved åpningen av Norges medlemskapsforhandlinger med EF', in *Stortingsmelding* 40, *Om medlemskap i Den europeiske union*, Oslo: Utenriksdepartementet, pp. 432–36.

Goldmann, K. (1988) *Change and Stability in Foreign Policy: The Problems and Possibilities of Détente*, Princeton, NJ: Princeton University Press.

Gourlay, C. (2004) 'European Union Procedures and Resources for Crisis Management', *International Peacekeeping* 11 (3): 404–21.

Gregory, F. (2003) 'The EU's Role in the War on Terror', *Jane's Intelligence Review*, 15 (1): 14–17.

Græger, N. (2002) 'Norway and the EU's Defence Dimension: A "Troops for Influence" Strategy', in N. Græger, H. Larsen and H. Ojanen (eds), *The ESDP and the Nordic Countries. Four Variations on a Theme*, Helsinki: Finnish Institute of International Affairs, pp. 33–89.

Gustavsson, J. (1998) *The Politics of Foreign Policy Change. Explaining the Swedish Reorganization on EC Membership*, Lund: Lund University Press.

Haas, E. B. (1958) *The Uniting of Europe: Political, Social and Economic Forces 1950–1957*, Stanford, CA: Stanford University Press.

Haas, E. B. (1964) *Beyond the Nation-State: Functionalism and International Organization*, Stanford, CA: Stanford University Press.

Haas, E. B, (1990) *When Knowledge is Power. Three Models of Change in International Organizations*, Berkeley, CA: University of California Press.

Haldén, E. (2001) 'Försvaret och det vidgade säkerhetsbegrepet', *Debattserien* FORBER0104, Stockholm: Försvarsberedningen.

Hallenberg, J. (2000) 'Swedish Foreign and Security Policy', in Lee Miles (ed.), *Sweden and the European Union Evaluated*, London and New York: Continuum, pp. 19–32.

Hanf, K. and B. Soetendorp (eds) (1998) *Adapting to European Integration. Small States and the European Union*, London: Longman.

Hansen, L. and O. Wæver (eds) (2002) *European Integration and National Identity. The Challenge of the Nordic States*, London: Routledge.

Heikka, H. (2003) 'Maintaining a Balance of Power that Favours Human Freedom', *UPI Working Papers* 39, Helsinki: Finnish Institute of International Affairs.

Heisbourg, F. (2000) 'Europe's Strategic Ambitions: The Limits of Ambiguity', *Survival* 42 (2): 5–15.

Herolf, G. (2000) 'The Swedish Approach: Constructive Competition for a Common Goal', in G. Bonvicini, T. Vaahtoranta and W. Wessels (eds), *The Northern EU. National Views on the Emerging Security Dimension*, Helsinki: Finnish Institute of International Affairs, pp. 141–60.

Herz, J. (1950) 'Idealist Internationalism and the Security Dilemma', *World Politics* 2: 157–80.

Heurlin, B. (2001) 'Danish Security Policy over the Last 50 Years – Long-Term Essential Security Priorities', *Working Papers* 7, Copenhagen: DUPI.

Hill, C. (1993) 'The Capability–Expectation Gap, or Conceptualizing Europe's International Role', *Journal of Common Market Studies* 31 (3): 305–28.

REFERENCES

Hillingsø, K. G. (2001) 'Det danske forsvaret i omstilling', *Det sikkerhetspolitiske bibliotek* 2, Oslo: Den norske Atlanterhavskomité.

Hoffmann, S. (2000) 'Towards a Common Foreign and Security Policy?', *Journal of International Affairs* 38 (2): 189–99.

Holbraad, C. (1991) *Danish Neutrality. A Study in the Foreign Policy of a Small State*, Oxford: Clarendon Press.

Hollis, M. and S. Smith (1990) *Explaining and Understanding International Relations*, Oxford: Clarendon Press.

Holm, H. H. (1997) 'Denmark's Active Internationalism. Advocating International Norms with Domestic Constraints', in B. Heurlin and H. Mouritzen (eds), *Danish Foreign Policy Yearbook*, Copenhagen: DUPI, pp. 52–80.

Holm, H. H. (2002) 'The Rise and Decline of Foreign Policy Activism: The Case of Denmark', in A. Dahl and N. Hillmer (eds), *Activism and (Non)Alignment*, Stockholm: Utenrikspolitiska institutet, pp. 83–102.

Holmen, B. and S. Ulriksen (2000) 'Norden i felt: På oppdrag for FN og NATO', *Report* 257, Oslo: NUPI.

Holst, J. J. (1983) 'The "Nordic Balance" and the Northern Flank: A Norwegian Perspective', *Working Papers* 287, Oslo: NUPI.

Honkanen, K. (2002) 'The Influence of Small States on NATO Decision-Making. The Membership Experiences of Denmark, Norway, Hungary and the Czech Republic', *Användarrapport* FOI-R-0548SE, Stockholm: Swedish Defence Research Agency.

Hopf, T. (2002) *Social Construction of International Politics. Identities and Foreign Policies, Moscow, 1955 and 1999*, Ithaca, NY, and London: Cornell University Press.

Howorth (2000) 'Britain, France and the European Defence Initiative', *Survival* 42 (2): 33–55.

Huldt, B. (1990) 'Svensk neutralitet – historia och framtidsperspektiv', in Ulla Nordlöf-laberkrantz (ed.), *Svensk neutralitet, Europa och EG*, Stockholm: Utenrikspolitiska Institutet, pp. 7–26.

ICG (2002) 'EU Crisis Response Capabilities: An Update', *Issues Briefing*, Brussels: International Crisis Group.

Ikenberry, J. G. and Charles A. Kupchan (1990) 'Socialisation and Hegemonic Power', *International Organization* 44 (3): 283–315.

Informationen (2001) 'EU klar til justering af forbehold', *Informationen*, 5 February.

Ingebritsen, C. (1998) *The Nordic States and European Unity*, Ithaca, NY: Cornell University Press.

Ingeniøren (2001) 'Nye tider, nye trusler – nyt beredskap?', 30 March (http://cph.in-g.dk/arkiv/).

Jagland, T. (2001) 'Utvidet sikkerhet', Speech given at NTNU in Trondheim, 19 April (http://odin.dep.no/ud/norsk/aktuelt/taler/index-b-n-a.html).

Jakobsen, P. V. (2000) 'Denmark at War: Turning Point or Business as Usual?', in B. Heurlin and H. Mouritzen (eds), *Danish Foreign Policy Yearbook*, Copenhagen: DUPI, pp. 61–85.

Jakobsen, P. V. (forthcoming) *The Nordic Approach(es) to Peace Operations After the Cold War: A New Nordic Model in Making?*, Copenhagen: DUPI.

Jakobson, M. (1998) *Finland in the New Europe*, London: Praeger.

Jensby, S. A. (2002) 'The Battle Against Terrorism – Global Challenges', *First Magazine* (January).

Jensen, R. (2003) *CIMIC i fredsstøttende operasjoner – en studie basert på erfaringer fra Kosovo*, Faglig fordypning, Oslo: Hovedstudiet, Forsvarets stabsskole, Oslo.

Jepperson, R. L., A. Wendt and P. J. Katzenstein (1996) 'Norms, Identity, and Culture in National Security', in P. J. Katzenstein (ed.), *The Culture of National Security. Norms and Identity in World Politics*, New York: Columbia University Press, pp. 33–75.

Joenniemi, P. (1992) 'Norden as a Mystery. The Search for New Roads into the Future', in J. Øberg (ed.), *Nordic Security Options in the 1990s, Options in the Changing Europe*, London: Pinter, for TFF, pp. 35–83.

Joenniemi, P. (1996) 'Finland i det nye Europa: Granne till en stormakt eller småstat bland småstater?' in I. Neumann (ed.), *Ny giv for nordisk samarbeid? Norsk, svensk og finsk sikkerhetspolitikk før og etter EUs nordlige utvidelse*, Oslo: Tano, pp. 106–30.

Joenniemi, P. (2002) 'Finland in the New Europe. A Herderian or Hegelian project?', in L. Hansen and O. Wæver (eds), *European Integration and National Identity. The Challenges of the Nordic States*, London and New York: Routledge, pp. 182–213.

Justisdepartementet (1999–2000) 'Om Norges deltakelse i internasjonalt politisamarbeid', *Stortingsmelding* 18, Oslo.

Justisdepartementet (2002) 'Samfunnssikkerhet. Veien til et mindre sårbart samfunn', *Stortingsmelding* 17, Oslo: Justisdepartementet.

Järvenpää, P. (2001) 'Security Perceptions and Defence Policy: Finland', in T. Ries and A. Hagelstam (eds), *Sweden and Finland: Security Perceptions and Defence Policy*, Helsinki: National Defence College, Department of Strategic and Defence Studies, pp. 8–16.

Kagan, R. (2003) *Of Paradise and Power*, New York: Alfred A. Knopf.

Karvonen, L. and B. Sundelius (1996) 'The Nordic Neutrals. Facing the European Union', in L. Miles (ed.), *The European Union and the Nordic Countries*, London and New York: Routledge, pp. 245–59.

Katzenstein, P. J. (1996a) *Cultural Norms and National Security. Police and Military in Postwar Japan*, Ithaca, NY, and London: Cornell University Press.

Katzenstein, P. J. (1996b) 'Introduction: Alternative Perspectives on National Security', in P. J. Katzenstein (ed.), *The Culture of National Security. Norms and Identity in World Politics*, New York: Columbia University Press, pp. 1–32.

Keane, R. (2004) 'The Solana Process in Serbia and Montenegro: Coherence in EU Foreign Policy', *International Peacekeeping* 111 (3): 491–507.

Keck, M. and K. Sikkink (1998) *Activists Beyond Borders. Transnational Advocacy Networks in International Politics*, Ithaca, NY: Cornell University Press.

Keohane, R. O. (ed.) (1986) *Neorealism and its Critics*, New York: Columbia University Press.

Knutsen, B. O. (2000) 'The Nordic Dimension in the Evolving European Security Structure and the Role of Norway', *Occasional Paper* 22, Paris: WEU ISS.

Kosmo, J. (1995) 'Norsk forsvars internasjoanle engasjement', Speech given at Bergen militære samfunn, 31 October.

Kowert, P. and Jeffrey Legro (1996) 'Norms, Identity, and Their Limits: A Theoretical Reprise', in P. J. Katzenstein (ed.), *The Culture of National Security, Norms and Identity in World Politics*, New York: Columbia University Press, pp. 451–97.

Krahmann, E. (2003) 'Conceptualizing Security Governance,' *Cooperation and Conflict* 38 (1): 5–26.

REFERENCES

Krasner, S. (1993) 'Westphalia and All That', in J. Goldstein and R. O. Keohane (eds), *Ideas and Foreign Policy. Beliefs, Institutions, and Political Change*, Ithaca, NY: Cornell University Press, pp. 235–64.

Kupchan, C. A. (2000) 'In Defence of European Defence: An American Perspective', *Survival* 42 (2): 16–32.

Kupchan, C. A. and C. Kupchan (1991) 'Concerts, Collective Security, and the Future of Europe', *International Security* 16: 114–61.

Kuusela, J. (2002) 'Security and Defence Policy' Virtual Finland(http://virtual.finland.fi/finfo/english/security.html).

Landerholm, H. (2001) 'Alliansfriheten döljer verkeligheten', *Internationella Studier* 1: 22–35.

Lapid, Y. and F. Kratochwil (eds) (1996) *The Return of Culture and Identity in IR Theory*, Boulder, CO: Lynne Rienner.

Larsen, H. (1997) *Foreign Policy and Discourse Analysis. France, Britain and Europe*, London: Routledge.

Larsen, H. (2000a) 'Danish CFSP Policy in the Post-Cold War Period. Continuity or Change?', *Cooperation and Conflict* 35 (1): 37–63.

Larsen, H. (2000b) 'Denmark and the European Defence Dimension in the Post Cold War Period: Opt-out or Participation?', in B. Heurlin and H. Mouritzen (eds), *Danish Foreign Policy Yearbook*, Copenhagen: DUPI, pp. 87–119.

Larsen, H. (2002a) 'Denmark and the EU's Defence Dimension: Opt-out across the Board?', in N. Græger, H. Larsen and H. Ojanen (eds), *The ESDP and the Nordic Countries*, Helsinki: FIIA, pp. 90–153.

Larsen, H. (2002b) 'The EU: A Global Military Actor', *Cooperation and Conflict* 37 (3): 283–302.

Lijphart, A. (1971) 'Comparative Politics and the Comparative Method', *The American Political Science Review* 65: 682–93.

Lindahl, R. (1995) 'Towards an Ever Closer Relation – Swedish Foreign Policy and the European Integration', in R. Lindahl and G. Sjöstedt (eds), *New Thinking in International Relations: Swedish Perspectives*, Stockholm: Utenrikspolitiska Institutet, pp. 163–82.

Lindh, A. (2001) 'Svensk utrikes- och säkerhetspolitik i ett nytt Europa', Speech given at Folk och Försvars rikskonferens in Sälen, 24 January (http://www.utrikes.regeringen.se/pressinfo/taloartiklar.htm).

Lindh, A. and E. Tuomioja (2000) 'Katastrofhjälpen duger inte', *Dagens Nyheter*, 30 April. (http://regeringen.se/galactica/service=irnews/action).

Lindh, A. and E. Tuomioja (2002) 'Combining New Threats with Deeper Solidarity', 18 December (http://www.utrikes.regeringen.se/inenglish/pressinfo/).

Lindh, A. and B. von Sydow (2000) 'Sverige bör ta ansvar även militärt', *Dagens Nyheter*, 12 November.

Lindley-French, J. and F. Algieri (2004) 'A European Defence Strategy. The Vision Document of the Venusberg Group', Guetersloh: Bertelsmann Foundation.

Lindström, G. (1997) 'Sweden's Security Policy: Engagement – the Middle Way', *Occasional Papers* 2, Paris: WEU ISS.

Lodge, J. (1993) 'From Civilian Power to Speaking with a Common Voice: The Transition to a CFSP', in J. Lodge (ed.), *The European Community and the Challenge of the Future*, London: Pinter, 2nd edition, pp. 1–36.

Lodge, J. and V. Flynn (1998) 'The CFSP after Amsterdam: The Policy Planning and Early Warning Unit', *International Relations* 14 (1): 7–21.

Lykketoft, M. (2001a) 'EU og NATO i samarbejde', *Jyllandsposten*, 18 March.

Lykketoft, M. (2001b) 'Europa og USA – et forhold under forandring', *Politiken*, 21 January.

Lykketoft, M. (2001c) 'Redegørelse om forsvarsforbeholdet op til det danske formandskab', Luxembourg, 8–9 October (http://www.um.dk/cgi-bin/dyn3nt/dyn3.exe?prog=showandpageid=270).

Lykketoft, M. (2001d) 'Udenrigsministerens besvarelse i Folketinget af F56 om europæisk forsvarsdimension', Copenhagen, 3 May (http://www.um.dk/cgi-bin/dyn3nt/dyn3.exe?prog=showandpageid=262).

Lykketoft, M. (2001e) 'Udenrigsministerens indlæg under åben debat på rådsmøde (udenrigsministre): Konfliktforebyggelse', Brussels, 22 January (http://www.um.dk/cgi-bin/dyn3nt/dyn3.exe?prog=showandpageid=262).

McSweeney, B. (1996) 'Identity and Security: Buzan and the Copenhagen School', *Review of International Studies* 22: 81–93.

McSweeney, B. (1999) *Security, Identity and Interests. A Sociology of International Relations*, Cambridge: Cambridge University Press.

af Malmborg, M. (2000) 'Neutraliteten och den svenska identiteten', *Internationella Studier* 1: 55–67.

Manners, I. (2002) 'European [Security] Union: From Existential Threat to Ontological Security', *Working Papers* 5, Copenhagen: COPRI.

Manners, I. and R. G. Withman (eds) (2000) *The Foreign Policies of European Union Member States*, London: Macmillan.

March, J. G. and J. P. Olsen (1989) *Rediscovering Institutions. The Organizational Basis of Politics*, New York: Free Press.

March, J. G. and J. P. Olsen (1998) 'The Institutional Dynamics of International Political Orders', *International Organization* 52 (4): 943–69.

Mathews, J. T. (1989) 'Redefining Security', *Foreign Affairs* 68 (2): 162–77.

Maull, H. W. (2000) 'Germany and the Use of Force: Still a Civilian Power?', *Survival* 42 (2): 56–80.

Mearsheimer, J. J. (1990) 'Back to the Future. Instability in Europe after the Cold War', in S. M. Lynn-Jones and S. E. Miller (eds), *The Cold War and After. Prospects for Peace*, Cambridge, MA, and London: The MIT Press.

Merriam, S. B. (1998) *Qualitative Research and Case Study Applications in Education*, San Francisco, CA: Jossey-Bass.

Miles, L. (ed.) (1996) *The European Union and the Nordic Countries*, London: Routledge.

Miles, L. (1997) *Sweden and European Integration*, Aldershot: Ashgate.

Missiroli, A. (2001a) 'EU–NATO Cooperation in Crisis Management: No Turkish Delight for ESDP [The extent to which NATO's "assets and capabilities" would be put at the disposal of "European-led" peace support operations + the legacy of the WEU]', *Security Dialogue* 33 (1): 9–26.

Missiroli, A., (ed) (2001b) 'Coherence for European Security Policy. Debates – Cases – Assessments', *Occasional Papers* 27, Paris: Western European Union Institute for Security Studies.

Møller, P. S. (2003) 'Udenrigsministerens besvarelse af forespørgsel i Folketinget om resultatene af det danske formandskab', Copenhagen, 8 January (http://www.um.dk/cgi-bin/dyn3nt/dyn3.exe?prog=showandpageid=207).

Mörth, U. (2000) 'Swedish Industrial Policy and Research and Technological Development: The Case of European Defence Equipment', in L. Miles (ed.), *Sweden and the European Union Evaluated*, London: Continuum, pp. 124–45.

NATO (1998) *NATO Handbook 1998*, Brussels: NATO.

Nehring, N. J. (2001) 'The Special Case of Denmark', in A. Pijpers (ed.), *On Cores and Coalitions in the European Union. The Position of Some Smaller Member States*, The Hague: Clingendael Institute, pp. 153–68.

Neumann, I. B. (1999) *Uses of the Other. The East in European Identity Formation*, Minneapolis, MN: University of Minnesota Press.

Neumann, I. B. (2001a) *Mening, materialitet og makt. En innføring i diskursanalyze*, Oslo: Fagbokforlaget.

Neumann, I. B. (2001b) *Norge – en kritikk : begrepsmakt i Europa-debatten*, Oslo: Pax.

Neumann, I. B. and S. Ulriksen (1995) 'Norsk forsvars- og sikkerhetspolitikk', in T. L. Knutsen, G. M. Sørbø and S. Gjerdåker (eds), *Norsk utenrikspolitikk*, 1st edn, Oslo: Cappelen Akademiske Forlag, pp. 80–105.

Neumann, I. B. and S. Ulriksen (1997) 'Norsk forsvars- og sikkerhetspolitikk', in T. L. Knutsen, G. M. Sørbø and S. Gjerdåker (eds), *Norges utenrikspolitikk*, 2nd edn, Oslo: Cappelens Akademiske Forlag AS, pp. 94–123.

Neumann, I. and S. Ulriksen (eds) (1996) *Sikkerhetspolitikk. Norge i makttriangelet mellom EU, Russland og USA*, Oslo: Tano Aschehoug.

Nielsen, R. R. (2001) 'Forsvarsforbeholdets fremtid efter 28. september 2000', *Reprint* 2, Copenhagen: DUPI.

NOU (1992) 'Forsvarskommisjonen av 1990', *NOU* 12, Oslo: Forsvarskommisjonen.

NOU (2000a) 'Et nytt forsvar', *NOU* 20, Oslo: Forsvarskommisjonen.

NOU (2000b) 'Et sårbart samfunn. Utfordringer for sikkerhets- og beredskapsarbeidet i samfunnet', *NOU* 24, Oslo: Sårbarhetsutvalget.

Nuttal, N. (1992) *European Political Cooperation*, Oxford: Clarendon Press.

Nye, J. S. and S. M. Lynn-Jones (1988) 'International Security Studies', *International Security* 12 (4): 5–27.

Ojanen, H. (1997) 'The Plurality of Truth. A Critique of Research on the State and European Integration', PhD thesis, Florence: European University Institute.

Ojanen, H. (1999) 'How to Customise Your Union: Finland and the "Northern Dimension of the EU" ', in *Northern Dimensions*, Helsinki: Finnish Institute of International Affairs, pp. 13–26.

Ojanen, H. (2002) 'Sweden and Finland: What Difference Does it Make to be Non-aligned?', in N. Græger, H. Larsen and H. Ojanen (eds), *The ESDP and the Nordic Countries. Four Variations on a Theme*, Helsinki: Finnish Institute of International Affairs, pp. 154–217.

Ojanen, H., G. Herolf and R. Lindahl (2000) *Non-alignment and European Security Policy*, Helsinki: Finnish Institute of International Affairs.

Olsen, G. R. (2001) 'Danmarks "fjerne" utenrikspolitik efter Golf-krigen: Alt ved det gamle eller en ny verdensorden?' *Militært Tidskrift* 123 (4): 311–22.

Olsen, J. P. (2002) 'The Many Faces of Europeanization', *Working Papers* 1, Oslo: Arena (on-line version: http://www.arena.uio.no/publications/wp02_2.htm).

Parsons, C. (2003) *A Certain Idea of Europe*, Ithaca, NY, and London: Cornell University Press.

215

Pastore, F. (2001) 'Reconciling the Prince's Two "Arms". Internal–External Security Policy Coordination in the European Union', *Occasional Papers* 30, Paris: Western European Union Institute for Security Studies.

Penttilä, R. E. J. (1994) 'Finland's Security in a Changing Europe', *Finnish Defence Studies* 7, Helsinki: National Defence College.

Petersen, F. A. (2000) 'The International Situation and Danish Foreign Policy 1999', in B. Heurlin and H. Mouritzen (eds), *Danish Foreign Policy Yearbook*, Copenhagen: DUPI, pp. 11–29.

Petersen, N. H. (1995) 'Post Maastricht Europe', Speech given at the University of Newcastle upon Tyne, 26 January, *DUPIDOK*, Copenhagen: DUPI.

Petersen, N. H. (1996) 'Udenrigsministerens artikel om den fælles udenrigs- og sikkerhedspolitik', October 1996, *DUPIDOK*, Copenhagen: DUPI.

Petersen, N. H. (1999a) 'Europahær er ikke aktuel', *Politiken*, 22 March.

Petersen, N. H. (1999b) 'Folkeret in en brytningstid', *Politiken*, 25 June.

Petersen, N. H. (1999c) 'Folketingets forhandlinger', *DUPIDOK*, Copenhagen: DUPI.

Petersen, N. H. (2000b) 'Forespørgsel om Dansk Udenrikspolitisk Instituts udredning om udviklingen i EU siden 1992 på de områder, der er omfattet af de fire forbehold', *DUPIDOK*, Copenhagen: DUPI.

Petersen, N. (2000c) 'Adapting to Change: Danish Security Policy after the Cold War', in B. Hansen (ed.), *European Security – 2000*, Copenhagen: Copenhagen Political Studies Press, pp. 99–116.

Peterson, J. and H. Sjursen (eds) (1998) *A Common Foreign Policy for Europe? Comparing Visions of the CFSP*, London and New York: Routledge.

Politiken (1999) 'Danmark foreslår EU-politistyrke', 19 October.

Politiken (2000a) 'Helveg angriber forsvarsforbehold', 19 June.

Politiken (2000b) 'Danske officerer til EU', 14 February.

Politiken (2000c) 'Hækkerup ønsker debat om EU-hær', 20 November.

Politiken (2001) 'Flere danskere i EUs politi', 8 May.

Prime Minister's Office (2004) *Finnish Security and Defence Policy 2004*, Government Report 6, Helsinki.

Prodi, R. (1999) Speech given in the European Parliament, Strasbourg, 4 May, (http://jpn.cec.eu.int/english/press-info/4–2–19.htm).

Prodi, R. (2000) *Shaping the New Europe*, Speech given in the European Parliament Strasbourg, 15 February (http://europa.eu.int/rapid/start/cgi/guesten.ksh?reslist).

Pursiainen, C. (1999) 'Finland's Security Policy Towards Russia: From Bilateralism to Multilateralism', *UPI Working Papers* 14, Helsinki: Finnish Institute of International Affairs.

Radaelli, C. M. (2000) 'Whither Europeanization? Concept stretching and substantive change', European Integration Online Papers (EIoP) 4 (8) (http://eiop.or.at/eiop/texte/2000–008a.htm.).

Ragin, C. C. (1987) *The Comparative Method: Moving Beyond Qualitative and Quantitative Strategies*, Berkeley, CA: University of California Press.

Ragin, C. C. and H. S. Becker (1992) 'Reflection on "What is a Case" ', in C. C. Ragin and H. S. Becker (eds), *What is a Case? Exploring the Foundations of Social Inquiry*, Cambridge: Cambridge University Press, pp. 1–18.

Rasmussen, P. N. (2001) 'Opening Address to the Danish Parliament', Copenhagen, 2 October (http://www.statsministeriet.dk/Index/dokumentoversigt.asp).

Rea, T. and J. Wright (1997) *International Relations 1914–1995*, Oxford: Oxford University Press.

Regelsberger, E. and W. Wessels (1996) 'The CFSP Institutions and Procedures. A Third Way for the Second Pillar', *European Foreign Affairs Review* 1: 29–54.

Rieker, P. (1998a) 'Frankrike og NATO i 1990-årene', *Internasjonal Politikk* 56 (4): 565–78.

Rieker, P. (1998b) 'Fransk NATO-politikk i 1990-årene. Kontinuitet eller endring?', *Report* 234, Oslo: NUPI.

Rieker, P. and S. Ulriksen (2003) *En annerledes supermakt? Sikkerhets- og forsvarspolitikken i EU*, Oslo: NUPI.

Ries, T. (2001) 'Finland – National, European or Atlantic Defence', in T. Ries and A. Hagelstam (eds), *Sweden and Finland: Security Perceptions and Defence Policy*, Helsinki: National Defence College, pp. 32–46.

Ries, T. (2002) 'Activism and Non-alignment: The Case of Finland', in A. Dahl and N. Hillmer (eds), *Activism and (Non) alignment*, Stockholm: Utenrikspolitiska Institutet (Conference Paper 31), pp. 71–82.

Risse, T. (2000) ' "Let's Argue!": Communicative Action in World Politics', *International Organization* 54 (1): 1–39.

Risse, T. (2001) 'A European identity? Europeanization and the Evolution of Nation-State Identities', in M. Cowles, J. Caporaso and T. Risse (eds), *Transforming Europe. Europeanization and Domestic Change*, London: Cornell University Press, pp. 198–216.

Risse, T. and K. Sikkink (1999) 'The Socialization of International Human Rights Norms into Domestic Practices: Introduction', in T. Risse, S. C. Ropp and K. Sikkink (eds), *The Power of Human Rights: International Norms and Domestic Change*, Cambridge: Cambridge University Press, pp. 1–38.

Riste, O. (2002) *Norway's Foreign Relations – A History*, Oslo: Universitetsforlaget.

Rometsch, D. and W. Wessels (eds) (1996) *The European Union and Member States. Towards Institutional Fusion?* Manchester: Manchester University Press.

Rosamond, B. (2000) *Theories of European Integration*, London: Macmillan.

Saryusz-Wolski, J. (2002) 'Looking to the Future', in J. Sediviny, P. Dunay and J. Saryusz-Wolski (eds), *Enlargement and the European Defence after 11 September (Chaillot paper)*, Paris: EU Institute for Security Studies, pp. 55–69.

Schimmelfenning, F. (1999a) 'The Double Puzzle of EU Enlargement. Liberal Norms, Rhetorical Action, and the Decision to Expand to the East', *Working Papers* 15, Oslo: Arena.

Schimmelfenning, F. (1999b) 'NATO Enlargement: A Constructivist Explanation', *Security Studies* 8 (2–3): 198–234.

Secretary General/High Representative and European Commission (2000) *Improving the Coherence and Effectiveness of the European Union Action in the Field of Conflict Prevention*, Report presented to the Nice European Council.

Sending, O. J. (2002) 'Constitution, Choice and Change: Problems with the "Logic of Appropriateness" and its Use in Constructivist Theory', *European Journal of International Relations* 8 (4): 443–70.

Singsås, Ø. (2000) *Et nytt forsvar for en ny tid*, Speech given at Tromsø Militære Samfunn, 11 April (http://odin.dep.no/odinarkiv/norsk/dep/fd/2000/taler/).

Sjursen, H. (1999) 'Med ryggen mot Europa? Endring og kontinuitet i norsk sikkerhetspolitikk', in D. H. Claes and B. S. Tranøy (eds), *Norge under EØS*, Oslo: Fagbokforlaget, pp. 39–79.

Sjursen, H. (2001a) 'The Common Foreign and Security Policy. Limits of Intergovernmentalism and Search for a Global Role', in K. A. Eliassen (ed.), *Making Policy in Europe. Europeification of National Policy-making*, London: Sage, pp. 187–205.

Sjursen, H. (2001b) 'New Forms of Security Policy in Europe', *Arena Working Papers* 4, Oslo: Arena.

Sjursen, H. (2004) 'Towards a post-national foreign and security policy?', *Arena Working Papers* 12, Oslo: Arena.

Sjöstedt, G. (1977) *The External Role of the European Community*, London: Saxon House.

Skogan, J. K. (2001) 'Sikkerhetspolitikk: mål, utfordringer og virkemidler', in J. Hovi and R. Malnes (eds), *Normer og makt*, Oslo: abstrakt forlag, pp. 57–94.

Smith, H. (2002) *European Foreign Policy. What it Is and What it Does*, London: Pluto Press.

Smith, K. E. (1999) *The Making of EU Foreign Policy. The Case of Eastern Europe*, London: Macmillan.

Smith, K. E. (2000) 'The End of Civilian Power EU?', *The International Spectator* 35 (2): 11.

Smith, K. E. (2003) *European Foreign Policy in a Changing World*, Cambridge: Polity Press.

Smith, M. E. (2004) *Europe's Foreign and Security Policy: The Institutionalisation of Cooperation*, Cambridge: Cambridge University Press.

Smith, S. (1996) 'Positivism and Beyond', in S. Smith, K. Booth and M. Zalewski (eds), *International Theory. Positivism and Beyond*, Cambridge: Cambridge University Press, pp. 11–46.

Soetendorp, B. (1999) *Foreign Policy in the European Union*, New York: Longman.

Solana, J. (2001) 'Europe: Security in the Twenty-first Century', Speech given at SIPRI, Stockholm, 20 June (http://about.sipri.se/activities/lect.html).

Solana, J. (2003) 'A Secure Europe in a Better World', Thessaloniki: June.

SOU (1994) 'Historiska vägval. Följderna för Sverige i utrikes- och säkerhetspolitisk hänseende av att bli, respektive inte bli medlem i Europeiske Unionen. Betänkande av EG/EU-konsekvensutredningarna: Utrikes- och säkerhetspolitik', *SOU* 8, Stockholm: Fritzes.

SOU (1999) 'Internationell konflikthantering – att förbereda sig tilsammans', *SOU* 29, Stockholm.

SOU (2000) 'Att verka for fred – et gemensamt fredscentrum i Sverige', *SOU* 74, Stockholm.

SOU (2001a) 'Samverkanscenter i Kramfors för katastrof- och fredsinsater', *SOU* 104, Stockholm.

SOU (2001b) 'Säkerhet i ny tid', *SOU* 41, Stockholm: Sårbarhets- och säkerhetsutredningen.

Strömvik, M. (1999) 'Sverige och EUs utrikes- och säkerhetspolitik: ett intensivt men hemligt förhållande?', in K. M. Johansson (ed.), *Sverige i EU*, Stockholm: SNS Förlag, pp. 248–65.

Study Group on Europe's Security Capabilities (2004) *A Human Security Doctrine for Europe. The Barcelona Report of the Study Group on Europe's Security Capabilities*,

REFERENCES

Presented to EU High Representative for Common Foreign and Security Policy Javier Solana: Barcelona, 15 September.

Sundelius, B. (2001) 'Totalförsvaret är överspelat – vi behöver et samhällsförsvar!', Stockholm: Försvarsberedningen.

Sundstøl, S. E. (2002) 'Comparing Constructions. Comparative Studies after the Constructivist Turn', Paper presented at a NUPI theory seminar.

Sverdrup, U. I. (1998) 'Norway: An Adaptive Non-Member', in K. Hanf and B. Soetendorp (eds), *Adapting to European Integration. Small States and the European Union*, London: Longman, pp. 149–66.

Sverdrup, U. I. (2000) 'Ambiguity and Adaptation. Europeanization of Administrative Institutions as Loosely Coupled Processes', *Arena Report* 12, Oslo: Arena.

Sæter, M. (1971) *Det politiske Europa*, Oslo: Universitetsforlaget.

Sæter, M. (1992) *Det Europeiske Fellesskapet: Institusjoner og Politikk*, Oslo: Universitetsforlaget.

Sæter, M. (1998) *Comprehensive Neofunctionalism: Bridging Realism and Liberalism in the Study of European Integration*, Oslo: NUPI.

Tamnes, R. (1997) *Oljealder 1965–1995*, Oslo: Universitetsforlaget.

Thune, H. and S. Ulriksen (2002) 'Prestige and Penance through Peace – Norway as an Allied Activist', in A. Dahl and N. Hillmer (eds), *Activism and (Non) Alignment*, Stockholm: Utenrikspolitiska Institutet (Conference Papers 31), pp. 113–37.

Tiilikainen, T. (1996) 'Finland and the European Union', in L. Miles (ed.), *The European Union and the Nordic Countries*, London: Routledge, pp. 117–32.

Tiilikainen, T. (1998) *Europe and Finland*, Aldershot: Ashgate.

Tonra, B. (2001) 'The EU and Small State Foreign Policy', Paper presented at the 4th Pan-European conference of the ECPR Standing Group on International Relations, University of Kent at Canterbury, 8–10 September.

Tunander, O. (1996) 'Norway's Post-Cold War Security: The Nordic Region Between Friend and Foe, or Between Cosmos and Chaos', in A. Orrenius and L. Truedson (eds), *Visions of European Security – Focal Point Sweden and Northern Europe*, Stockholm: Olof Palme International Center, pp. 48–63.

Tunander, O. (1999) 'The Uneasy Imbrication of Nation-State and NATO. The Case of Sweden', *Cooperation and Conflict* 34 (2): 169–203.

Tuomioja, E. (2002) 'Security Problems and the New Challenges', Speech given to the Vaasa Paasikivi Society, 11 February, Vaasa (http://formin.finland.fi/english/).

Udenrigsministeriet (2001a) 'Danmark og Europa. Utvidelse, Globalisering og Folkelig forankring', *Hvidbog*, Copenhagen: Udenrigsministeriet.

Udenrigsministeriet (2001b) 'Redegørelse om forsvarsforbeholdet op til det danske formandskab', *Redegørelse*, Copenhagen: Udenrigsministeriet.

Udenrigsministeriet (2003) 'The Goals and the Results of the Danish Presidency', Copenhagen (http://www.eu2002.dk/main/).

Udvalget for National Sårbarhedsudredning (2004) *Nasjonal Sårbarhedsudredning*, Copenhagen.

Ulriksen, S. (2002) *Den norske forsvarstradisjonen. Militærmakt eller folkeforsvar*, Oslo: Pax.

Utenriksdepartementet (1993–94) 'Om medlemskap i Den europeiske union', *Stortingsmelding* 40, Oslo: Utenriksdepartementet.

Utenriksdepartementet (2002) 'Samarbeidsregjeringens europapolitiske plattform. Utfordringer, målsetninger og virkemidler', Oslo, 21 February.

REFERENCES

Utrikesdepartementet (1998) 'Statement of Government Policy in the Parliamentary Debate on Foreign Affairs', Stockholm, 11 February (http://www.utrikes.regeringen.se/fragor/utrikespolitik/utrikesdek/index.htm).

Utrikesdepartementet (1999) 'Statement of Government Policy in the Parliamentary Debate on Foreign Affairs', Stockholm, 10 February (http://www.utrikes.regeringen.se/fragor/utrikespolitik/utrikesdek/index.htm).

Utrikesdepartementet (2000) 'Statement of Government Policy in the Parliamentary Debate on Foreign Affairs', Stockholm, 9 February (http://www.utrikes.regeringen.se/fragor/utrikespolitik/utrikesdek/index.htm).

Utrikesdepartementet (2001) 'Statement of Government Policy in the Parliamentary Debate on Foreign Affairs', Stockholm, 7 February (http://www.utrikes.regeringen.se/fragor/utrikespolitik/utrikesdek/index.htm).

Utrikesdepartementet (2002) 'Statement of Government Policy in the Parliamentary Debate on Foreign Affairs', Stockholm, 13 February (http://www.utrikes.regeringen.se/fragor/utrikespolitik/utrikesdek/index.htm).

Utrikesdepartementet (2003) 'Statement of Government Policy in the Parliamentary Debate on Foreign Affairs', Stockholm, 12 February (http://www.utrikes.regeringen.se/fragor/utrikespolitik/utrikesdek/index.htm).

Villaume, P. (1999) 'Denmark and NATO through 50 years', in B. Heurlin and H. Mouritzen (eds), *Danish Foreign Policy Yearbook*, Copenhagen: DUPI, pp. 29–61.

Vollebæk, K. (1998) 'Norsk sikkerhetspolitikk i et Europa i endring', Speech given at Johan Jørgen Holst minneforelesning, Oslo, 16 April (http://odin.dep.no/odinarkiv/norsk/dep/ud/1998/taler/).

Vollebæk, K. (1999) 'Statement on the Government's European Policy, with Emphasis on Relations with the EU', Stortinget, Oslo, 19 January (http://odin.dep.no/odin-arkiv/norsk/dep/ud/1999/taler/index-b-n-a.html).

von Sydow, B. (1999) 'Anförande i Riksdagen', Stockholm, 26 November (http://www.regeringen.se/galactica/service=irnews/owner=sys/action=oz_press_tal2).

Vaahtoranta, T. and T. Forsberg (1998) 'Finland's Three Security Strategies', in M. Jopp and S. Arnswald (eds), *The European Union and the Baltic States: Visions, Interests and Strategies for the Baltic Sea Region*, Kauhava: Ulkopolittinen Instituutti and Institut für Europäische Politik, pp. 191–211.

Wahlbäck, K. (1986) *The Roots of Swedish Neutrality*, Stockholm: Svenska Institutet.

Wallace, W. and A. Forster (2000) 'Common Foreign and Security Policy', in W. Wallace and H. Wallace (eds), *Policy-Making in the European Union*, Oxford: Oxford University Press, pp. 461–91.

Walt, S. M. (1991) 'The Renaissance of Security Studies', *International Studies Quarterly* 35: 211–39.

Waltz, K. (1979) *Theory of International Politics*, New York: Addison-Wesley.

Wendt, A. (1994) 'Collective Identity Formation and the International State', *American Political Science Review* 88 (2): 384–96.

Wendt, A. (1999) *Social Theory of International Politics*, Cambridge: Cambridge University Press.

Westing, A. (1986) *Global Resources and International Conflicts: Environmental Factors in Strategic Policy and Action*, Oxford: Oxford University Press.

Westing, A. (1988) 'The Military Sector vis-à-vis the Environment', *Journal of Peace Research* 25 (3): 257–64.

Westing, A. (1989) *Comprehensive Security for the Baltic: An Environmental Approach*, London: Sage.

White, B. (2001) *Understanding European Foreign Policy*, London: Palgrave.

Whitmann, R. (1998) *From Civilian Power to Superpower? The International Identity of the European Union*, Basingstoke: Macmillan.

Wæver, O. (1995a) 'Identity, Integration and Security: Solving the Sovereignty Puzzle in the EU Studies', *Journal of International Affairs* 48 (2): 46–86.

Wæver, O. (1995b) 'Securitisation and Desecuritisation', in Ronnie D. Lipschutz (ed.), *On Security*, New York: Columbia University Press, pp. 46–86.

Wæver, O. (1996) 'European Security Identities', *Journal of Common Market Studies* 34 (1): 103–32.

Wæver, O. (1997) 'Integration as Security: European International Identity and American Domestic Discipline', *Working Papers* 27, Copenhagen: COPRI.

Wæver, O. (1998) 'Insecurity, Security, and Asecurity in the West European Non-war Community', in E. Adler and M. Barnett (eds), *Security Communities*, Cambridge: Cambridge University Press, pp. 69–118.

Wæver, O. (2000) 'The EU as a Security Actor. Reflections from a Pessimistic Constructivist on Post-sovereign Security Orders', in M. Kelstrup and M. C. Williams (eds), *International Relations Theory and the Politics of European Integration: Power, Security, and Community*, London: Routledge, pp. 251–93.

Wæver, O. (2002) 'Identity, Communities and Foreign Policy. Discourse Analysis as Foreign Policy Theory', in L. Hansen and O. Wæver (eds), *European Integration and National Identity. The Challenge of the Nordic States*, London and New York: Routledge, pp. 20–49.

Wæver, O. and H. Wiberg (1992) 'Norden in the Cold War Reality', in J. Øberg (ed.), *Nordic Security Options in the 1990s. Options in the Changing Europe*, London: Pinter, pp. 13–34.

Wæver, O., B. Buzan, M. Kelstrup and P. Lemaitre (1993) *Identity, Migration and the New Security Agenda in Europe*, London: Pinter.

Youngs, R. (2002) 'The European Security and Defence Policy: What Impact on the EU's Approach to Security Challenges?', *European Security* 11 (2): 101–24.

Zielonka, J. (1998) *Explaining Euro-Paralysis. Why Europe is Unable to Act in International Politics*, Oxford: St Anthony's College.

Østergaard, U. (2000) 'Danish National Identity: Between Multinational Heritage and Small State Nationalism', in M. Kelstrup and H. Branner (eds), *Denmark's Policy towards Europe After 1945*, Odense: Odense University Press, pp. 139–84.

Åström, S. (2000) 'Efter Neutraliteten – Ny svensk doktrin behövs', *Internationella Studier* 2: 25–39.

INDEX

Europeanization and socialization 147–50, 187; external security 144–6, 183–4; from neutrality to NATO membership (1720–1949) 124–6; impact of EU's comprehensive security approach 140–6; instrumental adaptation or identity change 148–50; internal security 140–4, 182; Maastricht Treaty and 130–1, 132, 133, 135, 147, 148, 149, 179–80, 187, 192, 200 n. 1, 200 n. 3; NATO and 126–8, 129, 130, 131, 138, 139, 140, 144, 147, 149, 150, 187
Denmarkization 127
desecuritization 8, 29, 30
Dinkelspiel, Ulf 71
direct Europeanization 192
discourse analysis 18–20
dominant national security discourse 11
dominant security discourse 9–10, 195 n. 11
double-loop (complex) learning 53
drug-trafficking 39
Dublin Convention 161, 202 n. 12

Economic and Monetary Union (EMU) 4, 38, 67
EFTA (FINEFTA) 96, 97
Eksborg, Ann-Louise 82–3
Ellemann-Jensen, Uffe 128
Elysée Agreement 35
Euro-Atlantic Partnership Council (EAPC) 78
EUROJUST 44
Euro-Mediterranean Partnership 47
European Aerospace and Defence Company (EADC) 78
European arrest warrant 44
European Atomic Energy Community (Euratom) 34
European Coal and Steel Community (ECSC) 33, 127
European Council, establishment 35
European Defence Community (EDC) 33, 34, 39, 127
European Defence Strategy 48
European Economic Agreement (EEA) 68, 97, 158, 160, 197 n. 6, 202 n. 9
European Economic Community (EEC) 34
European Free Trade Area (EFTA) 67
European identity 52
European Mediterranean Partnership (EMP) 45
European Monetary Union (EMU) 131

European Political Co-operation (EPC) 35, 36, 67, 160
'European Programme for the Prevention of Violent Conflicts' 40
European Rapid Reaction Force 105–6, 166
European Security and Defence Identity (ESDI) 150, 159
European Security and Defence Policy (ESDP) 5, 12, 15, 17, 24, 30, 46, 178, 191; Denmark and 133–40, 145, 146, 147, 150, 180–1; Finland and 90, 103–10, 119, 120, 180–1; impact of 180–1; Norway and 158, 159, 160, 161, 162–7, 170, 173, 175–6, 180–1, 187, 192; Swedish participation in 74, 75–80, 87, 88, 180–1
European Security Strategy (ESS) 6, 41, 46, 47, 172
European Union (EU) 4; capacity to act 42–9; capacity to formulate goals 38–42; as comprehensive security actor 23–50; comprehensive security approach 87, 181–5; phases in development 5–6; security and integration 24–31; security identity of 3–6
European war, avoidance of 38–9
Europeanization 11–12; direct 192; indirect 192; national differences 188–9
Europeanization and socialization 51–62, 185–8; Denmark and 147–50, 187; Finland and 119–22, 186–7; Norway 172–6, 187–8; Sweden and 86–9
EUROPOL 44, 161, 168
external security 182–4; Denmark 144–6, 183–4; dynamics 39; Finland 115–19, 183; Norway 171–2, 183–4; Sweden and 84–6, 183

FCMA (Friendship, Co-operation and Mututal Assistance) Treaty 6, 66, 97
FINEFTA 96, 97
Finland 90–122; (1808–1945) 91–4; (1945–1975) 94–6; (1975–1990) 96–8; active neutrality 96–8, 110; CFSP and 99, 101, 102, 119, 120, 121; ESDP and 90, 103–10, 119, 120, 180–1; EU membership 98–102; Europeanization and socialization 119–22, 186–7; external security 115–19, 183; 'good pupil' strategy 103–6, 108, 121, 122; impact of EU's comprehensive

For Product Safety Concerns and Information please contact our EU
representative GPSR@taylorandfrancis.com
Taylor & Francis Verlag GmbH, Kaufingerstraße 24, 80331 München, Germany

www.ingramcontent.com/pod-product-compliance
Lightning Source LLC
Chambersburg PA
CBHW050425280326
41932CB00013BA/1996